Encountering Religion in the Workplace

Other Books by Raymond F. Gregory

Age Discrimination in the American Workplace: Old at a Young Age

Women and Workplace Discrimination: Overcoming Barriers to Gender Equality

Unwelcome and Unlawful: Sexual Harassment in the American Workplace

Norman Thomas: The Great Dissenter

ENCOUNTERING RELIGION
IN THE WORKPLACE

*The Legal Rights and Responsibilities of
Workers and Employers*

RAYMOND F. GREGORY

ILR PRESS

AN IMPRINT OF
CORNELL UNIVERSITY PRESS
ITHACA AND LONDON

First published 2011 by Cornell University Press
First printing, Cornell Paperbacks, 2011
Printed in the United States of America

Library of Congress Cataloging-in-Publication Data

Gregory, Raymond F., 1927–
    Encountering religion in the workplace : the legal rights and responsibilities of workers and employers / Raymond F. Gregory.
        p. cm.
    Includes bibliographical references and index.
    ISBN 978-0-8014-4954-3 (cloth : alk. paper)
    ISBN 978-0-8014-7660-0 (pbk. : alk. paper)
    1. Religion in the workplace—Law and legislation—United States.
I. Title.
    KF3466.5.G74 2011
    344.7301'256—dc22   2010027388

Cornell University Press strives to use environmentally responsible suppliers and materials to the fullest extent possible in the publishing of its books. Such materials include vegetable-based, low-VOC inks and acid-free papers that are recycled, totally chlorine-free, or partly composed of nonwood fibers. For further information, visit our website at www.cornellpress.cornell.edu.

Cloth printing   10 9 8 7 6 5 4 3 2 1
Paperback printing   10 9 8 7 6 5 4 3 2 1

For
Raymond, Pamela and John, George, and Dawn
and
Emma, Alanna, and George

CONTENTS

ENCOUNTERING RELIGION IN THE WORKPLACE

Introduction

The workplace is a community, a place where nearly all Americans spend a great deal of time, where friendships and relationships are initiated and developed, where life challenges are encountered, and where we find opportunities to contribute to society.[1] But the workplace is also a place where some workers pray with other workers and discuss their religious beliefs and practices. Many American workers refuse to conduct their lives in one way on their Sabbath and in an entirely different manner on the other days of the week, and thus they endeavor to integrate their religious and work lives. It should not surprise us, then, that an increasing number of Americans of all faiths find the workplace an appropriate and fitting site to express their religious and spiritual values.

Although American workers have traditionally taken advantage of their First Amendment rights to express their religious beliefs in the workplace, the heightened interest of some religious groups in expressing their faith while on the job has forced employers and coworkers to reconsider the appropriateness of certain aspects of religious conduct that now appear in offices and factories. Religion in the workplace does not sit well with all workers. From the employer's perspective, the presence of religious practice in the workplace may be distractive and at times divisive. While 96 percent of Americans assert a belief in God,[2] 30 percent feel that discussion of religious matters at work should always be avoided, and another 60 percent believe that care must be exercised when views on religious matters are exchanged with coworkers.[3]

A deeply held belief of many evangelical Christian denominations requires their adherents to spread the word of God whenever an opportunity presents itself. Though an increased desire of some workers to apply their faith at work may establish the workplace as a significant locus for spiritual expression and development, it may also set the stage for potential conflict with employers and coworkers. Rather than viewing evangelizing in a benign light, coworkers may consider it an intrusion.[4] How does a devoted Christian worker foster a workplace culture reflecting Christian values without impinging upon the rights of non-Christian coworkers? A thin line separates religious self-expression from unlawful proselytizing.

Several other factors have also effected a sharp increase in the incidence of religious practice and expression in the American workplace. Surveys show that as people grow older, religion often becomes a matter of greater significance and thus plays a more extensive role in many aspects of their lives, including their work. Since many employees do not become religiously observant until later in life, expression of their religious beliefs rarely creates workplace conflicts until that stage of their lives.[5] More than 80 million Americans now living were born during the two decades following World War II. The "baby boomer" generation, far more numerous than any generation either preceding or following it, will be the largest constituent of the national population during the next twenty-five to thirty years. The oldest baby boomers, who turned fifty in 1996, will be sixty-five in 2011. As the workforce grows older, the presence of religious practices and beliefs in the workplace will only intensify.

The increased incidence of religious expression in the workplace also is a product of a more diversified workforce, in turn an outgrowth of the global economy. Between 1970 and 2000, the foreign-born portion of the U.S. population more than doubled, increasing from just under 5 percent to 10 percent. A growing portion of the immigrants entering this country in 2000 originated in Latin America, Asia, the Middle East, and Africa, rather than in Europe, from which the majority of immigrants came in earlier eras. Two-thirds of that foreign-born population has joined the American workforce, thus introducing to the workplace disparate worldviews and religious customs wholly alien to most native-born American workers.[6] These have often clashed with more traditional views and customs, as divergent groups of employees attempt to adjust to rapidly changing work environments. Employees holding disparate and often competing worldviews vary not only in their spiritual, religious, or moral perspectives but also in the way they choose to express their convictions in the workplace. Similarly, they vary in the extent to which they will allow their coworkers, bosses, and subordinates to express their views, and when they are subjected to the influence of other religious beliefs, they may become annoyed or even offended.[7]

The expanded public role of personal religious experience constitutes a third factor that has greatly altered popular perceptions regarding the appropriate place for religious discussion. In recent years, personal religious faith has become a topic of general as well as public conversation. When a former president of the United States openly discusses his personal religious views on national television, it is not surprising that large numbers of Americans feel free to disclose their personal beliefs not just to their friends and acquaintances but to coworkers as well.

Employees are not alone in introducing religion to the workplace, as more than one employer has traveled that path. For example, an employer that inaugurates work practices designed to foster a Christian work ethic must then determine how best to accomplish that goal without violating the rights of its non-Christian employees; if it fails in that regard, one group or another of its workers may charge it with proselytizing. An employer that finds it advantageous to allow a group of workers greater leeway in expressing their religious beliefs may become a target of other groups of workers who charge it with favoritism, or even worse, with bias, prejudice, or intentional discrimination.

The growing presence of religion in the workplace has caused a number of other issues to surface, not the least of which is a dramatic increase in filings of Title VII religious discrimination charges levied against employers by their employees. Title VII of the Civil Rights Act of 1964 prohibits discrimination in employment based on race, color, national origin, sex, and religion. The Equal Employment Opportunity Commission—appointed by Congress to administer discrimination claims filed under Title VII—reported a 75 percent increase in the filing of religious discrimination charges between 1997 and 2008.[8] This increase reflects worker perceptions of the current status of the workplace. In a recent survey, 20 percent of the workers interviewed reported that they had either experienced religious prejudice while at work or knew of a coworker who had been subjected to some form of discriminatory conduct. Regardless of their religion, 55 percent of the workers surveyed believed that religious bias and discrimination commonly occur in the workplace.[9]

Title VII bars religious discrimination in both the private and public sector, while the free exercise and establishment clauses of the First Amendment also perform that function in the public sector. The free exercise clause bars the government from interfering with the exercise of religion by governmental employees, while the establishment clause bars it from adopting any law "respecting the establishment of religion." Public-sector workers may also rely on the free speech clause of the First Amendment to gain protection for the religious activities they engage in while at work.

Now that religion has been thrust into the workplace—to an extent those living in previous eras could not have imagined—workers are emboldened to assert their legal rights to protect themselves from acts of discrimination—real or merely perceived—that threaten the way they express their religious beliefs in office or factory. Consequently, workplace religious disputes are now more likely to be resolved only after lengthy and contentious litigation. Court cases arising under Title VII and the First Amendment must be closely studied if we are to fully understand the difficulties that arise for employers and employees alike when they become involved in workplace religious disputes. The study of these cases will be the task of the readers of this book.

Students studying for admission to the bar acquire knowledge of the law through the "casebook method"—they learn the law by reading groups of court cases assembled in book form. In this work I employ a modified form of that method. I have selected court cases illustrating various aspects of religious employment disputes and have summarized them for the reader. By reviewing these case summaries, readers should gain an understanding of the basic legal concepts applicable to the resolution of these disputes and thus be equipped to undertake measures appropriate to the circumstances they themselves encounter in the workplace.

The modified form of the casebook method is not without its limitations. While law students read actual court cases, readers of this book will read case summaries. Nearly every judicial decision examines more than a few relevant issues, but we will generally focus on the single issue in the case that is central to the point of law under consideration. Quoting the exact language of the court is the best approach to gaining a correct understanding of its ruling, but quoting the court is generally not feasible when we are examining only one of the many issues it considered. In most instances, these circumstances require the relevant aspects of the opinion to be summarized rather than cited word for word. In the interest of accuracy, when summarizing a ruling, I have closely tracked the court's language whenever possible.

The second limitation of the modified form of the casebook method may, in some instances, lead to a bit of frustration for the readers—they may learn the law relevant to the court's determination, but they may not always learn the ultimate outcome of the case under discussion. Actual trials of religious discrimination cases occur less frequently than the public supposes. More frequently, legal claims alleging religious discrimination are settled by the parties to the dispute at some point in the litigation process, most often before the case reaches the trial stage. Because jury trials present substantial risks for employers, they generally attempt to avoid the courtroom and a sitting jury whenever possible. The motion for summary judgment affords the employer the opportunity to procure an early dismissal of a worker's case, thus avoiding a trial before a jury. A motion for summary judgment requires the court to assess the evidence that the employer and the worker intend to offer during the course of the trial so as to determine whether a genuine need for a trial actually exists. If the court finds that the evidence to be offered is insufficient to allow a jury to reach a verdict for the worker, the court will grant the employer's motion for summary judgment. At that point, the court dismisses the worker's complaint. Unless the worker appeals, the case is over. But on the other hand, if the court finds the worker's evidence to be sufficient, it will deny the employer's motion for summary judgment and direct the parties to proceed to trial. In those circumstances, more often than not, an employer will opt to settle the dispute rather than face a jury.

Employers nearly always require that secrecy be maintained in the settlement process, demanding as a term of settlement that its provisions not be published. Some of the cases discussed in this book end in that posture, and thus the reader does not learn the details of the settlement. As stated, this can be frustrating, but readers may be assured that in nearly all instances of this nature, the terms of settlement are favorable to the worker. To avoid a jury trial, an employer will often make a far more generous settlement proposal at this point in the litigation than it would have made earlier in the proceedings. Although we do not learn the details of the settlement, we may conclude that the worker emerged victorious.

This book has been written for laypersons and those lawyers who do not specialize in employment law. Every attempt has been made to eliminate technical language and legal jargon and to preclude immersion in legal intricacies and technical data having less than general application. In the discussion of areas where some technical knowledge of the law is required, emphasis has been placed on the law's general applicability without regard to its exceptions. The broad picture takes precedence over special circumstances that may be relevant only in a limited number of instances.

None of the disputes reviewed in this work would have arisen except for the fact that American workers possess the right under Title VII of the Civil Rights Act of 1964 and the Constitution's First Amendment to express their religious and spiritual values while present in the workplace. Those rights need not be left behind when one enters the workplace. A worker, however, may not run roughshod over the rights of other workers. The right to practice one's religion in the work area comes with limitations. That is the primary subject matter of this book—limitations. Under what circumstances is a worker limited in practicing his or her religious beliefs in the workplace? We will closely examine issues emanating from the presence of religious practice and expression in the American workplace and study the perceptions of the parties involved in the religious disputes that so often occur. With studies of this sort, perhaps the resolution of such disputes in the future may be accomplished with a greater degree of intelligence and with far less contention than has been the case to this time.

Part I

RELIGIOUS DISCRIMINATION IN THE WORKPLACE

1

Is There a Place for Religion in the Workplace?

Does religion have a place in the American workplace? It is often argued that the presence of religion in the office and other work areas creates conflict and division and that employers and their workers would be far better off if it were barred from the work environs. Unquestionably, religion in the workplace may be disruptive and divisive. But should it be excluded?

In every era religion has been present in the American workplace. The Social Gospel movement of the late nineteenth and early twentieth centuries was active in spreading religion beyond the church door to all areas of life, including the workplaces of its followers. This religious social reform movement, the product of liberal Protestant groups who argued that industrialized society could not be improved without the application of religious principles, looked to prominent church leaders for guidance in pursuing their common goals. One of the most prominent of those leaders was Walter Rauschenbusch.

Rauschenbusch, the son of a Lutheran missionary to German immigrants living in the United States, was ordained a Baptist minister in New York City, where in a Hell's Kitchen parish he first observed the social problems common to depressed city neighborhoods. After the publication of his books *Christianity and the Social Crisis*[1] and *Christianizing the Social Order*[2] he rapidly gained recognition as a major spokesperson for the Social Gospel movement in the United States.

In advocating an equitable society, this movement was responding to the inadequacies, foibles, and failings of rapidly developing industrialization and urbanization of the nineteenth century. It endeavored to secure social justice for the poor through labor reforms, such as the abolition of child labor, and the enactment of legislation providing for a living wage and a shorter workweek. Those advancing the cause of the social gospel argued that the power of the business world must be set off and countered by the power of the workers.

Rauschenbusch held that the purpose of all that Jesus Christ did, said, and hoped for was the social redemption of human life. "His death was his greatest act of social service. His cross was the climax of world evil and the turning point of history toward a definite and permanent emancipation and redemption of the race."[3] The key to Rauschenbusch's theology lay in his concept of the Kingdom of God. For him, this kingdom was not located in some place called heaven. Rather, he viewed it as the "immanence of God in human life and in the interconnected, interacting, interdependent nature of the entire human species."[4] Relying upon Christ's proclamation in the Lord's Prayer, "Thy will be done on earth as it is in heaven," he maintained that the Kingdom of God was concerned not only with the immortal souls of men and women but also with their bodies, their homes, and their workplaces. Thus those who provided the fundamental necessities of human life were veritable ministers of God.[5]

Such an understanding of the Kingdom of God demanded a change in the role of the Christian Church. Whereas the chief purpose of the church in times past had been the salvation of souls, Rauschenbusch contended that societal needs required the church to focus more directly on group rather than individual issues, on social rather than personal matters:

> Our business is to make over an antiquated and immoral economic system; to get rid of laws, customs, maxims, and philosophies inherited from an evil

despotic past; to create just and brotherly relations between great groups and classes of society; and thus to lay a social foundation on which modern men individually can live and work in a fashion that will not outrage all the better elements in them. Our inherited Christian faith deals with individuals; our present task deals with society.[6]

Thus the Social Gospel movement conceived of Christian doctrine in social terms; Christ's ethical teachings should be directed to finding solutions to societal problems. The church must take the side of the people and heed their demands for social justice. It should focus on the solution of problems that would lead to the betterment of society, on issues pertaining to poverty, unemployment, education, health care, and civil rights. For advocates of the social gospel, Christianizing the social order meant humanizing it in the highest sense.[7] "A mature social Christian comes closer to the likeness of Jesus Christ than any other type [of Christian]."[8] Even if religion had never before made its presence known in the workplace, the Social Gospel movement and the teachings of Walter Rauschenbusch now convinced workers that they were free—indeed, compelled—to introduce religious beliefs to their coworkers.

At about the same time that the Social Gospel movement was gaining momentum in the United States, the Catholic Church disseminated Pope Leo III's 1891 encyclical, *Rerum Novarum* (*The Condition of Labor*), which had much in common with the teachings of the Social Gospel movement. The pope spoke of the dignity of work and workers, of the special consideration that must be provided the poor and the marginalized, and of workers' right to a just wage.

Jewish workers arrived in the American workplace with similar traditions. Judaism taught that the law, originally given by God, bound rulers as well as the ruled, a small step from holding that it also bound the rich as well as the poor, employers as well as employees. Other religious beliefs similarly entered the American workplace when the forces released by globalization and massive immigration initiated contact between Americans and deeply ingrained religious cultures of other parts of the world, and this in turn led to the appearance at American work sites of beliefs held by adherents of Islamic, Buddhist, Hindu, and other belief systems.

Another religious force that has more recently entered the workplace originated with Christians belonging to evangelical churches. A 2001 survey showed that a huge segment of the American population—24 percent—identify themselves as evangelical Christians.[9] More than half of the evangelicals report that their religious faith is "the most important influence" in their lives.[10] Their worldview is vastly different from that of the rest of the American populace. Eighty-six percent of evangelicals believe that the Bible is the actual word of God and should be taken literally, and nearly all of those also believe that Satan opposes religion in public life. More important for our purposes, over 60 percent of the evangelical followers believe they are required to share their faith with others and spread the word of God wherever possible.[11] "Wherever possible," of course, includes the workplace.

The evangelical belief in and dedication to spreading the faith parallels in some respects the traditional concept of mission, an indispensable aspect of Christianity. Theologian David Bosch defines "mission" as "that dimension of our faith that refuses to accept reality as it is and aims at changing it."[12] Undoubtedly, the Christian worker who engages in the process of transforming reality will aim at changing the workplace as well.

The Faith at Work movement is still another force that has made its presence felt in the workplace. As described by Professor David W. Miller of the Yale Divinity School, this movement has arisen largely outside the churches and has emerged as a loosely connected network of laypersons who "focus on integrating spirituality and work." The result has been the growth of a plethora of voluntary associations that shun doctrinal disputes and transcend denominational boundaries "to focus on a host of issues, including identity, meaning, purpose, calling, discipleship, witness, evangelization, and transformation in and of the business world."

> What draws most people to the Faith at Work movement is the desire to live an integrated life, where faith teachings and workplace practices are aligned. Workers of all types, whether data entry clerks or senior executives, are no longer content to leave their souls in the parking lot. Business people today want to find moral meaning and purpose in their work. Regardless of job level or salary, today's employees want their work to be more than just a way to put bread on the table and pay the rent.... Most people involved in the...movement refuse to accept marketplace reality as it is; they wish to change or transform it in some fashion, driven by the teachings of their faith.[13]

The Faith at Work movement is composed of more than 1,200 groups, institutions, and organizations located throughout the country.[14]

Other forces that have introduced religion to the workplace are also lay-initiated. As noted, many workers believe that faith and work are not meant to stand separately, and they have no desire to isolate their home lives from their work lives. This may be true particularly of younger workers who appear less willing to compartmentalize their lives. Here again is Professor Miller: "Business people want the ability to bring their whole selves to work—mind, body, and soul—and are no longer satisfied with sacrificing their core identities or being mere cogs in the machine, nor do they want a disconnected spirituality."[15] For many workers the workplace has become a community where they endeavor to practice their faith while striving, as in church and home, to resolve their emotional and spiritual problems.

Some workers attempt to achieve an integration of faith and work by applying their ethical tenets to workplace situations. Those with evangelical leanings see their work sites as places to spread the faith, while those who tend to experience work in spiritual terms search for greater meaning and purpose in their work lives. But these lay-initiated endeavors have one thing in common—they seek to remove the moral conflicts that religious workers perceive as existing between the claims of their faith and the demands of their work.[16]

Unquestionably, the introduction of religion to the workplace creates conflict. Christian workers, motivated by their religious beliefs to spread the faith among their fellow workers, frequently confront strongly voiced opposition from both non-Christian and Christian coworkers. Isolated instances of such conflicts are often overlooked, but on some occasions they may lead to the disruption of workplace procedures and practices. A worker's persistent overtures to change one's way of life may be perceived by coworkers as religious proselytization, often resulting in heated responses.

A worker subjected to a coworker's proselytizing initiatives may ask his or her employer to bar such conduct. Such a request creates a dilemma for the employer for which there exists no ready solution. If the employer accedes to the worker's request and directs the proselytizer to desist from such conduct, the employer may then be charged with harassment and failure to accommodate the proselytizer's religious beliefs. On the other hand, if the employer decides not to interfere with such conduct, the worker subjected to proselytization may charge the employer with religious discrimination.

Any concession by an employer to a worker engaged in religious activities may be considered discriminatory by other workers. Increasing

cultural and racial diversity in the American workplace will undoubtedly cause even greater conflict. Employers therefore must travel an ever-
narrowing path when resolving workplace religious disputes.

Acceding to employee demands to bar expressions of religious faith in
the workplace may create still other problems for an employer. Employers frequently perceive religious workers as more productive than nonreligious workers, and they consider it a good business practice to hire them.
Moreover, according to a 2003 survey, a growing number of employers believe that the existence of a religiously diversified workforce improves the
corporate culture, attracts new workers, improves client relations, and is
generally a favorable development for their companies.[17] Any action undertaken by an employer opposing the religious activities of its employees
may thus prove counterproductive.

The worldview favored by evangelical workers may also give rise to
workplace conflict. Assertions that the Bible should be taken literally, that
Satan opposes religion in public life, and that workers are bound to share
their faith with their coworkers inevitably engender opposition, often culminating in bitter conflict among workers. Conflict occurring as a consequence
of the expression of religious belief has led to demands that employers act
to bar all religious practices and expressions of religious content from the
workplace. Taking such a step would, however, be not only wholly imprac-
ticable but also unlawful. General legal principles regarding discrimination
and harassment in matters of religious conduct in the workplace are the
same as those that apply to similar disputes involving race, sex, or national
origin. Religion in the workplace, therefore, is here to stay.

Conflicts evolving from religious conduct in the workplace are best resolved at the corporate level, before the involved parties proceed to litigation. Unfortunately, such efforts often prove unsuccessful. Although
the courts are not the best arbiters of these conflicts, judicial proceedings
provide an indispensable guide for those who are required to deal with
such problems on the corporate level. The body of law that has developed
as a consequence of these proceedings is the subject of the chapters that
follow.

2

WHAT IS RELIGION AS DEFINED
BY LAW?

What is religion? This is not merely a rhetorical question. In a surprising number of cases, courts have been called upon to decide whether particular practices are in fact religious, thus requiring the law's protection. As an example, Christopher Lee Peterson was a member of the World Church of the Creator. Pursuant to a system of beliefs referred to as "Creativity," church members were taught that all people of color are "savage" and intent upon mongrelizing the white race, that African Americans are subhuman and should be sent back to Africa, that the Jews control the nation and have been responsible for instigating all wars within the past one hundred years, and that the Holocaust never occurred, but even if it did, Nazi Germany did the world a great favor. This church was established solely for the survival, expansion, and advancement of the white race and stated as its basic belief that "what is good for the White Race is the highest virtue, and what is bad for the White Race is the ultimate sin." Although it considered itself a religion, it did not espouse a belief in God or in any sort of Supreme Being.

Peterson, a minister in the church, supported himself and his family by working for Wilmur Communications as a day-room manager, a position that entailed the supervision of eight employees, three of whom were not white. In March 2000, an article appeared in the Sunday edition of the *Milwaukee Journal Sentinel* dealing with the World Church of the Creator and exhibiting a photograph of Peterson wearing a T-shirt bearing the picture of a man who had recently targeted African American, Jewish, and Asian people in a two-day shooting spree in Indiana. When Peterson arrived for work the day after the publication of the article, he was suspended and demoted to a lower-paying position having no supervisory duties. The company's letter that relieved Peterson of his supervisory functions read in part:

> On Sunday...an article appeared in the Milwaukee Journal Sentinel disclosing that you were a member of the World Church of the Creator, a White supremacist political organization. On Monday...the information in the newspaper was known by everyone in our office. Our office has three...employees who are not white.... As a supervisor, it is your responsibility to train, evaluate, and supervise [these workers]. Our employees cannot have confidence in the objectivity of your training, evaluation, or supervision when you must compare Whites to non-Whites. Because the company, present employees, or future job applicants cannot be sure of your objectivity, you can no longer be a supervisor and you are hereby notified of your demotion.

Peterson then filed suit against Wilmur Communications alleging that it had demoted him because of his religious beliefs in violation of Title VII of the Civil Rights Act of 1964.[1]

In the chapters that follow, Title VII will be examined in some detail, but the bare essentials of this federal legislation are set forth here so that the reader may understand the court's ruling in the *Peterson* case. Title VII makes it unlawful for an employer to discriminate against an individual with respect to compensation, terms, conditions, or privileges of employment because of the individual's race, color, sex, national origin, or religion. The statute defines religion to include "all aspects of religious observance and practice as well as belief," and it imposes upon an employer an affirmative duty to reasonably accommodate "the religious observances and practices of its employees unless such accommodation causes undue hardship" to the conduct of the employer's business.[2]

The first order of business in cases such as Peterson's is for the plaintiff to establish that his beliefs constitute a religion. This is an issue the courts have traditionally found difficult to resolve. As one court put it, "[F]ew tasks that confront a court require more circumspection than that of determining whether a particular set of ideas constitutes a religion."[3] In 1990 the Supreme Court commented that theological pronouncements that exceed the knowledge and expertise of the court must always be avoided.[4]

Over time, the courts have devised a test to determine whether a specified set of beliefs actually constitutes a religion. The test requires the court to determine whether the plaintiff's beliefs actually function as a "religion" in his or her life. Does that person's beliefs occupy the same place in his or her life as an orthodox belief in God holds in the life of a member of one of the traditional religions? In answering that question, the Supreme Court has instructed the courts to give "great weight" to the plaintiff's own characterization of those beliefs.[5]

Religious beliefs need not be generally acceptable, logical, consistent, or even comprehensible to others.[6] Moreover, to be religious under this test, a belief system need not be based on a concept of God,[7] as the courts have consistently refused to restrict the law's protections to mainstream and organized religious institutions. In the end, Peterson had little to prove— only that his beliefs were sincerely held and that they occupied a place in his life similar to the place that religious beliefs held in the lives of his Catholic, Protestant, Jewish, or Muslim coworkers.

Unquestionably, Peterson's beliefs were sincerely held. He stated as much, and his employer had no contrary evidence to offer the court. The court then turned to the second issue. Did the World Church of the Creator play a central role in Peterson's life? Did his belief in this church and its teachings occupy a place in his life parallel to that held by a belief in God by believers of one of the traditional churches? Because Peterson had served as a minister in the World Church of the Creator for more than three years, the court closely examined the oath he had taken at the time of his elevation to the ministry:

> I hereby affirm my undying loyalty to the White Race and the World Church of the Creator ...; that I will fervently promote the Creed and Program of Creativity as long as I live ...; that the World Church of the Creator is the only pro-White organization of which I am a member so that my

energies may not be diverted ...; and lastly, that I will aggressively convert others to our Faith and build my own ministry.

After Peterson told the court that he tried to put the teachings of Creativity into practice every day of his life, the court ruled that the beliefs of the World Church of the Creator occupied a place in his life similar to the position that a belief in God occupied in the lives of members of mainstream religions. Thus Creativity functioned as a religion for Peterson.

This seemed to have ended the matter, but Wilmur's attorneys were not yet finished. They argued that the World Church of the Creator could not be considered a religion because it was similar to other white supremacist groups that courts had previously found to be political rather than religious organizations. One of those groups was the Ku Klux Klan.

Several courts, confronted with the claim that the KKK was a religious organization, had ruled that the racist and anti-Semitic ideology proclaimed by the KKK assumed a narrow temporal and political character inconsistent with religious teaching. Those courts held that the KKK was a political and social organization, not a religion.[8]

The *Peterson* court agreed that the World Church of the Creator, as demonstrated by its doctrines, shared the white supremacist positions of the KKK, but it noted that while these doctrines might in some respects be categorized as political, they might also be considered by some as religious. Peterson's beliefs could very well be thought of as political by others and still function as religious beliefs for him. But Wilmur's lawyer also argued that Creativity's assumptions could not be religious because they were immoral and unethical. The court again sided with Peterson:

> Creativity teaches that followers should live their lives according to what will best foster the advancement of white people and the denigration of all others. This precept, although simplistic and repugnant to the notions of equality...is a means for determining right from wrong.... Plaintiff has shown that Creativity functions as religion in his life; thus Creativity is for him a religion regardless of whether it espouses goodness or evil.

The court then proceeded to rule that Peterson had been demoted solely because of his religious beliefs and granted judgment in his favor.[9]

The court's rulings in this case are difficult to accept. They are contrary to traditional conceptions of religion, and the repugnant and offensive beliefs promulgated by Peterson and his church lead most of us to conclusions rejected by the court. Wilmur Communications not only suffered defeat in this litigation but was forced into a hopeless position. In effect, the court's decision compelled Wilmur to employ an individual, who had adopted and espoused an extremist, racist ideology, to supervise a multiracial staff of workers. After this decision, Wilmur would have no legal recourse if Peterson's racist theories led to disruption in its workplace. Moreover, the decision left the company vulnerable to legal action by its African American employees, who undoubtedly could successfully allege that a racist supervisor, employed by the company, had unlawfully discriminated against them. This case records a state of affairs we will find too often in this book: the litigation of a workplace religious dispute may culminate in an unjust conclusion.

The *Peterson* case is nonetheless noteworthy as it points up a basic legal premise. In nearly all instances, the courts will reject efforts to denominate an individual's personal beliefs as nonreligious. The fact that no religious group accepts such beliefs is not decisive. Rather, the courts have endeavored to determine the issue by asking a single question: Do the person's beliefs occupy the same place in his or her life as an orthodox belief in God holds in the life of a member of one of the traditional religions? Answering that question is not always a simple matter, but the courts have refused to retreat from the rulings in the *Peterson* case.

William Frazee refused a temporary retail position because the job would have required him to work on Sundays. He then applied for unemployment benefits, but his application was denied because, as the Illinois authorities announced, a refusal to accept a position on account of religious conviction must be based upon "some tenets or dogma accepted by...some church, sect, or denomination," and a refusal based solely on an individual's personal belief is irrelevant. Therefore, the Illinois officials ruled, Frazee's contention that as a Christian he believed it wrong to work on Sunday was not enough. As you might expect, this reasoning did not sit well with the Supreme Court, which dismissed the Illinois ruling with one sentence:

Undoubtedly, membership in an organized religious denomination, especially one with a specific tenet forbidding members to work on Sunday, would simplify the problem of identifying sincerely held religious beliefs, but we reject the notion that to claim the protection of the [law], one must be responding to the commands of a particular religious organization.[10]

Although the courts have steadfastly held to the position that legal protection for personally held nonreligious beliefs must be denied, they rarely enter the "judicial thicket" that would require them to distinguish between a personal or nonreligious belief and a religious belief.

In *Thomas v. Review Board of the Indiana Employment Security Division,* the Supreme Court held that a person's constitutional right to the free exercise of religion is not limited to the beliefs shared by all members of that person's religious sect. Thomas, a Jehovah's Witness, worked for Blaw-Knox Foundry & Machinery Co. in its roll foundry department, which fabricated sheet steel for various industrial uses. About a year after Thomas began his employment, Blaw-Knox closed its roll foundry department and transferred Thomas to a department that produced turrets for military tanks. Once Thomas realized that his new job assignment was weapons-related, he resigned his position because, as he later testified, his religious beliefs barred him from participating in the production of war materials. After leaving the employ of Blaw-Knox, Thomas applied for unemployment compensation benefits, but his application was denied on the ground that he had quit his job voluntarily for personal reasons. The Indiana Supreme Court later held that although Thomas's reasons for leaving his employment were described by him as religious, the religious basis of his beliefs was unclear since he was unable to articulate his beliefs precisely; thus it appeared that he had merely made a personal philosophical choice rather than a judgment based on religious conviction.

When the case finally reached the United States Supreme Court, the Court noted that the Indiana court had given significant weight to the fact that another Jehovah's Witness worker employed by Blaw-Knox had testified that he had suffered no religious scruples about working on tank turrets. But, the court noted, this is not the proper test:

> The guarantee of free exercise [of religion] is not limited to beliefs which are shared by all of the members of a religious sect. Particularly in this sensitive area, it is not within the judicial competence to inquire whether [Thomas] or his fellow worker more correctly perceived the commands of their common faith. Courts are not arbiters of scriptural interpretation.

The narrow function of a court in circumstances such as these is to determine whether the worker terminated his employment because of an honest conviction that such work was forbidden by his religion. Unquestionably, Thomas's religious convictions were honestly held, and thus his application for unemployment benefits should not have been denied by the Indiana authorities.[11]

The Equal Employment Opportunity Commission has also wrestled with this issue and has promulgated guidelines that in general reflect the court rulings we have just considered. The commission has stated that it will not confine the definition of religious practices "to theistic concepts or to traditional religious concepts" but instead will define them to include "moral or ethical beliefs as to what is right or wrong" that are held by a person "with the strength of traditional views."[12] EEOC guidelines also provide that "the fact that no religious group espouses [an individual's personal] beliefs or the fact that the religious group to which the individual professes to belong may not accept such belief will not determine whether the belief is a religious belief [of that individual]."[13]

Because each individual articulates his beliefs in a manner unique to that person, an individual's claim that his beliefs constitute an element of his religious faith must be given great weight. Religious experiences real to some may be incomprehensible to others. But the Supreme Court has clearly specified that the judiciary is not free to reject a belief merely because it is considered incomprehensible. Rather, the task of a court is to decide whether a belief is sincerely held and whether it is, in that person's general scheme of things, religious.[14]

The courts, however, rarely question the sincerity of an individual's beliefs. If a plaintiff testifies that these beliefs are sincerely held, that ordinarily ends the matter. Even in the cases of an outrageous set of beliefs, such as those of Christopher Lee Peterson, the courts nearly always refrain from questioning their sincerity. There is one set of circumstances, however, where the courts are more apt to cast aside their reluctance to enter into an examination of the sincerity of an individual's beliefs, and that is where the evidence tends to show that the employee acted in a manner clearly inconsistent with his professed beliefs.[15]

Gwendolyn Cooper, a Seventh-day Adventist, refused to work on Saturday, the day she observed the Sabbath. Cooper worked for Oak Rubber Company, a manufacturer of industrial vinyl gloves. Oak operated six production machines around the clock. Each machine required three shifts of workers, composed of six glove strippers and one packer. The machines operated continuously, not stopping for employee breaks or lunch periods, and Oak maintained a staff of workers to cover those on break or lunch as well as those absent from work or on vacation. In order to alleviate problems caused by absences from work, Oak instituted a point system that penalized workers for unexcused absences. The accumulation of points led first to a warning, then to suspension, and ultimately to termination.

Oak hired Cooper as a glove stripper to work the night shift. Nine years after her hire, she attended her first Seventh-day Adventist service and thereafter regularly attended those services. Although Cooper knew that her church prohibited all work from sundown on Friday until sundown on Saturday, she continued to work on Saturdays whenever Oak required her attendance on those days. About three years later, she exercised her seniority rights to transfer to the day shift. Coincidentally, after one day in her new position she was notified she would be required to work the upcoming Saturday. She immediately notified her supervisor that because of her religious beliefs, she would be unable to work on Saturdays. As a result of her subsequent absences from Saturday work, Cooper began to accumulate penalty points that eventually would lead to her termination. When her point total was about to reach a critical level, Cooper resigned and sued Oak for religious discrimination, alleging that she had been forced to resign because of her adherence to religious beliefs that barred work on the Sabbath.

In the ensuing litigation, Oak centered its defense to Cooper's discrimination charge on its allegation that she did not sincerely hold any religious belief that prevented her from working on Saturdays. Oak contended that Cooper could not have sincerely held such a belief since she continued to work on Saturdays after she joined the Seventh-day Adventist Church. Cooper countered by testifying that her religious beliefs had grown more fervent in the years after she joined the church, and ultimately she concluded she no longer could work on her Sabbath. Oak was unable to contest that testimony, and since Cooper's later actions were entirely consistent with her expressed beliefs, the court ruled that her religious beliefs were sincerely held.[16]

The court in this case undertook the initial step of questioning the sincerity of Cooper's beliefs. Instead of accepting without question her expressions of sincerity, the court looked to the underlying facts to determine whether her actions were consistent with her beliefs. Ultimately, it accepted Cooper's testimony that her faith had deepened during the course of her employment, thus compelling her to reconsider her Sabbath obligations. The court thus had no alternative but to reject Oak's attack on the sincerity of her beliefs.

In another case involving an employee's refusal to work on the Sabbath, the terminated worker sued his employer, and again the sincerity of the worker's belief was placed in issue. This time the challenge to the worker's sincerity was based on evidence that after his termination, he had obtained new employment and had acquiesced to the demands of the new employer that he work on Saturdays. The worker explained, however, that this change in heart regarding Saturday work followed upon his loss of faith. The court rejected the employer's position that actions occurring after the worker was discharged were relevant to a determination of issues arising prior to the discharge. It then ruled that the worker's actions before his termination were wholly consistent with his expressed religious beliefs, and it rejected the employer's position.[17]

A claimed loss or change in intensity of faith has not always worked in the employee's favor. When Mirtis Hansard was fired because he refused to work on Sundays, he claimed that his religious conviction requiring him not to work on Sundays was "lifelong," and although he admitted that he had not always acted in accordance with that conviction, he testified that his religious beliefs had recently been revived after a near-miraculous recovery of his ill son. Even then Hansard had not always refused to work on Sundays. As he explained it, he "just didn't have the faith" on those occasions. The court had little difficulty in finding that Hansard's reliance on his religious beliefs appeared to be grounded on convenience rather than conviction, and it dismissed his case.[18]

Some courts refuse to consider workplace conduct as evidence of the sincerity or lack of sincerity of a worker's religious convictions. For example, a Jewish worker was fired because he insisted upon absenting himself from work to attend Yom Kippur services. When he sued for religious discrimination, his employer asked the court to consider the depth of the worker's religious conviction, but the court declined:

> The court will not closely scrutinize the extent to which plaintiff celebrated other Jewish holidays or his knowledge about Judaism in general. In order

for plaintiff to succeed on his claim, it is not necessary that this court find plaintiff to be devout in his observance of all aspects of Judaism. It is enough that plaintiff has attended Yom Kippur services in the past and wanted to attend [again].[19]

Even a court reluctant to question the sincerity of a worker's religious beliefs will make certain that the assertion of such beliefs is bona fide. Moreover, a court may question a worker's motivation in making the assertion. Both those issues arose in the religious discrimination case alleged by Mary Tiano against her former employer, Dillard Department Stores, located in Phoenix.

Tiano, a salesperson in the women's shoe department, was considered a productive employee—a "pacesetter"—because her sales exceeded $200,000 per year. Tiano was a devout Catholic, and, as she testified, her religion played a significant role in her life. In late August of 1988, she learned of a pilgrimage to Medjugorje, Yugoslavia, that was scheduled to take place in mid-October of that year. This piqued her interest as she was aware that several persons had claimed that visions of the Virgin Mary had appeared to them in Medjugorje, although she also knew that the Catholic Church had not designated Medjugorje as an official pilgrimage site of the church. She later testified that at the time she learned of the pilgrimage she experienced "a calling from God" to participate in it: "I felt I was called to go....I felt that from deep in my heart that I was called. I had to be there at that time. I had to go." When asked if she could have gone at another time, she responded, "No."

Tiano met with her supervisor and requested unpaid leave to travel with the October pilgrimage. For a number of reasons, her request was denied, including the fact that her presence on the sales floor was required during an anniversary sale that Dillard had scheduled for October. Tiano's supervisor advised her that if she persisted in her intention to absent herself from work so as to participate in the pilgrimage, she would not have a job when she returned. Tiano, claiming that Dillard was discriminating against her, departed with the pilgrimage.

In Tiano's absence her supervisor was forced to spend a significant amount of time on the sales floor as the staff was unable to cope with increased customer traffic during the course of the October sale. When Tiano returned from the pilgrimage, she was advised that Dillard considered her employment to have been voluntarily ended. Tiano then sued Dillard, alleging it had terminated her because she had attended a religious pilgrimage.

Tiano claimed that her religious beliefs required her to go to Medjugorje. But the court questioned whether her calling from God required her presence in Medjugorje *in October, 1988?* Was she called by God to go to Medjugorje on pilgrimage, or was she called to go to Medjugorje on that particular pilgrimage? The only evidence offered by Tiano to establish the timing of the pilgrimage was her own testimony. "I felt that from deep in my heart that I was called. I had to be there at that time. I had to go." But she offered no corroborating evidence to support her claim that she had to join that particular pilgrimage. As the court noted, she offered no testimony that visions of the Virgin Mary were expected to occur at that time or that her church advocated her attendance at the time of this pilgrimage rather than at another time.

Much of the other evidence introduced in the case appeared to contradict Tiano's testimony. First, it was learned that she had complained about religious discrimination only after she learned that her flight ticket for the pilgrimage was nonrefundable. Second, her friend and pilgrimage companion testified that she and Tiano had decided on that particular pilgrimage after they obtained information about the trip, discussed it, and concluded that it would be an interesting venture. She also testified that Tiano had never supplied a specific reason for her desire to go on that particular pilgrimage: "No, not a definite reason. I don't recall a definite reason; just [that] we both had a strong desire to go."

Thus the friend's testimony suggested that the timing of the trip was a personal preference, not an element of a bona fide religious belief. Both women talked about the trip and thought it would be an "interesting venture," hardly a religious calling. Since other pilgrimages were scheduled, Tiano could have selected one of them that would not have conflicted with her employment duties. In light of this evidence, the court dismissed her claim of religious discrimination.[20]

On first examination, the court in the *Tiano* case appears to have taken a radical turn. Unlike the courts in cases cited earlier in this chapter, the *Tiano* court questioned the sincerity of her religious beliefs. However, a major element absent from the other cases drove the court in that direction. Tiano failed to present the court with a complete and accurate description of her beliefs. She failed to advise the court that she might very well have been motivated to attend the October pilgrimage not only because of a calling from God but also because she would have been unable to recover the cost of her airline ticket if she had canceled the trip. Second, her friend's testimony differed markedly from Tiano's representations that her calling from God required her to travel to Medjugorje at that particular time. Faced with these facts, the court had no alternative but to question the sincerity of Tiano's religious beliefs, and this led to a dismissal of her religious discrimination claim.

The cases discussed in this chapter clearly show that historically courts have rarely disputed a worker's assertion that she acted on the basis of a religious belief. They are reluctant to question a worker's belief system even if it is offensive or not readily acceptable by others. Personal preferences, however, are not considered religious beliefs. Except when workers are shown to have failed to act consistently in accordance with their beliefs, the courts have generally assumed that those beliefs are sincerely held and, accordingly, have granted them the protection of the law.

3

Religious Discrimination and the Civil Rights Act of 1964

After experiencing adversity in the workplace, a worker who decides to seek legal relief generally frames a legal complaint that falls within the parameters of Title VII of the Civil Rights Act of 1964.

In 1963 President John F. Kennedy proposed civil rights legislation barring discrimination in places of public accommodation, in voting rights, in the nation's schools, and in employment, and the following year Congress passed and President Lyndon Johnson signed into law the Civil Rights Act of 1964. Title VII of the act proscribes discrimination in employment and endeavors to achieve true equality in the American workplace by eliminating discriminatory employer practices. Title VII provides:

> It shall be an unlawful employment practice for an employer:
> (1) to fail or refuse to hire or to discharge any individual, or otherwise discriminate against any individual with respect to his [or her] compensation, terms, conditions, or privileges of employment, because of such individual's race, color, religion, sex, or national origin; or

(2) to limit, segregate, or classify his [or her] employees or applicants for employment in any way which would deprive or tend to deprive any individual of employment opportunities or otherwise adversely affect his [or her] status as an employee, because of such individual's race, color, sex, religion, or national origin.[1]

At the time of the adoption of Title VII, Congress also created the Equal Employment Opportunity Commission (EEOC) to administer the title and process claims made pursuant to its provisions. Initially most of the claims filed with the EEOC alleged acts of racial discrimination, but with the passage of time, increasing numbers of sex, national origin, and religious claims have been lodged with the commission. In recent years the number of religious discrimination charges filed with the EEOC has increased dramatically. In contrast, the filing of race and sex discrimination charges, while remaining far more numerous than religious claims, have declined rather than increased.[2] Since those trends appear to be holding,[3] experts in this area of the law predict that conflicts involving religion in the workplace will in the years to come continue to plague workers and their employers.[4]

The primary reasons for the continuing growth in religious discrimination claims were mentioned in the Introduction: (1) the desire of workers to practice and apply their religious beliefs at work, (2) the "spread the faith" rationale of evangelical Christians, (3) the aging of the workforce, (4) the growth of a more diversified workforce, and (5) the expanded public role of religious experience. For these reasons it appears that the workplace will continue to be more religiously oriented, and that conflicts will continue to proliferate as a result.

A 2003 survey disclosed that although up to 75 percent of American workers believe they have been subjected to some form of religious bias at work, they have chosen to suffer in silence rather than report those incidents.[5] It appears certain that as greater numbers of workers find themselves involved in religious conflicts, they will be less inclined to remain silent, and this will lead to a still greater expansion in the filings of EEOC religious discrimination complaints.

As earlier noted, workers who elect to sue their employers for damages suffered as a consequence of adverse employment actions generally rely upon Title VII as the legal basis for claims asserted against their employers.

Because Title VII provides workers with basic protections against acts of religious discrimination, it is incumbent upon all workers who believe they have been subjected to acts of religious bias to attain a general understanding of its provisions.

Title VII's bans against acts of discrimination based on a person's race, sex, or national origin relate to particular classes of workers, such as African Americans, women, and Latinos, whereas its ban against religious discrimination applies to all workers, regardless of their race, sex, or national origin. Title VII obligates an employer to act in a specified manner in two designated areas. First, an employer must eliminate all religious discriminatory animus from employment decisions involving the hiring, promotion, layoff, transfer, discipline, job assignment, compensation, discharge, and other working conditions of its employees. Second, it must reasonably accommodate workers who notify it of the existence of a conflict between their religious observances and practices and the employer's work rules and directives, unless in doing so it would incur an undue hardship. At this point we will examine the employer's first obligation to its workers, reserving for later discussion its obligation to accommodate a worker's beliefs and practices (chapters 15–17).

A worker alleging workplace religious discrimination may establish a Title VII claim by submitting direct or indirect evidence of the employer's discriminatory intent in advancing an employment decision adverse to the worker's interests. In the majority of cases an employer manages to conceal its religious prejudice, and thus it remains wholly or partially hidden from the view of the worker. To successfully establish a legal claim where there is no direct evidence of prejudice, the complaining worker must rely on indirect evidence of the employer's discriminatory bias.

There are exceptions, however: in rare circumstances an employer may make no attempt to conceal its religious prejudice. Those were the circumstances that confronted Wallace Weiss when he was subjected to acts of religious discrimination by a supervisor and one of his coworkers. Weiss, who was Jewish, was employed as a research analyst by the U.S. Defense Logistics Agency (Logistics). His supervisor, who was not Jewish, was not aware at the time he hired Weiss that he was Jewish. After his hire, Weiss was the only Jew working in the Logistics office.

Soon after Weiss started working at the agency, his supervisor and a coworker openly used religious slurs in his presence. They referred to him as the "resident Jew," "Jew faggot," and "rich Jew" and daily taunted him, accusing the Jews of having killed Christ. Although continuously subjected to anti-Semitic remarks of that nature, Weiss still achieved high performance evaluations and, as a consequence, salary increases.

After suffering in silence for many months, he developed stress and anxiety-related disorders. Ultimately, after deciding that enough was enough, he complained to company executives about the anti-Semitic remarks. When his supervisor learned of those complaints, he immediately changed course, stopping the remarks and making certain that the coworker did also. His prejudice against Jews, however, resurfaced in another mode. He severely criticized Weiss's job performance, gave him unreasonably difficult assignments, unfairly blamed him for delays in the completion of work projects, and subsequently lowered his job performance evaluation.

Although the agency's executive personnel were aware of these occurrences, they neither ordered disciplinary action taken against Weiss's supervisor nor directed him to cease his harassing conduct, and even though they could have readily arranged Weiss's transfer to another supervisor, they declined to take that step. As Weiss's anxiety-related disorders intensified, his job performance deteriorated, and eventually he was fired. Weiss then sued Logistics for religious discrimination under Title VII.

An occasional offensive religious epithet most often will not rise to the level justifying a Title VII claim. But when a worker is repeatedly subjected to demeaning and offensive religious commentary, the conditions of his employment are necessarily altered, and thus this type of conduct almost always gives rise to a valid discrimination claim against the employer. The Logistics executives took no action to eliminate religious discriminatory animus from Weiss's work environment or from decisions made with respect to his working conditions. They simply ignored his complaints. After considering this evidence, the court ruled that the supervisor's conduct violated Weiss's right to work in an environment governed by the nondiscriminatory terms and conditions of employment guaranteed by Title VII.[6]

The offensive work conditions Weiss experienced were directly and flagrantly imposed upon him, allowing no conclusion other than that he had been subjected to conduct proscribed by Title VII. In other cases, however, the evidence of discriminatory bias is generally less direct. A case in point involved Paul Rosen's discrimination claims against his employer, the Drug Enforcement Administration (DEA).

Rosen was offered a position as a DEA special agent, contingent on successful completion of a twelve-week training program. A resident of New York, he was sent to the DEA's training center in Georgia and was assigned to participate in one of the first activities in the training program, an exercise that required him to drive around a track at high speed while executing a series of turns. Rosen was later advised he had failed the exercise and consequently would be required to attend a remedial training program.

The remedial driving session consisted of two hours of instruction and a demonstration of proper driving skills and techniques. Rosen was then retested but again was informed he had failed. DEA officials decided that Rosen lacked basic driving skills, that further remedial training would be of no value, and that he should be dismissed from the training program. Soon afterward he was terminated.

According to the DEA, this was a case of an employee who was unable to demonstrate the skills required to handle the position for which he had been hired. But Rosen claimed that because he was Jewish, his instructors had prevented him from satisfying the driving test, and had it not been for their discriminatory conduct, he would have successfully completed the training program and been designated a special agent.

Rosen's version of what had occurred in Georgia differed markedly from that related by DEA officials. According to Rosen, a DEA training center counselor derisively stated that she did not like the name "Rosen" and that henceforth she would call him "Franklin." One of Rosen's instructors asked him whether he enjoyed lox and bagels and repeatedly referred to New York as "Rosenland." During the course of a lecture devoted to various cultural differences often encountered by special agents, an instructor noted in passing that Jews were concerned only about money. Still another instructor derogatorily referred to the Jewish residents of Miami. A fellow classmate called him "a half-breed Jew bastard" and uttered other religious slurs whenever their paths crossed. DEA counselors and instructors were aware of these slurs and insults and, in ignoring Rosen's objections, appeared to condone the classmate's attacks on him.

Rosen also disputed DEA's evaluation of his driving skills. Before applying for employment with the DEA, he had been a licensed driver in New York with a ten-year unblemished record. Moreover, during previous employment with the New York State Division of Parole, he had been involved in several high-speed auto chases, all without incident. Rosen claimed that the driving test he purportedly failed had been improperly administered by a DEA staff that was motivated by an anti-Jewish animus.

He filed a Title VII suit, claiming that the DEA had unlawfully terminated his employment because of his religious beliefs. DEA attorneys immediately filed a motion with the court asking it to dismiss Rosen's suit on the ground that he would be unable to prove at trial that religion had been a motivating factor in the termination of his employment. In ruling on the motion, the court observed, "Employment discrimination is often accomplished by discreet manipulations and hidden under a veil of self-declared innocence. An employer who discriminates is unlikely to leave a 'smoking gun'…attesting to a discriminatory intent." Noting that the indirect evidence elicited by Rosen pointed to the presence of an anti-Semitic bias among training center staff, the trial court denied DEA's motion to dismiss Rosen's suit.[7]

Rosen, unlike Wallace Weiss, was not subjected to flagrant anti-Semitic remarks. From the perspective of an outside viewer, his coworkers' remarks—certainly uttered in poor taste—might or might not have had their origin in a discriminatory animus. But when Rosen's instructors, acting in highly suspicious circumstances, claimed that he had failed the driving test, the discriminatory prejudice existent at the Georgia facility fully came into view.

As noted, direct evidence of religious discrimination, similar to that offered by Wallace Weiss, is most often unavailable to a Title VII complainant. Because of current legal and social sanctions, employers generally repress demonstrations of overt discrimination and bias. As a consequence, evidence of discriminatory conduct rarely appears in the form of an employer's direct and unequivocal admission that an adverse decision affecting the employee was based on his or her religious beliefs or practices. Even if a fellow worker of a complainant were to observe a discriminatory act committed by their employer and thus be in a position to offer the court direct eyewitness testimony of discriminatory intent, he may be reluctant to come forward to testify on behalf of the complainant for fear of jeopardizing his own job or future advancement. As a result, cases that turn on direct evidence of discrimination, such as the Weiss case, are clearly the exception rather than the norm. Discrimination cases are far more likely to involve claims supported solely by indirect evidence of religious discrimination.

When direct evidence of discrimination is unavailable, a Title VII plaintiff has no option other than to offer indirect evidence to support his or her claim. Indirect evidence, however, is generally less persuasive than direct evidence and at times may be insufficient to establish an employer's discriminatory intentions. Those were the circumstances that confronted Wamiq Sattar, a native of Bangladesh who came to this country for his college education, married an American Lutheran girl, and gave up his Muslim faith. Subsequently he began working as an engineer for Motorola in Illinois and was assigned to work under the supervision of Arif Pardesi, a native of Pakistan and an orthodox Muslim. According to Sattar, Pardesi issued him unwarranted negative performance reviews and caused other supervisors to follow suit. Sattar claimed that Pardesi was motivated to ruin his reputation at Motorola because of his abandonment of the Muslim faith and marriage to a Lutheran woman. When Sattar was later fired, he sued Motorola for religious discrimination, alleging Title VII violations.

Sattar buttressed his claim of religious bias by disclosing to the court that Pardesi had sent hundreds of e-mail messages containing passages from the Koran and the sayings of Muslim prophets to Muslim workers at the Motorola plant. Because Sattar was no longer a practicing Muslim, Pardesi soundly criticized him, warning him that he had no future at Motorola. In order to determine whether Sattar had lost his job because of Pardesi's religious bias, the court was required to closely examine these and all the other underlying facts.

Pardesi's first evaluation of Sattar's job performance was unsatisfactory, but a later review culminated in a satisfactory evaluation and a certificate of outstanding achievement. At that point Sattar was transferred to the supervision of David Yen, who later evaluated Sattar's performance as satisfactory but ranked him at the bottom of his division. Yen, acting in accordance with a plan previously initiated by Motorola to improve the performance of the lowest-rated employee in each of its divisions, placed Sattar under a performance improvement plan that required him to perform a series of projects while being evaluated at thirty-, sixty-, and ninety-day intervals. If he failed to satisfactorily perform these projects, the plan required his dismissal. Before completing the plan, Sattar was again transferred to another supervisor, who fired him at the end of the ninety-day period.

In order for Sattar to establish his Title VII claim against Motorola, he had to proffer either direct evidence of religious discrimination, as in the *Weiss* case, or indirect evidence of religious bias, as in the *Rosen* case. Since he had no direct evidence showing that he had been discharged because he had abandoned his Muslim faith, he had to rely solely on indirect evidence.

Before continuing our discussion of the *Satter* case, let us examine the rules of law that the courts have developed to prove the existence of discriminatory conduct solely through the submission of indirect evidence. Soon after congressional enactment of Title VII, the Supreme Court established ground rules for evaluating indirect evidence of discrimination. These rules were based on the Court's observation that an employer invariably responds to a charge of discriminatory behavior with the argument that the employment decision adversely affecting the worker was based upon a legitimate, nondiscriminatory reason. In those circumstances, if the worker is able to show that this reason simply is not credible or is based on false premises, the court may assume that the employer proffered such a reason only to cover up an unlawful motive.[8] The Supreme Court explained why it was justified in making such an assumption:

> We are willing to presume this largely because we know from our experience that more often than not people do not act in a totally arbitrary manner, without any underlying reasons, especially in a business setting. Thus when all legitimate reasons for an [employer's decision] have been eliminated as possible reasons for [its] actions, it is more likely than not the employer, who we generally assume acts only with *some* reason, based [its] decision on an impermissible consideration such as race [or religion].[9]

Thus the task of an attorney representing a Title VII claimant is to prove that the employer's stated reasons for its actions were false or not credible. He must show that the employer, rather than disclosing its real reasons, concealed them and that the reasons given were in fact pretextual, offered only to cover up discriminatory intent.

As thus prescribed by the Supreme Court, a Title VII claim may be established by submitting indirect evidence demonstrating that the employer offered a false explanation for its decision adversely affecting the plaintiff worker. A court or jury may infer from the falsity of that explanation that the employer intentionally dissembled or misrepresented the facts in order to cover up a discriminatory purpose.

Because the employer is in the best position to assert the actual reason for its decision, once the employer's explanation is shown to be false, the most likely alternative explanation is that the employer committed a discriminatory act. A court or jury, therefore, may infer the ultimate fact of discrimination from the falsity of the explanation.[10] A federal appellate court succinctly explained that rationale: "Resort to a pretextual explanation is like flight from the scene of a crime, evidence indicating consciousness of guilt, which is, of course, evidence of illegal conduct."[11] Thus, in a pretext case, the worker is required to prove that the employer opted not to express its true reasons for acting as it did, that the employer's reasons were "pretextual" and would not have been offered by the employer except to cover up its discriminatory intent.

Since nearly all Title VII religious discrimination claims depend upon the submission of indirect evidence, the primary focus of the trial of a religious discrimination lawsuit is directed to the employer's motivation in implementing the decision that adversely affected the employment status of the plaintiff worker. Are the reasons expressed by the employer for that decision its actual reasons, or was the decision motivated by an impermissible factor, such as the worker's religious practices or beliefs? Are the reasons advanced by the employer credible? Even if an employer's reasons did in fact serve as one of the bases for the decision adversely affecting the worker, was the employer also motivated to make that decision because of the worker's religious beliefs or practices? Are the reasons asserted by the employer merely pretexts, proffered for the purpose of covering up the true nature of its decision? These are the questions that typically confront juries hearing Title VII religious discrimination cases.

The Supreme Court formalized this method of proving workplace discrimination through indirect evidence by establishing a three-step procedure. In a religious discrimination case, the procedure is generally described as follows:

1. The plaintiff worker must show that he was subjected to an adverse employment decision under circumstances that give rise to an inference of unlawful religious conduct. In satisfying this first element of proof, the plaintiff may offer evidence showing that he adhered to a religious belief system and that although he performed his job tasks satisfactorily, he nonetheless suffered an adverse employment action or decision. When a

plaintiff worker has sustained this burden of proof, it is said that he has
presented a prima facie case of religious discrimination.

2. If the plaintiff's evidence gives rise to an inference of religious discrimination, the defendant employer may rebut the plaintiff's prima facie case
   by submitting evidence showing that it had a legitimate, nondiscriminatory reason for taking adverse action against the plaintiff worker.

3. When an employer offers evidence tending to show that its actions were
   nondiscriminatory, the worker must then establish that the reasons given
   by the employer for its actions were pretexts designed to cover up the discriminatory conduct.

Thus, when relying upon indirect evidence, a plaintiff worker sustains his
burden of proof if, at the conclusion of the three-step procedure, he has established that the reasons given by the employer for its actions were false.
The court may then infer that religious discrimination was the real reason
for its conduct. This procedure was announced in *McDonnell Douglas v.
Green* and is generally referred to as the *McDonnell Douglas* rule.[12]

The Supreme Court did not intend the three-step procedure to constitute an inflexible rule, as the facts in a particular case may call for modification if this procedure is to work properly. Regardless of the modification,
in the end a Title VII plaintiff must show that the actions undertaken
by the employer were such that the trier of fact—either the court or the
jury—may infer they were based on a discriminatory criterion illegal
under Title VII.[13]

We may now return to Mr. Sattar and an examination of his case in light
of the *McDonnell Douglas* rule. In step 1, after Sattar submitted evidence
relating to his troubled employment at Motorola, the court ruled that the
circumstances surrounding his termination gave rise to an inference that
religiously motivated criticisms and negative performance evaluations
might have influenced the employer's decision to terminate him. Sattar
had established a prima facie case of religious discrimination. In step 2,
Motorola was required to articulate a legitimate, nondiscriminatory reason for firing Sattar. In that regard, it relied on Sattar's poor performance
record—that he was ranked at the bottom of his division, that his supervisors found his performance in need of improvement, and that he had failed
to successfully complete the performance improvement plan. The court
ruled that Motorola had articulated a legitimate, nondiscriminatory reason

for terminating Sattar's employment, thus sustaining its burden required by step 2 of the *McDonnell Douglas* procedure.

Under step 3, the burden shifted back to Sattar. It is at this point that a Title VII plaintiff's case is most likely to fall short. Sattar was required to show that Motorola's reasons for firing him were either false or unworthy of belief—that its reasons were nothing more than pretexts for unlawful religious discrimination. But in this respect, Sattar failed. He was unable to establish that the reasons given for his termination were false. Even though he was able to establish that Pardesi was motivated by discriminatory religious animus, he could not prove that the supervisors who actually made the decisions adverse to him were similarly motivated or, in the alternative, acted at Pardesi's behest. The supervisor who gave him the lowest ranking in his division and the supervisor who later ordered his termination were not accused of acting from a religious motive, and since Sattar was unable to establish that Pardesi had influenced these other supervisors in the decisions adversely affecting him, his case was fatally flawed. The court ruled that Motorola had articulated a legitimate, nondiscriminatory reason for terminating Sattar's employment, and it dismissed his case.[14]

The *Sattar* case illustrates how difficult it is to prove religious discrimination through indirect evidence. If Pardesi had been directly involved in Sattar's dismissal, the final result most likely would have been in Sattar's favor, but because the evidence failed to show that the other supervisors were also motivated by a religious bias, Sattar was unable to satisfy his burden of proof in accordance with the *McDonnell Douglas* rule, and thus the court could do nothing other than dismiss his claims.

Although attempts at proving discrimination through indirect evidence frequently fail, a plaintiff who offers persuasive evidence of discriminatory intent will most likely succeed. Kent Nielson's Title VII claim is a case in point. Nielson began his employment with AgriNorthwest as a plant geneticist and later was promoted to various positions and ultimately to vice president of farm operations. Over the succeeding five years, AgriNorthwest's CEO issued a series of written reprimands criticizing Nielson's performance. When his CEO finally demoted him, Nielson resigned and commenced legal proceedings against the company, alleging that he had been subjected to acts of religious discrimination.

The discrimination claim was based on a series of events that coincided with the CEO's reprimands. Nielson, a lifelong member of the Mormon Church, had been excommunicated following disclosure of his affair with his secretary. Subsequently, he separated from his wife, was divorced, and began keeping company with a woman who was a Seventh-day Adventist. AgriNorthwest's CEO then convened a meeting at his home for all company officers except Nielson to discuss Nielson's sexual and romantic affairs. It was at approximately this time that the written reprimands first surfaced. Within days of Nielson's announcement of his plans to marry the Seventh-day Adventist, he was demoted. At nearly the same time, another AgriNorthwest worker was demoted following excommunication by the Mormon Church after church officials had charged him with having committed adultery. A few months later, after Nielson remarried, he was presented with a written warning, purportedly issued because he was performing poorly as vice president of farm operations. As he later testified, at that point he saw the handwriting on the wall, and after more than thirty years on the job, he resigned and started looking for other employment.

After filing religious discrimination claims against AgriNorthwest, Nielson provided the court with substantial evidence demonstrating that his job performance had not deteriorated as his CEO had asserted and that allegations of his unsatisfactory job performance were wholly pretextual. Although Nielson was unable to offer direct evidence tying the CEO's reprimands to his excommunication by the Mormon Church and his subsequent marriage to a Seventh-day Adventist, the issuance of the reprimands simultaneously with the occurrence of those events appeared to have been more than merely coincidental. The indirect evidence Nielson proffered, showing that the CEO's decisions regarding Nielson's employment status were closely connected with his perceptions regarding Nielson's relationship with the Mormon Church, was compelling.[15]

Pretext cases not buttressed by direct evidence of discrimination may fail if the evidence of pretext is unclear or unpersuasive. Evidence that an employer treated its workers unfairly or unequally will often turn jurors against that employer, as they may be reminded of episodes of unfair or unequal treatment they endured during their own work careers. Such evidence, linked to evidence tending to show the presence of a discriminatory intent, may be sufficient to persuade a jury to decide in the worker's favor.

Pretext appears in a myriad of forms and is often detected only through the vigilance of the affected worker. My experience in these types of cases has led me to conclude that because the worker is better informed than anyone else regarding the particulars of her own job, she generally is in the best position to evaluate the accuracy and truthfulness of the reasons advanced by her employer to justify its employment decision adversely affecting her.

The worker's ability to root out the facts underlying the employer's decision often determines whether a pretext case succeeds or fails. This was vividly demonstrated in an age discrimination case litigated in the federal district court in New York. This case involved an employer charged with intentionally engaging in age bias when it selected my client for termination. Virginia Green (a pseudonym, used here because of privacy reasons) created television commercials and magazine advertisements for a large advertising agency. After a lengthy career in the world of advertising, she found herself the oldest of twenty-three associate creative directors employed in the agency's creative department. When the agency experienced financial difficulties, it conducted a reduction-in-force, culminating in the termination of a number of workers, including Green, who was sixty-four at the time.

About one year before the terminations, as Green was making a presentation of a proposed television commercial, one of the agency's executive directors, on hand to view the presentation, began chanting, "We know how old you are, we know how old you are." Green, then sixty-three (with gray hair verging on near white), appeared in stark contrast to the surrounding younger work staff. Frightened and humiliated by the incident, from that point onward Green feared for her job. Later, when the reduction-in-force terminations were announced, it was disclosed that the chanting executive director had designated Green as one of those to be terminated. Green sued for age discrimination.

The agency defended against Green's age discrimination suit on the ground that she had been terminated not on account of her age and not because she was the oldest of the twenty-three associate creative directors but because her productivity was allegedly lower than that of the other associate creative directors. In short, the agency purported to justify Green's dismissal on the ground that in the three years prior to her termination, she had produced very few television commercials and magazine advertisements that were ultimately sold to the agency's clients. The criterion for termination, according to the agency, was productivity, and those workers who were most productive and generated work acceptable to clients survived the reduction-in-force while the less productive workers did not.

When the agency claimed that Green was less productive than her coworkers, it opened the door to her demand that she be allowed to analyze the agency's production records for all twenty-three creative directors. To the casual observer, those records were all but indecipherable, but Green's long tenure in the advertising business enabled her to pull from them a wealth of information helpful to her case:

1. Data showed that the agency had neglected to maintain an accurate count of magazine advertisements sold to clients. Thus worker productivity could not be measured by magazine ads but only by television commercials sold to clients.

2. In the three years prior to Green's termination, eighteen of the twenty-three associate creative directors had produced fewer client-approved television commercials than Green. In fact, during the last two years of her employment, Green produced and sold more television commercials than all but one of the associate creative directors, and in the last year she was employed, no one produced and sold more television commercials than she did.

With this type of information in hand, we were able to argue forcefully that the agency had misrepresented her productivity in an attempt to justify her termination. When an employer misrepresents, exaggerates, understates, overstates, distorts, or tampers with the facts, it opens itself to claims of a cover-up of its discriminatory conduct as the real reason underlying an employment decision adverse to the interests of its employees.

Green's ability to evaluate the accuracy and truthfulness of the reasons advanced by her employer to justify its decision to terminated her ended in a substantial monetary settlement of her age discrimination suit.[16] If Green's employer had been motivated by elicit religious considerations and had offered its flawed productivity allegations in defense of a religious discrimination claim, it would have been no more successful than it was in the age suit.

A subset of the type of Title VII violation we have been reviewing has been labeled "hostile environment" religious discrimination. A work environment may be delineated as hostile under a number of circumstances. For example, when a worker was required to work in an area where photographs of nude women were openly displayed, he informed his supervisor that the presence of these photographs violated his religious beliefs, and as a consequence he could not continue to work unless they were removed. The supervisor fired him. The worker then filed a Title VII suit alleging that because of his religious beliefs, the presence of sexually explicit photographs in the workplace created a hostile work environment. When the employer tried to block the litigation from proceeding, the court held that the worker had established a prima facie case and permitted the case to go forward.[17]

The courts have long held that a worker has the right to work in an environment free of intimidation, ridicule, and insult. An employer who allows workplace behavior that is sufficiently severe or pervasive to alter the conditions of a worker's employment creates an abusive and hostile (and hence unlawful) work environment.[18]

Whether the conduct in question actually creates a hostile work environment is determined through the application of two standards of analysis, one subjective—does the worker believe the conduct complained of is hostile?—and the other objective—would a reasonable person also believe it to be hostile? Among the factors the court will consider in determining whether a reasonable person would consider the conduct to be offensive or hostile are the severity and persuasiveness of the conduct, its frequency, and the length of time the worker is required to endure it.[19]

Hostile-work-environment issues arise in a myriad of circumstances. Workplaces that are hostile to the religious beliefs and practices of various groups of workers will appear as a continuing subject of examination in the chapters that follow.

4

Religious Discrimination at Various Stages of the Employment Relationship

A worker who intends to pursue a religious discrimination claim against his or her employer initiates that process by filing a charge of discrimination with the Equal Employment Opportunity Commission. Once the worker files a charge, EEOC procedures call for the agency to investigate the allegations of discrimination. That investigation typically leads to a determination that (1) reason exists to believe the worker was subjected to discriminatory conduct—a "for cause" finding—or (2) no reason exists to believe the employer engaged in such conduct—a "no cause" finding. A no-cause finding effectively terminates the EEOC's involvement in the charge. Conversely, a for-cause finding generally leads to further EEOC actions, such as conciliation, settlement, or on occasion, litigation.

Of the 2,700 religious discrimination charges resolved by the EEOC in 2008, it dismissed 63 percent as its investigators found no reason to believe that the complainants had been discriminated against. Another 22 percent were summarily dismissed for various administrative reasons—that the claims had not been timely filed or that the complainants had failed to pursue their claims. Nine percent of the charges were settled. In only 6 percent of the resolved cases did EEOC investigators actually find that the complainant had been discriminated against.[1] Thus a relatively small number of religious discrimination charges reach the stage at which the EEOC ventures either to negotiate a settlement of the worker's claims against the employer or, alternatively, proceeds against that employer in the courts.

If the EEOC fails to settle or conciliate the claim and subsequently decides not to proceed against the employer in litigation, the worker may elect to pursue his or her claim in the courts. In fact, once the EEOC has had an opportunity to investigate the charge, the worker is free to commence legal proceedings against the employer.

A no-cause finding does not bar a worker from litigating his or her claim in the courts, but it may weaken the case because courts tend to place great weight on EEOC findings. As reflected in the cases analyzed in this and the following chapters, this factor and others render it more likely than not that a court will decide a Title VII religious discrimination case in favor of the employer.

A worker's prosecution of a religious discrimination claim that ends in defeat adds to the pain already suffered as a consequence of the alleged discriminatory conduct. Moreover, because litigation is expensive, time-consuming, and often frustrating, the worker's decision to proceed or not proceed with it is a difficult one to make.

Religious discrimination may occur in the life of a worker at any time from hiring to termination. Discrimination claims asserted during the employment relationship are examined in this chapter, while those advanced after termination are reviewed in chapter 5. The cases discussed in both chapters illustrate the problems workers typically confront as they pursue their religious discrimination claims before the EEOC and the courts.

Hiring

The reported cases disclose few instances of religious discrimination claims asserted during the job application process. Of those claims that have been made, most have failed, often on the ground that the employer was simply unaware of the applicant's religious beliefs or church affiliation and thus could not have acted in a discriminatory manner. Those, however, were not the circumstances that confronted Ellie Jordan in her discrimination claim alleged against WilTel, Inc. Company executives maintained that the refusal to hire Jordan was based on a decision of its hiring personnel that she was unqualified for the position for which she had applied. Jordan, on the other hand, claimed she had been rejected for employment because she was an evangelical Christian and a member of the Southern Baptist Church.

While working in a temporary secretarial position in WilTel's customer service department, Jordan expressed an interest in obtaining a permanent position as a customer service representative. After interviews by several supervisory employees, Jordan's application for the position was rejected when the interviewers concluded she was unqualified for the position.

During the course of one of the interviews, Julie Hackett, the department manager, questioned Jordan about personal aspects of her life. These inquiries later raised questions about the propriety of the hiring process. Hackett questioned Jordan about her "goal in life," and Jordan responded that her "purpose in life is to please the Lord and to serve my employer and the people that I work with." When Hackett followed with a question regarding how Jordan dealt with frustration, she answered that she "prayed and asked the Lord for guidance and wisdom and strength to deal with whatever was causing the frustration." Sometime after Jordan had been rejected for the position, Hackett was heard to say: "I don't like Ellie because she is into all that Jesus shit and she doesn't fit in." It was this statement that the court focused on in considering the merits of Jordan's Title VII discrimination suit.

The court assessed the relevancy of Hackett's post-interview comment in the context of three indisputable facts: (1) Jordan was clearly unqualified for the position she sought, (2) Hackett's statement was made after the decision had been made to reject Jordan's application, and (3) on a previous occasion Hackett had recommended the hire of an evangelical Christian. The court noted that the evidence failed to show that Hackett had expressed a bias against evangelical Christians, and thus one might infer that rather than expressing religious bias, she was commenting on what she felt was inappropriate conduct—namely, that Jordan, a job applicant, had improperly asserted her religious views during the interview process. The court suggested that Hackett was merely expressing disapproval of Jordan's business judgment rather than of her religious views. But if one were to reject this approach and instead infer that Hackett was biased against Jordan because she was an evangelical Christians, such an inference, the court noted, would have to be rejected since Hackett previously had recommended the hire of an evangelical Christian. The court dismissed Jordan's claim.[2]

Several members of the supervisory staff participated in evaluating Jordan's application for permanent employment and the evidence indicated, at best, that only one of those interviewers had exhibited a bias toward her religious views. Moreover, the trial testimony failed to show that Hackett's comment—the only statement that might have been viewed as an expression of religious discriminatory animus—actually infected or influenced the attitudes of the other interviewers. Jordan's evidence of religious bias was weak and unpersuasive, thus resulting in the rejection of her claim.

Proving that an employer's rejection of an applicant for employment occurred as a result of its discriminatory intent has nearly always been difficult. Over the history of Title VII, worker allegations of discrimination during the hiring process have more often failed than have allegations of discrimination occurring at other points in the employment relationship. Various reasons have been offered to explain this lack of success. My own experience in representing workers who have filed discrimination claims after having been rejected for employment is that the worker does not possess sufficient information regarding the hiring process in question to support the bias claim. Terminated workers generally have a fair amount of information available to them concerning the circumstances existing at the time of their terminations. Even after being discharged, a worker may have a rich source of information in the friends and coworkers left behind in the workplace. A job applicant, on the other hand, has none of these advantages. Thus an employer's discriminatory conduct is more readily concealed from the applicant than from its terminated workers.

Jordan would not have learned about Hackett's comment had one of her interviewers not been a personal friend. Her friend overheard Hackett's comment concerning her negative perception of Jordan's religious life, and she in turn reported the remark to Jordan. It was only in these unusual circumstances that Jordan learned anything that might have lent support to her allegations of religious animus.

The employer's invariable defense to a failure-to-hire claim is that the job applicant was unqualified for the position or that another applicant was better qualified. A myriad of factors generally present themselves in connection with the decision to hire Ms. X rather than Ms. Y, many of which are wholly subjective. Subjective employer decisions are rarely upset by the courts because judges have historically been extremely reluctant to substitute their judgment for that of the business person. In such circumstances, it is readily apparent that an employer bent on discriminating against a job applicant may easily conceal its illegitimate intentions.

When a rejected applicant suspects that a discriminatory bias has played a role in her rejection, she may be reluctant to file a discrimination claim with the EEOC and even more hesitant to become later involved in litigation. Obtaining a job is the primary interest of the unemployed worker, and in most instances, the worker will not allow the mere suspicion of unlawful employer behavior to deflect her from the job search. Also, the bitterness suffered by the wrongfully discharged long-term worker is less often experienced by the unsuccessful job applicant, and thus the latter's motivation to involve herself in proving allegations of employment discrimination is less compelling. And, as many workers have experienced, an employer's rejection is invariably accompanied by the promise that the applicant's resume and application will remain on file in the event another position becomes available. It almost never does, but hope springs eternal. Why charge an employer with discrimination when, if you don't, it may offer you another position next week?

The reluctance of a worker to file a failure-to-hire suit, combined with the difficulties ordinarily encountered in prosecuting such a legal action, serves to insulate employers from liability. Since employers are clearly aware that the prospect of a successful prosecution of a failure-to-hire discrimination charge is remote, they are less inclined to concern themselves with the demands of Title VII in making hiring decisions.

In most instances, a failure-to-hire discrimination case will not succeed unless the rejected applicant is able to provide the court with direct and convincing evidence that religious discrimination was responsible for the employer's rejection of her application. Absent such evidence, the rejected worker and her attorney are well advised to proceed with great caution.

Promotions

The successful prosecution of a failure-to-promote case is as difficult to achieve as that of a failure-to-hire case. The reasons underlying an employer's decision to promote a worker or deny him that promotion are generally as subjective as its reasons underlying a decision to hire or reject a job applicant. Thus an unscrupulous employer, intent upon masking its religious bias, may engage in the process of promoting one worker rather than another with little fear that the religious discriminatory intentions underlying its decision will ever be revealed. But on occasion employer religious discriminatory animus surfaces in plain view.

Leon Weiss was employed as a warehouseman by Parker Hannifan at its distribution center in Trenton, New Jersey. Weiss, the only Jewish warehouseman working at that facility, had greater seniority than any other employee. Because of his lengthy experience and highly honed job skills, he was charged with training newly hired workers. When a vacancy occurred in a position designated "warehouse lead person," George Altmeyer, manager of the Trenton distribution center, interviewed several employees, including Weiss, for the position. Although it was generally known throughout the facility that Weiss was the best-qualified candidate, Altmeyer selected another worker, Robin MacNeal. When a coworker angrily confronted Altmeyer on his rejection of Weiss for the promotion, he responded, "As long as I'm the manager, no Jew will run the warehouse for me." When Weiss was informed of Altmeyer's outrageous remark, he filed a Title VII religious discrimination case against Parker Hannifan.

In analyzing the case, the court used the three-step procedure announced by the Supreme Court in the *McDonnell Douglas* case (chapter 3).[3] In step 1, Weiss was required to establish the following:

1. He was a member of a protected group.
2. He was qualified for the higher position.
3. He was considered for and was denied promotion to that position.
4. Another worker with the same qualifications who was not a member of the protected group was promoted to the higher position.

The court noted that as a Jew, Weiss was a member of group entitled to the protection of the statute, that he clearly was qualified to fulfill the responsibilities of the warehouse lead person, that he was denied the promotion, and that another worker, who was not Jewish, was awarded the position. The court thus held that Weiss had satisfied the step 1 requirements and had established a prima facie case of religious discrimination.

Turning to step 2—the employer's assertion that it had a legitimate, nondiscriminatory reason for its decision—the court noted that Altmeyer had advanced three reasons for promoting MacNeal rather than Weiss: (1) MacNeal had a better attendance record, (2) Weiss had no supervisory experience and MacNeal did, and (3) Weiss was less able than MacNeal to communicate with other employees. These reasons were all legitimate and nondiscriminatory considerations for denying the promotion to Weiss, and thus Parker Hannifan satisfied the requirements of step 2 of the procedure.

In step 3 Weiss was required to show that the reasons advanced by Parker Hannifan for not promoting him were pretextual, that is, that they were false or not worthy of credence. In light of Altmeyer's anti-Semitic remark that no Jew would ever run the warehouse on his watch, the court had little difficulty in ruling that the reasons advanced by Parker Hannifan were indeed pretextual:

> We find that Altmeyer's anti-Semitic statement, which was said in direct reference to Weiss and contemporaneous to the decision to promote MacNeal, strong evidence of the defendant's discriminatory intent. There may exist a more unequivocal way to express an intent to exclude [a Jewish person] from consideration from promotion, but none comes readily to mind.

The court expressed no doubt that the reasons given for the refusal to elevate Weiss to the leadership position were clearly pretextual.[4]

Absent Altmeyer's anti-Semitic remark, Weiss would have faced the nearly insurmountable task of demonstrating that the three reasons for not promoting him were false or not worthy of belief. Some of the evidence supported Altmeyer's positions. MacNeal's attendance record was better than Weiss's but only insignificantly. MacNeal had prior supervisory experience, as Altmeyer claimed, but Weiss had previously served for a time as the acting warehouse lead person. The assertion that MacNeal was better than Weiss in communicating with other workers was a subjective evaluation that was not readily disputed. Thus the evidence directly relating to the three reasons for the decision not to promote would have been insufficient to carry the day for Weiss, but when the court evaluated this evidence in light of Altmeyer's blatantly anti-Semitic remark, it concluded that his testimony was in all respects untruthful and that the reasons given for denying the lead-person position to Weiss were not worthy of belief. In this rare win for a worker alleging religious discrimination in a failure-to-promote case, the court granted Weiss a substantial monetary award.

Dress Codes, General Attire, and Personal Appearance

Carol Grotts, a member of a Pentecostal church, was hired by Brink's as a relief messenger at its Peoria, Illinois, facility. She was assigned to an armored-car crew and in that capacity was required to wear a Brink's uniform. Grotts's religious beliefs, however, precluded her from wearing pants, a standard part of the uniform. When she requested permission to wear culottes, made of the same material as the uniform, Brink's refused her request and terminated her.

Grotts filed a charge of discrimination with the EEOC. After investigating the matter, the EEOC found "reasonable cause" to believe that Brink's had discriminated against Grotts by refusing to reasonably accommodate her religious beliefs by allowing her to wear culottes rather than pants. Ultimately the company reversed course, rehired Grotts, and allowed her to wear culottes while on the job. Commenting upon this outcome, the EEOC reminded employers that "in our pluralistic society, employers cannot unreasonably create inflexible policies that infringe upon an individual's ability to live in accordance with his or her religious beliefs."[5]

Disputes arise in this area over seemingly innocuous items of dress. Although the Christian cross may generally be worn in the workplace without causing alarm, other religious symbols are often barred. Muslims in particular have in recent years confronted problems of this sort. Elijah Karriem insisted upon wearing on his security officer uniform an Islamic pin, circular in shape and in size measuring between a quarter and a half dollar. His employer's regulations provided that "no security officer shall wear...a metal or metallic appearing badge," but the regulations did not suggest that the wearing of religious symbols or pins was banned. Thus, after Karriem rejected a direct order to remove the pin from his uniform, his employer was unable to advance a reasonable basis to support its decision to terminate him. When Karriem later sued the company, the court determined that he had been a victim of religious discrimination.[6]

Other employers have encountered similar problems after ordering workers to shave off their beards as a condition of continued employment. Title VII comes into play in those cases if a worker's beard has religious meaning for him. A typical case involved Ulysses Carter, who agreed to accept employment with the Bruce Oakley company provided

he was allowed to practice certain religious beliefs, including those relating to his beard. When he reported for work on his first day of employment, his supervisor ordered him to trim his beard in a way that
Carter deemed in conflict with his religious beliefs. After Carter filed a
Title VII claim, Bruce Oakley defended the supervisor's action by arguing that Carter's beliefs with regard to his beard did not constitute a religious belief within the meaning and protection of the statute. The court,
however, ruled that Carter held a sincere belief in a Supreme Being who
had revealed his will in scripture and that his religious beliefs were based
on that scripture. The company countered that if Carter were allowed
to wear his beard in the style he preferred, he would project an unpro-
fessional appearance. The court found this argument unpersuasive in
light of the fact that Carter had been hired for a position that did not
require contact with the public, and thus his appearance was irrelevant.
Ultimately, Bruce Oakley's president admitted while testifying that the
company's policy regarding beards had initially been instituted by his
father and that he was determined to continue his father's rule. On the
basis of that testimony, the court decided the Title VII case in Carter's
favor and awarded him monetary damages.[7]

In cases of this sort, an employer is unlikely to prevail unless it is able to
demonstrate that a beardless face is a necessary element of the job in question. Any employer that pursues a no-beard employment policy that in
effect eliminates candidates for employment for reasons unrelated to specified job functions will likely end up paying damages to those workers.

Women who insist upon wearing head coverings for religious reasons
have probably asserted as many Title VII discrimination claims as have
men claiming religious beliefs relating to their beards. Deborah McGlothin
had worked for more than three years as a teacher's aide in a Jackson, Mississippi, school district when she was terminated for subordination stem-
ming from her refusal to conform to a dress code promulgated by school
officials. McGlothin alleged that she had been fired because her head wraps
and hairstyles, which she claimed were expressions of her religious beliefs,
conflicted with the dress code.

At the trial of the discrimination suit she later initiated, McGlothin testified that she held a deep spiritual belief that she was required to cover
her head as a means of demonstrating modesty and humility, as well as to
protect herself from external disruptive influences. She explained that she

did not groom her hair by any artificial means, limiting herself to combing it with her fingers alone, because she believed her hair should be allowed to appear as a source of spiritual strength, demonstrating the depth of her religious commitment.

In contrast to this testimony, the school principal testified that soon after McGlothin was hired, she began to wear a red beret in the classroom, and when she was directed not to wear any head covering while teaching, she said nothing about religious conviction as the reason for wearing the beret. Subsequently, during Black History Month, she wore African-style head wraps, and her principal again reminded her of the dress code requirements. Eventually McGlothin complied with the principal's directions and ceased wearing berets and head wrappings but then proceeded to let her hair grow and ceased combing it, allowing dreadlocks to form. In addition, she stopped washing her hair so that it began to appear, as her principal described it, "linty and matted." The following year during Black History Month, McGlothin resumed wearing a head wrap and dressed in full African garb. After that she alternated periods when she wore the head wrap with periods when she did not comb her hair. When the principal again complained, McGlothin responded that her actions reflected her African American heritage and were thus consistent with the school district's multicultural educational directives. At that time she did not indicate that any of her actions were religiously motivated.

The court had to sift through this conflicting testimony to determine whether McGlothin had provided the school district with adequate notice of her religious beliefs as they related to hair grooming and head coverings. It was persuaded that her beliefs were sincerely held but not that she had communicated the religious nature of these beliefs to the officials of the school district. Rather, it appeared to her principal and others that McGlothin's practices were reflective of the African culture and her African heritage. Culture and heritage, however, do not equate with religion. The court thus held that McGlothin had failed to sustain her claims, and it dismissed her discrimination complaint.[8]

If an employee or a candidate for employment clearly informs an employer that he or she wears a head covering for religious reasons, the employer will be hard-pressed to justify rejection of that person for employment, and if it persists in following that course, it will undoubtedly be held to have acted in violation of Title VII.

Work Assignments

After serving several years as an assistant professor of history at Jackson State University in Mississippi, Leslie Citron complained that his department head and other university officials had made several decisions that proved adverse to his interests and reflected a bias against his Jewish faith. Among other complaints, Citron alleged he had been denied the opportunity to teach in the graduate school and that other professors, who were not Jewish and were less qualified, were granted those assignments. The university rebutted his claim with evidence that those assignments had been made in favor of professors who possessed a particular form of academic training that Citron lacked.

Citron also claimed he had been discriminated against when he was assigned to teach a disproportionate number of freshman courses, while non-Jewish professors were permitted to limit their assignments to these courses. But again the university easily rebutted his claim by showing that department heads exercised professional judgment in determining the needs of their particular departments and in assessing the capabilities of their faculty. Commenting that no faculty member had a vested right to teach any course he desired, the court ruled that Citron had failed to sustain his burden of proving that discrimination played any role in the university's decisions with regard to work assignments.[9]

Employer decisions regarding work assignments, as with those relating to hiring, promotions, and other actions involving the exercise of professional judgment, are generally immune to attack unless the complaining worker is capable of proffering direct evidence that religious bias infected the decision-making process. Without persuasive evidence of that nature, religious discrimination claims involving work assignments usually end in defeat for the worker.

Discipline

Angelo Rodriguez served as a patrol officer in the Chicago Police Department's Fourteenth District. Two abortion clinics were located in that district. After a mass demonstration at one of the clinics, the department assigned officers to protect the clinic and its employees. Rodriguez was one of the officers assigned to that duty.

At first he fulfilled this assignment without complaint, but he later grew concerned that his presence at the clinic facilitated the performance of abortions and, consequently, that his police duties conflicted with his Catholic beliefs. Rodriguez informed his watch commander that his religious beliefs holding that an abortion constituted the intentional killing of a human being prohibited his further participation in protecting the clinic. His commander agreed that he should be excused from further clinic assignments except, of course, in those circumstances where an emergency situation demanded his presence. Contrary to the watch commander's direction and despite Rodriguez's protestations, one of his supervisors insisted upon assigning him to serve at one of the clinics. When Rodriguez informed the supervisor of his agreement with their commander, the supervisor responded that he was unaware of any such agreement but that in any event Rodriguez's religious beliefs were irrelevant and were not factors to be considered when making duty assignments. The supervisor forcefully stated that he made assignments solely on the basis of professional ability and that he would not change Rodriguez's assignment. Rodriguez reiterated his objection to the assignment, citing his deeply held religious convictions, but ultimately accepted the clinic assignment under protest. He then filed suit, alleging that the police department's refusal to excuse him from the abortion clinic detail violated Title VII.

To establish a religious discrimination claim of this nature, Rodriguez had to show (1) that his religious beliefs conflicted with the requirements of his employment, (2) that he had informed his employer of those beliefs, and (3) that he had been discharged or disciplined or had otherwise suffered an adverse employment action as a consequence of asserting his beliefs. Unquestionably Rodriguez's religious views conflicted with police department policy, and its officials had been notified of the conflict. Thus the only question to be resolved was whether he had actually suffered an adverse employment action.

Police department attorneys argued that Rodriguez's Title VII claim should be dismissed because he had failed to show that he had been discharged, disciplined, or otherwise disadvantaged as a result of his efforts to avoid the abortion clinic duty and, moreover, that he had impliedly

consented to the assignment when he complied with his supervisor's orders, even though he advised the supervisor that he was doing so under
protest. But the court rejected this position:

> It is nonsensical to suggest that an employee who, when forced by his em-
> ployer to choose between his job and his faith, elects to avoid potential finan-
> cial and/or professional damage by acceding to his employer's religiously
> objectionable demands, has not been the victim of religious discrimination.
> An employee does not cease to be discriminated against because he tempo-
> rarily gives up his religious practice and submits to the employment policy
> [he finds to be objectionable].

The court concluded that Rodriguez could well have believed that he
would have been disciplined had he refused the assignment. He thus satisfied the third element of his religious discrimination claim and therefore
successfully pleaded a valid Title VII claim.[10]

Discipline cases, unlike claims relating to hiring, promotion, and work
assignments, less frequently present issues involving questions of professional judgment and thus are more amenable to resolution through application of a less rigorous standard of proof. Here the supervisor made it
clear that he would not allow Rodriguez's religious beliefs to interfere with
the way he assigned police department personnel to the tasks at hand and
that if Rodriguez failed to accede to his demands, he would be disciplined.
For him religious belief was an irrelevancy. He made it easy for Rodriguez
to establish his claim.

Wages and Benefits

Occasionally workers will claim that an employer's discriminatory intent
culminated in a diminution in their wages or other employee benefits, but
these claims rarely succeed. Some religious discrimination claims are so de-
void of any substantiating evidence that one wonders what led the worker
to assert the claim in the first place. For example, Manohar Singh, a follower
of the Sikh religion, claimed that in a number of instances his employer had
denied him employee benefits that were provided other workers, but he
offered no evidence to support his claims.

Singh, who had a Ph.D., worked for several years as an evaluator for the United States General Accounting Office in Washington, D.C. He alleged that he had been unfairly treated with regard to awards of commendations and honors, and he attributed this unfair treatment to the supervisory staff's aversion to his religious convictions. During the course of his employment, Singh had published several articles in both national and international journals, and he claimed that those articles should have brought him recognition and cash awards. But he could offer no evidence showing that the General Accounting Office had ever adopted a policy that granted commendations or cash awards for articles published by its employees. Singh also alleged that he had been denied opportunities to attend training conferences, but he failed to demonstrate that other employees in similar circumstances had been granted permission to attend such conferences. The court dismissed all of his claims, noting that his allegations were "woefully" inadequate.[11]

Transfers

Bertrand Simmons was employed by Sports Training Institute in New York City as a maintenance worker on its morning shift (6:00 a.m. to 2:00 p.m.), working Monday through Friday and occasionally on a Saturday. After two years on the job, Simmons converted to the Seventh-day Adventist faith, which prohibits its members from working on the Sabbath, a period extending from sundown Friday until sundown Saturday. Simmons notified the company's owner, Michael O'Shea, that because of his religious beliefs he could no longer work on Saturdays.

Some time later O'Shea transferred Simmons to the graveyard shift (10:00 p.m. to 6:00 a.m.), and in order to accommodate Simmons's Sabbath obligations, O'Shea revamped his shift schedule to run from Sunday through Thursday. Apparently things worked out well for about a year, but Simmons then insisted upon taking a three-week vacation when he was entitled to only two weeks off. When O'Shea later confronted Simmons about his absence from work for a week without authorization, Simmons stated that he was no longer willing to work the graveyard shift and demanded that he be transferred back to the morning shift. At this point O'Shea fired Simmons, who then filed a Title VII action alleging that religious bias had motivated his transfer to the graveyard shift. But where was the bias? Rather than objecting to that transfer, Simmons had readily consented to it. Moreover, the shift exchange had occurred more than a year before Simmons was fired and was irrelevant to O'Shea's decision to terminate him.

The evidence overwhelmingly established that Simmons was discharged for insubordination. After having taken an unauthorized week of vacation, he simply refused to continue working the graveyard shift and demanded reassignment to the morning shift. His insubordination led directly to his dismissal. Religious discrimination played no role in O'Shea's decision to fire him.[12]

All too often a worker will attribute a discriminatory intent to an adverse employment decision, even in circumstances where the evidence of religious bias is wholly absent. A claim of workplace discrimination should never be advanced unless the complaining worker possesses persuasive evidence supporting it. In this case, Simmons had no evidence to offer, persuasive or unpersuasive. The decision to proceed to litigation should never have been made.

In another case a worker alleged that his employer's failure to transfer him to a newly established position was motivated by religious prejudice, but the evidence in the case showed that the worker had failed either to apply for the transfer or to seek the approvals necessary to effect it. Consequently, his supervisors assumed he wished to remain in the position he then held. When another employee was selected for the transfer, the complainant, rather than expressing objection, requested changes in the duties of his current position. As in the *Simmons* case, the worker had no evidence to support his allegations of religious bias.[13]

Decisions involving job transfers often surface in the context of the appropriateness of steps undertaken by an employer to accommodate a worker's religious beliefs and practices. Kwasi Opuku-Boateng, a devout member of the Seventh-day Adventist Church, held a temporary position as a grain inspector for the California Department of Food and Agriculture. After applying for several permanent positions, he was named plant inspector at a border inspection station in Yermo, California. After his selection for the position, Opuku-Boateng moved his family to Yermo and reported for work, prepared to assume his new duties. On his first day on the job, he learned he was slated to work on the forthcoming Saturday. He immediately informed his supervisor that his religious beliefs precluded him from working on his Sabbath, that the tenets of his church held that repeated violations of the Sabbath observance imperiled his salvation, and that he had never previously worked on the Sabbath and refused to do so under any circumstances. Opuku-Boateng and representatives of the local Adventist parish then negotiated with department personnel in an attempt to find a solution to the Sabbath issue, but ultimately the department determined there was no solution, and Opuku-Boateng was dismissed.

Although officials of the Department of Food and Agriculture investigated several proposals designed to obviate the need for Opuku-Boateng to work on his Sabbath, they found none feasible and thus argued that they had fulfilled their responsibility to attempt to accommodate his religious beliefs. After reviewing their attempts at accommodation, however, the court ruled that they had not proceeded far enough, holding that they should have allowed Opuku-Boateng to remain employed in a temporary status, thus providing the parties additional time to investigate the possibility of transferring him to another job in the department or in some other state agency.[14]

As will become evident in later chapters, a job transfer is often suggested, sometimes by the worker and other times by the employer, as a method of accommodating a worker's religious beliefs relating to work on the Sabbath.

Layoffs

Barton Mann was working in the produce department of a Milgram Food Store in Missouri when he experienced a religious conversion that culminated in his becoming a Seventh-day Adventist. After he notified his supervisors that he could no longer work on his Sabbath, Milgram transferred him to another store to work as a grocery clerk. Two years later, when Mann was laid off, he claimed that the order relieving him of his position constituted an act of religious discrimination. The facts, however, failed to support his position.

Other workers were laid off at the same time, all in accordance with the workers' seniority rights, as required by Milgram's collective bargaining agreement. Neither Mann nor any other laid-off worker filed a union grievance with regard to the layoffs. When Mann later sued Milgram alleging Title VII violations, he was unable to offer any evidence to substantiate his religious discrimination claim, and thus the court had no alternative but to dismiss his case.[15] This is still another case that never should have seen the light of day.

5

Religious Discrimination Claims Arising Out of the Termination of Employment

As reflected in the cases analyzed in previous chapters, the courts often reject Title VII religious discrimination claims alleged by workers, deciding a majority of those cases in favor of employers. The most often-cited reason for this occurrence is the failure of the complaining worker to provide the court with persuasive evidence demonstrating the presence of a discriminatory intent on the part of the employer in advancing decisions that disadvantage the worker. Evidence establishing the employer's intent to discriminate is frequently unavailable, since employers, rather than broadcasting their religious prejudices, ordinarily undertake all available measures to conceal them. The quantum and types of evidence that are more likely to persuade a court to decide a religious discrimination case in favor of the worker are discussed in the cases that follow, each involving the discharge of the worker involved.

Since an employer will nearly always structure its defense to a Title VII unlawful-discharge case upon allegations that the worker's poor job performance or workplace misconduct justified his discharge, the worker must always be prepared to offer evidence demonstrating that his job performance was not a factor relevant to the decision to terminate him. The court will quickly reject a religious discrimination claim unless the worker is able to submit evidence demonstrating that the reason underlying his dismissal was the employer's discriminatory intent, rather than the inadequacy of the worker's job performance.

Glenda Beasley, a Christian fundamentalist who fervently believed that her worship of God was the most important aspect of her life, worked as a supervisor for Blue Cross. At a weekend company-sponsored training session designed to improve supervisory communication and management skills, Beasley and other attendees were told that they had to make Blue Cross their first life priority. Beasley's priorities, however, were God first, family second, and job third.

Soon after the training session, Beasley's performance began to deteriorate. After several workplace incidents led to conflicts with her supervisors, she took a three-month disability leave, purportedly because of an arthritic knee condition. While on leave she undertook a missionary trip to China. Beasley's fellow supervisors were angered when they learned of the trip, since in her absence they had been required to assume her unit's workload. Shortly after her return to the office, company officials discovered that Beasley's unit had erroneously entered computer data, an error that could be corrected only with a recalculation of customer payment levels, thus requiring Blue Cross to incur substantial additional costs. The decision was then made to terminate Beasley. She later claimed that her discharge had been ordered not because of any purported performance problems but on account of her religious beliefs.

At the trial of her Title VII action, Beasley alleged that Blue Cross's "requirement" that she make her job her first priority created a conflict between her religious beliefs and her employer's demands and that this conflict affected her behavior at work and hence the quality of her job performance. But she offered no evidence specifically connecting this conflict to her performance. On the other hand, it was clear that she constituted a disruptive force among her subordinates and supervisors and that she had been responsible for a major error in the entry of computer data. The court concluded that her deficient job performance and not her religious beliefs had motivated Blue Cross to terminate her employment.[1]

To have any chance of success in a discharge case, the worker must prove that the reasons given by the employer for her discharge had no basis in fact. Since these reasons generally relate to the worker's job performance, the worker must be prepared to offer probative evidence clearly showing that her performance could not have been an essential factor in the employer's decision to discharge. A worker who approaches the trial of her lawsuit against her former employer without having first gathered evidence rebutting allegations of poor performance will more often find her claim dismissed. Marvin Evans learned that lesson the hard way.

Evans worked in the credit division of Bally's Health and Tennis Club in Maryland and was also enrolled as a student at the New Hope Bible Crusade College and Seminary. His religious beliefs were well known to those with whom he worked, and his fellow employees were accustomed to seeking his advice on religious matters. Two years into his employment, Evans was charged by a female employee with having sexually harassed her by making unwelcome physical advances. She further claimed that his behavior had been witnessed by a number of other female workers. This was not the first time Evans had been charged with sexual harassment as three other women had previously complained of similar conduct. Although Evans adamantly denied the harassment charges, Bally's nonetheless terminated his employment. Evans immediately responded by filing a Title VII claim against the health club, alleging that his discharge had arisen solely out of acts of religious discrimination committed by members of its supervisory staff.

Evans's Title VII suit was fatally flawed in three respects. First, he was unable to offer any probative evidence refuting the sexual harassment charges, thus leaving Bally's defense to the discrimination charge unchallenged. Second, other than self-serving assertions that his religion was a factor in his termination, Evans failed to offer any evidence that his religious beliefs or practices led Bally's to treat him differently from its other employees. Finally, he also failed to establish that his assertions of discrimination, even if substantiated, would have been sufficient to establish intentional discriminatory conduct on Bally's part. The court dismissed Evans's Title VII action.[2]

Despite the enormous difficulties confronting a discharged worker who sues an employer for religious discrimination, some workers have met with success. Jennifer Venters was employed as a radio dispatcher by the police department of Delphi, Indiana. She answered emergency telephone and police radio calls and then initiated appropriate responses, such as alerting the police or fire departments or directing an ambulance to the scene of an accident. She was responsible for providing emergency teams with the information they needed to respond to the crisis at hand, and if she were ineffective in carrying out her duties, lives would be lost. After Venters had served as a radio dispatcher for more than six years, the town appointed a new police chief, who thereafter served as Venters's direct supervisor.

Beginning with his first day on the job, the new police chief, Larry Ives, made it clear to Venters that his decisions as chief would be guided by his born-again Christian faith, and that he had been sent by God to Delphi to save as many people as possible from damnation. From that point onward, Ives was accustomed to interjecting his religious beliefs into his conversations with Venters, often quoting from the Bible, and speaking to her in terms that led her to believe he considered her to be living an immoral life.

Ives was persistent. He informed Venters that he would consider her a good employee only if she became "spiritually whole." He spoke to her about being saved, advising her that she had a limited number of chances to accept God and she might be running out of chances. He also informed her that the police station was "God's house" and that if Venters was unwilling to play by God's rules, Ives would have to "trade" her. He provided her with a copy of the Bible and other religious materials and directed her attention to a religious videotape entitled "Hell's Fire and Heaven's Gate," which he had placed with the police department's training materials.

Venters unswervingly resisted Ives's attempts to save her soul, but his religious harangues only increased in frequency and intensity. He urged her to attend church services and informed her that she had to choose between God's way and Satan's way and that she could not continue working in the police department if she chose the latter. Venters never wavered in opposing Ives's religious overtures, and eventually he fired her, purportedly for deficiencies in her job performance.

Venters then commenced a Title VII action against the police department, claiming that her discharge had occurred only because she had refused to subscribe to Ives's particular views of Christianity. Although Ives argued that he had fired Venters because of problems with her performance, the police department records failed to disclose any performance deficiencies. When the defendants asked the court to dismiss Venters's claims, the court sided with Venters:

> Venters need only show that her perceived religious shortcoming (her unwillingness to strive for salvation as Ives understood it, for example) played a motivating role in her discharge.... In that sense, Venters' Title VII claim presents a very straightforward question no different in kind from that presented in the familiar cases of race, sex, and age discrimination.... Simply put, the question is whether [Venters] has established a logical reason to believe that the decision to terminate her rests on a legally forbidden ground.

It was clear that she had established such a reason. Ives had warned her that if she did not choose "God's way over Satan's way," she would lose her job. Ives evaluated Venters in terms of his own religious beliefs, and thus religion clearly played a role in her discharge.[3] Venters later agreed to settled her Title VII claim for $125,000.

In lieu of firing a worker, an employer may resort to forcing him to resign, and under those circumstances a termination of employment is referred to as a "constructive discharge." A worker may demonstrate that he was constructively discharged by showing either that he was forced to resign because his working conditions grew unbearable or that he resigned only after his employer communicated, in one form or another, that he was about to be terminated. In a leading constructive discharge case, a worker was told repeatedly that he had no future with the company and that he would no longer receive salary increases. The court later ruled that the worker, who resigned after concluding that continued employment would be inconsistent with even a minimal sense of self-respect, was constructively discharged.[4]

Victoria Leyva found herself in similar circumstances. A recruiter for the University of Chicago Hospitals, she repeatedly received high marks on her performance evaluations until hospital executives replaced the director of human relations, the person to whom Leyva reported. The newly appointed director, JoAnn Shaw, was a Catholic while Leyva was an evangelical Christian Baptist. Before officially undertaking her new duties, Shaw met with Leyva in her office, where she noticed on Leyva's desk a calendar entitled "Treasures of Inspiration: A Woman's Guide to Daily

Living." She also noted the presence of a clock inscribed "Armitage Baptist Church, Chicago, Illinois. Pastor Charles Lyon." Shaw told Leyva that these articles were "too religious" and had to be removed. She recorded the event by placing a note in Leyva's personnel file, stating "Baptist church referrals off desk." Shaw subsequently commented to another employee that she had a problem with Leyva because she insisted upon bringing religion into the workplace. Later Shaw was heard to say that she wanted Leyva fired as she was a religious fanatic. She graded Leyva's next performance evaluation as "needs improvement."

Not long afterward Leyva departed for her vacation, but she was not long out of the office when she received a phone call notifying her to be prepared to discuss her job performance when she resumed work. Upon her return to the office, Leyva found her desk materials had been removed and her office used as a storage area. Leyva immediately resigned.

When Leyva later sued for religious discrimination, the court ruled that she had been constructively discharged on account of her religious beliefs:

> It has been sufficiently demonstrated that a reasonable employee standing in Leyva's shoes would have believed that had she not resigned, she would have been terminated. Most significantly, when Leyva arrived at work [after her vacation], her belongings were packed and her office was being used for storage.... This environment in which her employer made reasonably clear to her that she had reached the end of the line...and the axe was about to fall...[was] to a reasonable employee, unbearable.

Clearly this constructive discharge was motivated by discriminatory intent. Shaw labeled Leyva a "religious fanatic," stated that she had problems with Leyva's religious beliefs, and criticized her for bringing religion into the workplace. The court ruled that Leyva had established the necessary elements of a constructive discharge case motivated by a religious discriminatory animus.[5]

An employee of a Texas bank also successfully claimed that she had suffered a constructive discharge motivated by illicit religious intentions. When Martha Young first began working for the Bellaire, Texas, branch of the Southwestern Savings and Loan Association, she was aware that all Southwestern employees were required to attend monthly staff meetings in the Houston office. She knew that various business matters were considered at these meetings—organizational policies, current economic conditions, and plans for the future—but she did not know that these business discussions were preceded by religious homilies, followed by prayers, both led by a local Baptist minister. Young was an atheist.

At first she attended these meetings without complaining, but later she concluded that her forced attendance violated her freedom of conscience. Instead of registering a complaint, she simply stopped going to the meetings, but after a time her absence was noted and reported to the Bellaire branch manager. When confronted, Young admitted she had repeatedly skipped the meetings because of their religious content. Her manager reminded her of her obligation to attend these meetings and that if she objected to the religious content, she should "close her ears" during those portions of the meetings. When Young persisted in not attending the meetings, the manager again reminded her that her attendance was mandatory. Young then notified him that she was leaving Southwestern. When he asked her for a letter of resignation, she refused his request, noting that she was not resigning but was in fact being fired.

Several months later Young filed suit against Southwestern, demanding reinstatement, back pay, and reimbursement of her attorney's fees. In a constructive discharge case, the plaintiff worker must show that her employer deliberately made her working conditions so intolerable that she was forced into an involuntary resignation. Young enjoyed her work, and Southwestern valued her services. The only possible reason for her resignation was her resolution not to attend religious services that were repugnant to her conscience, coupled with the knowledge that her attendance at the monthly staff meetings was mandatory and that if she failed to attend, she would be terminated. In these circumstances, the court noted, Young did not have to wait for the ax to fall:

> Surely it would be too nice a distinction to say that Mrs. Young should have borne the considerable emotional discomfort of waiting to be fired instead of immediately terminating her association with Southwestern. This is precisely the situation in which the doctrine of constructive discharge applies, a case in which an employee resigns in order to escape intolerable and illegal employment requirements.[6]

The cases cited in this and preceding chapters demonstrate what has long been recognized—defendant employers most often prevail in litigated religious discrimination cases. If an employer is willing to sustain the costs of litigation and suffer the adverse publicity these cases at times generate, its chances of prevailing after a trial are quite high. But there exists some risk of defeat, and rather than confront that risk, employers frequently adopt another tactic—prior to the trial they request the court to grant them summary judgment. If the court grants the employer's motion, it orders the dismissal of the worker's case, thus eliminating the need to proceed to trial. It is the motion for summary judgment that affords the employer the opportunity to procure an early dismissal of the worker's case while reducing its costs of litigation, minimizing adverse publicity, and avoiding a trial before a jury or judge. It is not surprising, therefore, that employers and their counsel generally regard this motion as the most important aspect of a Title VII case.

A motion for summary judgment allows the court to assess the evidence that the employer and the worker intend to offer during the course of the trial and then determine whether there is a genuine need for a trial. Employers' counsel use several techniques in structuring a record in support of the motion. Typically the worker will be required to endure several days of deposition questioning, the primary purpose of which is to obtain admissions that may then be used to support the employer's purported reasons for rendering a job-related decision adverse to the worker. For example, if the employer intends to defend its discharge of the worker on the ground that his performance had materially deteriorated over time, its counsel will attempt to elicit from the worker testimony admitting, in some respects, that his performance had indeed become deficient, thus buttressing the employer's case.

Another tactic used by company counsel is to attempt, during the course of the worker's extended deposition, to educe inconsistencies in the testimony. Variations, gaps, and disparities in testimony may persuade a court to dismiss it as not credible and therefore enhance the chances that the employer's position will be accepted by the court. Still another tactic is to attempt to demonstrate through the testimony that little or no evidence exists to support his charge that the employer was guilty of religious discrimination.

Even if the employer's counsel successfully weaves a pattern of testimony and other evidence that tend to support the company's position, a motion for summary judgment will fail unless the employer first demonstrates to the court's satisfaction that there are no unresolved issues of fact in the case. On a motion for summary judgment, the court is barred from deciding factual issues in favor of one side or the other. That is a task reserved for the jury. If the court is faced with issues of fact it considers material to its decision, it must deny the motion for summary judgment and order the parties to proceed to trial.

The employer and the worker almost always disagree on the basic fact issues in the case. For example, the employer argues that the worker was fired not because of religious bias but because of serious performance problems. The worker responds with evidence showing that his employment record demonstrates an extended history of excellent performance evaluations and that it was not until the employer decided to terminate the employment relationship that it suddenly became overly critical of his performance and downgraded his ratings. A material issue of fact thus surfaces. Since material issues of fact must always be resolved at the trial stage of the case, the court cannot grant the summary judgment motion. Thus the worker's basic strategy in defending against such a motion is apparent: he must elaborate as many issues of fact as the circumstances permit.

A basic element of a worker's religious discrimination case is proof that the employer intended or was motivated to discriminate against the worker because of his or her religious beliefs or practices. Because it is highly unlikely that any employer will ever freely admit to a discriminatory intent, proof establishing intent almost always depends upon inferences that are drawn from the relevant facts in the case. Thus an issue of intent is generally dependent upon the resolution of issues of fact, issues that must be reserved for the trial of the case.

If the facts as presented by the parties are in some respects ambiguous, all factual inferences must be drawn in favor of the party opposing the motion—in this case, the worker. In addition, all the evidence must be viewed in a light most favorable to the worker. This places the employer at a tremendous disadvantage, and as one court described it, twenty bishops testifying on behalf of the employer will not eliminate a genuine issue of fact.[7]

Flooded with issues of fact, the court will turn aside the employer's attempt at an early dismissal of the worker's case. To avoid this result, the employer may utilize another tactic: it eliminates issues of fact entirely by assuming the worker's version of the facts to be true. The employer in effect says to the court, "We won't dispute the facts as the worker alleges them to be. For the purpose of this motion, we will assume the worker's version of the facts to be true. But even assuming the worker's factual contentions are truthful and accurate, his case must nevertheless be dismissed because the evidence fails to show that the worker's religion was a factor in the decision to fire him."

When confronted with this argument, the court must view the worker's factual assertions from the perspective of a typical jury. If the worker has failed to present any evidence of discriminatory motive on the part of the employer, then the motion for summary judgment should be granted. If the worker has submitted some evidence of a discriminatory bias, but the court nonetheless believes that no reasonable, fair-minded jury could possibly reach a verdict in the worker's favor, then again the motion should be granted. But on the other hand, if the worker presents evidence sufficient at least to raise an inference of discriminatory intent on the employer's part, then the motion should be denied.

The burden of proving discriminatory animus is upon the worker. It bears repeating that this is a basic element of her case. To defeat a motion for summary judgment, however, the worker merely has to demonstrate to the court's satisfaction that the factual issues pertaining to the employer's intent are in dispute and thus cannot be resolved at that stage of the proceedings. But if the employer is able to show that the worker lacks probative evidence to support her claim of discrimination and there are no issues of fact to be resolved, the case should be dismissed.

In summary, if material facts are in issue, the court will not dismiss the case at this stage of the proceedings. If the facts are not in issue but the evidence raises an inference of discriminatory conduct on the part of the defendant employer, the court will not order the case dismissed unless it finds the worker's case so weak that no jury could possibly rule in her favor. Even with these difficulties confronting every employer that files a motion for summary judgment, employers invariably opt to proceed with the motion and, as noted, occasionally meet with success. The employer wins when the worker's job performance record is so poor that no reasonable jury would question the decision to fire her. It wins when it appears that the worker will fail to establish an essential element of her case. It wins when the evidence shows that the worker cannot prove that the employer intended to discriminate against her.

It may appear that the worker has little if anything to gain from the employer's motion for summary judgment. Unless reversed on appeal, a decision awarding the employer summary judgment constitutes total defeat for the worker. Conversely, a decision denying summary judgment leaves the employer and the worker in the same positions as before the motion since the worker still must prove his case at trial. The worker has nothing to gain procedurally other than avoidance of total defeat. But contrary to appearances, the employer's decision to ask the court to summarily dismiss the case affords the worker advantages and opportunities not otherwise attainable.

Even though an employer may have been advised by its attorneys that the court is more likely than not to deny its motion for summary judgment, the impact of a defeat upon the employer is no less devastating. No immediate appeal follows from the denial of the motion, and thus the employer at that point must confront the prospect of a trial, a prospect it may not have previously permitted itself to seriously consider. After the denial of the motion, many employers appear psychologically unprepared to continue the battle. For the first time, settlement appears a more expedient option than continuing the litigation, and it is at this stage of the proceedings that many religious discrimination cases are in fact settled. This is precisely what happened after the city of Delphi and Police Chief Larry Ives were denied a summary dismissal of Jennifer Venters's religious discrimination claims. Rather than proceeding to trial, they elected to settle her claims with the payment of a substantial sum.

Although a motion for summary judgment may not always be the best thing to happen to a worker alleging acts of religious discrimination, it frequently presents opportunities for a conclusion favorable to the worker, and thus these motions are generally welcomed by experienced litigators retained by worker plaintiffs to prosecute their religious discrimination claims.

6

Employee Proselytization

Most people tend to keep their religious beliefs to themselves, refraining from open discussions of a matter they consider wholly private. Other are less inhibited and at times freely engage in open discussions of religious beliefs and practices. Still others feel obligated to express their deeply held religious beliefs to those with whom they come in contact during the day's normal course. This is especially the case with evangelical Christians, who are dedicated to the concept of conversion of one's neighbor and are frequently cited as those more likely to engage their coworkers in religious discussion.[1]

Title VII of the Civil Rights Act of 1964 requires an employer to reasonably accommodate its workers' religious observances and practices unless such accommodation imposes an undue hardship upon the conduct of its business. An employer must try to balance the religious commitments of its workers with its normal business needs, and although it can often accommodate a worker's religious practices without inconveniencing or unduly burdening other employees, on occasion this is a difficult feat to achieve, as executive personnel of the Tulon Company of Richmond discovered.

Tulon, a manufacturer of drill bits and routers used in the printed circuit board industry, maintained several service centers throughout the
United States, including one in Richmond, Virginia. Charita Chalmers, a
star employee in the Richmond office, rapidly rose through the employee
ranks to the top management position in that office. Her immediate supervisor, Richard LaMantia, was in charge of all of Tulon's sales in the
eastern part of the United States and customarily visited Richmond only
occasionally. In LaMantia's absence, Chalmers was responsible for the office's operations.

Chalmers was a lifelong member of the Baptist Church. During the
course of her employment with Tulon, she also adopted the beliefs held by
evangelical Christians and publicly accepted Christ as her personal savior.
She felt compelled to share the Gospel and her beliefs with others and became convinced that the time had come for LaMantia "to accept God," as
she believed he had been guilty of misrepresenting delivery times to certain
of Tulon's customers. Accordingly, she wrote to him at his home:

Dear Rich,

The reason I'm writing you is because the Lord wanted me to share somethings [*sic*] with you. After reading this letter you do not have to give me
a call, but talk to God about everything. One thing the Lord wants you to
do is get your life right with him. The Bible says in Roman 10:9 that if you
confess with your mouth the Lord Jesus and believe in your heart that God
hath raised him from the dead, thou shalt be saved—vs 10—for with the
heart man believeth unto righteousness, and with the mouth confession is
made unto salvation. The two verse are [*sic*] saying for you to get right with
God now.

The last thing is, you are doing somethings [*sic*] in your life that God is
not please [*sic*] with and He wants you to stop. All you have to do is go to
God and ask for forgiveness before it is too late....I have to answer to God
just like you do, so that's why I wrote you this letter. Please take heed before
its too late. In his name,
  Charita Chalmers.

After receiving the letter, LaMantia advised the company's vice president of administration that he could no longer work with Chalmers,
and he recommended her termination. While investigating LaMantia's

complaint, company officials discovered that Chalmers, on the same day that she had written to LaMantia, had sent a second letter to another Tulon employee, Brenda Combs, who was convalescing at her home, suffering from an undiagnosed illness after giving birth to a child out of wedlock.

> Brenda,
>
> You probably do not want to hear this at this time, but you need the Lord Jesus in your life right now. One thing about God, He doesn't like when people commit adultery. You know what you did was wrong, so now you need to go to God and ask for forgiveness. Let me explain something about God. He's a God of Love and a God of wrath. When people sin against Him, He will allow things to happen to them or their family until they open their eyes and except [sic] Him. God can put a sickness on you that no doctor could ever find out what it is.... All I'm saying is you need to invite God into your heart and live a life for him and things in your life will get better.... Please take this letter in love and be obedient to God. In his name,
>   Charita Chalmers

Combs later told company officials she felt the letter was cruel, that she had been "crushed by the tone of the letter," as she believed Chalmers had implied that an immoral lifestyle had caused her illness.

After being apprised of these occurrences, upper management concluded that the letters had inappropriately invaded the privacy of other employees and negatively impacted the working relationships in the Richmond office. They ordered Chalmers's dismissal. She responded by filing suit, alleging that Tulon had discriminated against her by failing to accommodate her religious beliefs. In effect, she claimed that Tulon was required to accommodate her belief that God wanted her to convince her coworkers to live without sin.

The court that ruled on Chalmers's case noted that a worker forces her employer into a difficult position when she imposes her religious beliefs upon her fellow employees. If Tulon were to allow a worker to act freely in that manner, her coemployees could claim that the company was engaging in religious harassment. On the other hand, Title VII required Tulon to endeavor to accommodate that worker's religious beliefs and practices.

To effectively operate its Richmond office, Tulon had to assure its staff that management would not tolerate a coworker's actions that adversely impacted the religious beliefs of others and that the privacy of its employees would be protected from the meddling of a coworker professing religious beliefs generally unacceptable to those other employees. Concluding that Tulon could not accommodate Chalmers's religious beliefs and practices without incurring undue hardship in the conduct of its business, the court dismissed her suit.[2]

Employee proselytization of other employees often requires the employer to engage in a delicate balancing act. While an employer is required to attempt to accommodate the religious beliefs of an employee committed to persuading other workers to adopt his or her religious beliefs, it must also endeavor to accommodate the religious beliefs of the workers targeted by the proselytizer. Thus the employer may be confronted with demands for accommodation by both the proselytizer and the targeted employees, and if it accedes to the demands of one, it may face harassment charges asserted by the other.

In another case of employee proselytization, the employee targeted for conversion could have lost his life in the process. The proselytizer, Ned Cary, was employed by Anheuser-Busch as a maintenance operator in its Williamsburg, Virginia, plant. During the course of his employment, Cary claimed to have had a religious experience, after which his primary goal in life was to become an ordained minister. Sometime after he claimed to have had this experience, a coworker, Claude Gilmer, informed his supervisor that Cary had approached him and informed him that he had been "called" by the Lord, that the Lord had told him that he could take two people with him "to the other side," and that he had selected Gilmer as one of the two to go with him. Greatly frightened by this encounter, Gilmer filed a complaint against Cary.

In response to the complaint, management directed Cary to confer with the Anheuser-Busch Employee Assistance Program counselor. After a meeting with Cary, the counselor referred him to a local psychiatrist. Cary then filed a charge of religious discrimination against Anheuser-Busch, alleging that because of his religious beliefs he had been coerced into receiving psychiatric treatment.

If Anheuser-Busch had been motivated by a rejection of Cary's religious beliefs to force him to undergo psychiatric treatment, it would have been guilty of an act of religious discrimination in violation of Title VII. But in seeking psychiatric treatment for Cary, the company was moved to act not because of his religious beliefs but because his conduct in the workplace that was clearly threatening to other employees. Had Anheuser-Busch taken no action after receiving the Gilmer complaint, it might have incurred liability to Gilmer or—in the worst case—to his survivors. The court dismissed Cary's discrimination suit.[3]

Outlandish or extreme behavior such as that exhibited by Ned Cary leaves little room for maneuver by an employer engaged in protecting the religious rights of its workers. A worker who forces his religious beliefs upon his fellow employees against their wishes is a worker who will not long remain in that workplace.

Christine Wilson was employed by U.S. West Communications in its offices in Omaha, Nebraska, as one of nine information specialists and supervisory personnel charged with maintaining records pertaining to the location of telephone cables. After nearly twenty-one years on the job, Wilson, a Catholic, made a religious vow that she would wear a particular. antiabortion button "until there was an end to abortion or until [she] could no longer fight the fight." The button, which she wore at all times while at work, depicted a fetus at the early developmental stage and contained the words "Stop Abortion," and "They're Forgetting Someone." She had chosen this particular button because she wanted to be an instrument of God as the Virgin Mary had been, and she believed that Mary would have chosen this particular button since the photograph of the fetus was not "offensive or grotesque." The button also reminded her of a time when her mother miscarried, which led to Wilson's conviction that "no one will ever be able to tell [her] that [a fetus] is not a baby."

Wilson held particularly strong views about abortion and apparently felt she could influence the views of other U.S. West employees by continuously exhibiting a picture of a fetus to all those who interacted with her in the workplace. Her antiabortion views had their source in her religious beliefs, and thus when she exhibited the picture of the fetus she also presented her religious convictions for the other workers to consider. The other workers, however, did not appreciate her attempt at proselytization. The graphic nature of the button caused immediate and emotional reactions from coworkers, thus causing disruptions in office procedure. When asked by coworkers to desist from wearing the button, Wilson refused, advising them that wearing it was a matter of principle and a promise to God and that she would never stop wearing it.

When they first viewed the pictured fetus, coworkers were distressed, mostly because of private concerns—an inability to have their own children, having suffered a miscarriage, and, in at least one instance, the death of a prematurely born infant. Workers tended to expend time talking about the button rather than performing their jobs, and at one point it was estimated that the office experienced a 40 percent decline in productivity.

Two employees filed grievances. Others charged management with harassment because they had failed to promptly resolve the issue. On five occasions Wilson's supervisors met with her to discuss employee complaints relating to the button, advising her that her coworkers found it offensive and that some were even refusing to remain on the job. Wilson responded that she felt she was being singled out for criticism as the company did not have a dress code that would bar her from wearing the button, and that if some employees did not like it, they simply should not look at it. She made it clear that she was not about to alter her conduct, regardless of the circumstances. She persisted in refusing to remove or cover the button or compromise on the issue in any respect.

U.S. West, aware of its obligations under Title VII to accommodate Wilson's religious beliefs, offered her three options: (1) wear the button only in her work cubicle, leaving it at her desk whenever she moved about the office, (2) cover it while at work, or (3) wear a different button with the same message but without the picture of the fetus. Wilson refused each option as in each case she felt she would be breaking her promise to God. Instead, she suggested that her coworkers be instructed to "sit at their desks and do the job U.S. West was paying them to do." After she rejected each option, Wilson was terminated. She then filed a religious discrimination suit against U.S. West.

After a trial, the court, ruling in favor of U.S. West, dismissed Wilson's complaint, and she appealed. The appellate court first noted that the position adopted by Wilson—that complaining workers should simply have been directed to ignore the button and do their jobs—would have required U.S. West to allow Wilson to impose her beliefs on others as she chose. To simply instruct her coworkers to work in an environment they found unacceptable was antithetical to the concept of reasonable accommodation. Requiring Wilson to cover the button while at work, however, was a reasonable accommodation that she should have accepted. The appeals court affirmed the lower court's decision in favor of U.S. West.[4]

U.S. West was unsuccessful in finding an accommodation that Wilson found acceptable. If it had simply been a matter of her belief that she was required to wear the button in order to fulfill her vow to God, she could have acceded to the company's suggestion that she cover the button while at work, but because she was engaged in proselytizing her coworkers— attempting to persuade them to adopt her position on abortion—she rejected that proposal. Clearly she was engaged in imposing her religious beliefs on her coworkers. Management could not allow her to proceed in that endeavor without violating the rights of its other workers. When Wilson refused to accept a reasonable accommodation that would have protected the rights of other employees, U.S. West had no alternative but to terminate her employment.

The courts have been particularly sensitive to the presence of employee proselytization in the workplace where the proselytizer targets a captive audience, and this is especially true in cases involving teachers and their students. Peter Helland, a substitute teacher for the South Bend Community School Corporation in Indiana, distributed religious pamphlets and read aloud Bible passages to middle and high school students. While teaching a science course, he professed a belief in the biblical version of creation. After these matters were brought to the attention of the school corporation, Helland was warned that the improper interjection of religion into the classroom constituted grounds for removal of his name from the substitute teacher list. When he persisted in presenting his religious views to his students, the corporation barred him from receiving further teaching assignments. Helland cried foul, alleging that he had been removed from the list solely because of his religious beliefs, and he sued the corporation pursuant to Title VII, charging it with religious discrimination.

Title VII required the corporation to accommodate Helland's religious beliefs provided it could do so without incurring undue hardship in the conduct of its business, but Helland's proselytizing of his students could not be tolerated. He was clearly violating school regulations and was well aware that he was doing so. The court rejected his claim of religious discrimination.[5] It's highly unlikely that any court—under any circumstances—will ever give its approval to the proselytization of public school students by their teachers.

In a Michigan county jail, the site of another captive audience case, inmates were subjected to unlawful efforts to bring God into their lives.

Robert Spratt, in his capacity as a social worker, provided counseling and therapy for inmates of the Kent County Jail. He described himself as a believer in "Pentecostal Christianity," a belief system that obligated him to spread the Gospel "whenever an opportunity presented itself." Spratt used a counseling technique described as "treatment by spiritual means," which purportedly allowed the spirit of God to administer to both the counselor and the inmate. Among the methods he employed were Bible reading, prayer, and in at least one instance, the "casting out of demons." He claimed that he utilized treatment by spiritual means only when requested, although he admitted that he encouraged his subjects to adopt this manner of treatment.

The Kent County Sheriff's Department, which operated the jail, directed Spratt to refrain from carrying his Bible into the jail, but he circumvented that order by arranging for inmates to be brought to his office, where he freely used his Bible during counseling sessions. Spratt continued to engage in sessions of that nature even though he had been advised that he was not to intermix religious and psychological counseling and should refer inmate requests for religious counseling to chaplains who were available to render that service.

Spratt had offered this type of counseling for about six months when several women inmates complained to sheriff's department personnel that he was functioning as a religious counselor. The sheriff advised him that this type of counseling was inappropriate, that inmates offended by his methods could sue the department for religious harassment, and that he was immediately to cease his religious counseling. Spratt was not deterred. A few months later, the mother of an inmate complained to the sheriff that Spratt had tried to cast a demon from her son. But Spratt did not stop there. Lacking all authority, he prepared printed forms on which inmates could grant their consent for him to treat them by spiritual means. "Enough," declared the sheriff, who then proceeded to fire Spratt.

Spratt allowed his enthusiasm for proselytizing jail inmates to run amok. He disregarded his employer's reasonable and lawful directives and endeavored to fulfill his counseling duties in a manner he felt was appropriate rather than in accordance with the sheriff's directions. He left no room for the accommodation of his religious views. The sheriff did not ask Spratt to shed his Pentecostal Christian beliefs when he entered the jail, but he did instruct him to suppress those views when counseling inmates.

But Spratt believed that he could not separate his religious beliefs from his role as a counselor. When his Title VII claim was litigated, the court ruled that Spratt had used his position as a counselor simply as a means of evangelizing the inmates, and in those circumstances it was not possible to accommodate his religious beliefs and practices.[6]

Not all employee proselytization is unlawful; it is only unlawful if it is unwelcome. If the fellow workers of an employee bent on converting them to his system of religious beliefs do not resist his efforts, the employer need not intervene. But if a single worker objects to religious conduct he considers proselytizing, the employer must step in. As earlier observed, in these circumstances the employer may be confronted with trying to accommodate the religious views of both employees.

The line demarcating the division between acceptable and unacceptable employee religious practices may not always be clear. As a general rule, however, conduct that intrudes less directly upon the workplace environment is more likely to be found acceptable than conduct that directly clashes with that environment, and thus highly provocative behavior is unlikely to attain court approval. Two cases, each involving workers who insisted upon using religious greetings when communicating with others in their workplaces, illustrate the point.

In accordance with its contract with General Motors, Service America Corporation operated a cafeteria at GM's plant in Kansas City, Kansas. This operation represented a significant portion of Service America's business, and thus it took pains to make certain that GM and its workers remained satisfied with its operation. It employed eighteen workers to serve daily meals to approximately three thousand GM workers, and they were trained to greet cafeteria customers in a friendly fashion, such as "Hello. What can I get for you today?" But two of its food service employees—Lee Ray Banks and Marcus Horton—on occasion greeted their customers with such phrases as "God Bless You" or "Praise the Lord," and at times when they claimed to have been moved by the Holy Spirit, they greeted all their customers in that fashion.

Because of what they perceived God had done for them and the joy he had provided them by dramatically altering their lives, Banks and Horton were convinced they were obligated to greet others in a positive, uplifting, and inspiring manner. Although they were always careful in conveying these greetings in a polite, pleasant, and nonconfrontational manner, some

GM workers complained about them. Service America warned Banks and Horton that unless they ceased greeting cafeteria customers in that manner, they would be terminated. The two refused to comply, stating that honoring God through their speech, such as in their greetings to GM employees, was a deep-seated religious belief they could not abandon. When they were later discharged, they filed a Title VII lawsuit against Service America.

Service America had made no attempt to accommodate Banks's and Horton's religious practices, arguing that the appropriate performance of their food service jobs was incompatible with their religious greetings; the only possible accommodation would have involved keeping Banks and Horton separate from cafeteria customers, but that would have left the company shorthanded or have required it to hire other employees to replace them on the food line. Moreover, it argued, if it had not removed Banks and Horton from the cafeteria, it confronted a possible boycott by the GM workers, and that could have led to a material diminishment in the profitability of its business.

The court was unmoved. It observed that Service America had failed to establish the loss of any business by reason of Banks's and Horton's religious practices. The fear of a GM worker boycott was groundless, since complaining GM workers could easily avoid Banks and Horton by choosing another of the eighteen Service America food servers. The court noted that Banks and Horton were not attempting to proselytize GM workers or impose their beliefs on others, and in these circumstances, it was compelled to rule in their favor.[7]

In the second case, an employee of a retail business in Missouri often prefaced her greetings to customers with the phrase "In the name of Jesus of Nazareth." Her employer was fearful that this language would offend some of its customers, thus undermining its business. Although it attempted to accommodate the employee's religious practice, she refused to make any effort to cooperate in resolving the problems confronted by her employer. A court later ruled that the employer could not accommodate her religious practices without incurring undue hardship, and it dismissed her claims.[8]

The religiously oriented language used by this employee was more likely to offend her customers than the phrases used by Banks and Horton, since "God bless you" and "Praise the Lord" are clearly less likely to offend non-Christians, and even some Christians, than the phrase "In the name of Jesus of Nazareth." It is not surprising, then, that the first court ruled that greetings such as "God bless you" and "Praise the Lord" were acceptable, whereas the second court held that "In the name of Jesus of Nazareth" was inappropriate and should be barred.

The *Banks* case points up another matter that the courts focus on in determining whether an employee's religious practice amounts to unlawful proselytization and should be barred from the workplace. The court ruled that the evidence submitted in that case did not compel a finding that Banks and Horton were attempting to proselytize or impose their religious views on the GM employees. The daily encounter between them and the cafeteria customers was at best fleeting, and these religious greetings did not adversely affect the job performance of any GM worker. These religious practices may have been bothersome to some, but they did not constitute an undue hardship for Service America.[9]

As the preceding cases demonstrate, it is impossible to formulate universal guidelines definitively establishing the acceptability or nonacceptability of particular workplace religious practices. When unlawful proselytization is defined too broadly, the curtailment of lawful religious expression may follow, and when it is defined too narrowly, the rights of targeted employees may remain unprotected. For those working at the side of a fellow worker who, as a central tenet of his identity, believes that he is compelled to share his faith with them, the problem will persist.

7

Employer Proselytization

An employer's proselytization of its employees may constitute a particularly egregious violation of Title VII because workers who find themselves in those circumstances are more likely to endure repeated violations of their rights rather than risk losing their jobs by reacting negatively to efforts to convert them. Similarly, a job applicant made aware of the religious beliefs and practices of an employer may decide to ignore its proselytization endeavors, hoping thereby to gain employment.

An employer's proselytization efforts may be directed at a single employee, a small group of employees, or its entire staff. The larger the group, the greater the likelihood the employer will be taken to task for its efforts.

Arthur Owens, Marc Crevier, and Forest Larson owned and operated seven sports and health clubs, located in the Minneapolis-St. Paul area, providing recreational and exercise facilities for eighteen thousand members. All three of the owners were born-again Christians, publicly expressing deeply held fundamentalist religious convictions while proclaiming they were required to act in accordance with the teachings of Jesus Christ in their business relationships as in their personal lives.

The owners' religious convictions led them to initiate certain employment practices seldom found elsewhere. They questioned prospective employees about their religious practices and beliefs, whether they believed in God, attended church, or read the Bible. Job applicants were also questioned about their marital status and whether they had engaged in premarital or extramarital sexual relations. They justified interviews of this nature as a method of informing prospective employees of their fervent religious beliefs and as a means of determining whether an applicant possessed a "teachable spirit" and pursued a disciplined lifestyle. They refused to hire an applicant living with a person of the opposite sex unless the two were duly married, and they denied employment to a single woman without her father's consent and to a married woman without her husband's consent. They also refused to consider for employment anyone antagonistic to the teachings of the Bible, which in their view included homosexuals. They agreed to hire Jews and Catholics "so long as [they] are not offended by the owners' faith, are not antagonistic toward the Christian gospel and [promise] to comply with management's work rules in a cheerful and obedient spirit."

After employees were hired, the owners promoted them primarily on the basis of their religious beliefs, elevating only born-again Christians to manager and assistant manager positions because, as they argued, they were forbidden by God to work with "unbelievers." Bible studies comprised a substantial portion of weekly business meetings held for managerial personnel, while voluntary Bible studies were conducted for all sales personnel. At the entrances of each club were copies of religious screeds and texts unquestionably designed to persuade their employees to accept the owners' fundamentalist religious beliefs.

Eventually some of the employees objected to these practices and complained to the Minnesota Department of Human Rights. In the litigation that ensued, it was established that Owens, Crevier, and Larson had inaugurated a number of practices that were clearly discriminatory, including questioning job applicants about their religious beliefs and marital status, promoting employees on the basis of their religious affiliation, and terminating workers because of changes in marital status. They were also found guilty of using their positions as owners of the company to force their religious beliefs and practices upon their employees. As born-again Christians, they favored those employees who joined the born-again ranks, and during the hiring process they searched out applicants who they believed would be amenable to conversion to fundamentalist religious beliefs. Once hired, a worker had to agree to become a born-again Christian in order to be eligible for promotion to manager or assistant manager, and after elevation to one of those positions, he or she was compelled to attend weekly Bible study meetings. Owens, Crevier, and Larson had designed a work environment dedicated to the conversion of their employees to Christian, fundamentalist beliefs and practices. Nearly every aspect of that environment violated applicable antidiscrimination laws. The owners possessed the right to practice their religious faith in the place and manner they wished, but that right did not extend to the workplace. The workplace they created was dominated by religious bias and unquestionably had to be dismantled.[1]

Fundamentalist Christians and others who openly center their daily lives on their religious beliefs, firmly believing that all persons should similarly direct their lives, not infrequently find themselves in violation of antidiscrimination laws. Although they honor and respect what they perceive to be God's law, they often demonstrate a lack of respect for human law, always granting greater priority to the former while rejecting the latter whenever they view it as conflicting with or standing in opposition to their religious beliefs. Those charged with the responsibility of enforcing the antidiscrimination laws must then act to make certain that those who purport to follow God's law also fulfill their responsibilities to the laws designed by human beings to govern the workplace. Those purporting to act on God's law, however, at times strongly resist efforts to bring them within the confines of those workplace laws.

The founders of the Townley Manufacturing Company ran their company in accordance with what they perceived to be God's law while ignoring the proscriptions of Title VII. When Jake and Helen Townley first organized their company to manufacture mining equipment in Florida, they covenanted with God that the company would always stand as a "Christian faith-operated business." The Townleys were "born again believers in the Lord Jesus Christ," convinced that they were wholly unable to separate God from any portion of their daily lives, including the activities of their manufacturing company. As the company flourished, it expanded its activities to other states, including Arizona, where a plant was established in the town of Eloy.

In keeping with its covenant with God, the company enclosed a Gospel tract in every piece of its outgoing mail and printed biblical verses on all company invoices, purchase orders, and other commercial documents. It gave financial support to various churches and missionaries and initiated a weekly devotional service for its employees, a move that became particularly significant in later years.

From its inception, the company's Florida plant conducted these weekly services. Typically lasting from thirty to forty-five minutes, the services included prayer, singing, giving testimony, and scripture readings, as well as discussion of business matters. Failure to attend a weekly service was regarded as equivalent to missing work.

These devotional services had not yet been inaugurated at the Arizona plant at the time that Louis Pelvas was hired, but subsequently the company distributed to its workers at that plant a handbook stating that all employees were required to attend weekly nondenominational devotional services. At first Pelvas attended those services without complaint, but later he asked to be excused from attendance because he was an atheist. His supervisor advised him that attendance was mandatory, regardless of his religious beliefs or lack of such beliefs, but if he wished, he could read his newspaper or sleep through the service. This was not good enough for Pelvas. He filed a religious discrimination charge with the Equal Employment Opportunity Commission and resigned his position with the company.

In the litigation that followed, Pelvas argued that the Townleys should have accommodated his atheist beliefs by relieving him of the obligation to attend the devotional meetings. The Townleys responded that their covenant with God required them to share the Gospel with all their employees, and the accommodation sought by Pelvas would have caused them "spiritual hardship." The court rejected this argument, noting that Title VII states that the employer must show undue hardship in "the conduct of [its] business." The mere assertion that excusing Pelvas from the services would have inflicted spiritual costs on the company or on the Townleys was not enough:

> It follows that Townley's attempts to link the alleged spiritual hardship to
> the conduct of the business must fail. It is not enough to argue that Townley
> was founded to "share with all of its employees the spiritual aspects of the

company,"...and that the proposed accommodation would have a "chilling effect" on that purpose. To "chill" its purpose has no effect on its economic well-being.

While the court did not question the Townleys' assertion that their covenant with God compelled them to share the teachings of the Bible with all their employees, it observed that the strength of the government's interest in eradicating discrimination through the application of the principles of Title VII was clear:

> Congress' purpose to end discrimination is equally if not more compelling than other interests that have been held to justify legislation that burdened the exercise of religious convictions....Protecting an employee's right to be free from forced observance of the religion of his employer is at the heart of Title VII's prohibition against religious discrimination.

The court refused to allow the Townleys to override a worker's objections to forced attendance at devotional services solely on the basis of their assertion that their covenant with God obligated them to share their faith with all their employees. The Townleys had to accept Title VII's proscriptions over their covenant with God.[2]

Title VII did not require the Townleys to suspend their religious beliefs when they opened their Arizona plant, but it prohibited them from forcing those religious beliefs upon their workers. They were free to operate their company in accordance with their covenant with God, but they were not free to compel unwilling employees to accede to the terms of the covenant. Attendance at the devotional services should have been made optional, and adverse consequences should not have been levied against workers who opted not to participate in them.

God's law, as the Townleys perceived it, was wrongly preempted by human law—Title VII—and this concept led them to commit violations of that law. The Townleys, however, were not unique in their concerted efforts to bring religion into the workplace. Other employers have engaged in even more pervasive invasions of the private lives of their employees. A prime example involved Jackie Steuerwald and her company, Preferred Home Health Care.

Steuerwald and her husband owned Preferred and several related companies that provided home health care services. Steuerwald identified herself as a practicing Christian who adhered to a literal interpretation of the Bible while professing a concept of salvation that called her to be born again. She also believed that God had directed her to establish the Preferred companies and that Preferred was God's home health care agency. She openly shared those beliefs with her employees by distributing to them a narrative entitled "The Transfiguration of Preferred," a brief history of God's involvement in the company's formation and his continued participation in its direction.

Steuerwald firmly believed in the precepts of the "The Great Commission," a religious directive requiring a believer to go into the world and share the faith. Believing without doubt or reservation that this directive required her to share her faith in the workplace, she proclaimed that "in Him I live and breathe and have my being, and I don't leave my faith at the door when I go to work. It's who I am. It permeates my thinking, my decisions."

When the company expanded its operations, she anointed new branch offices with olive oil, asking for God's blessing. When she purported to have discovered that demons were causing strife and discord in two of the company's offices, she rid them of their presence by anointing the offices. On occasion she also anointed individual employees.

Steuerwald defined Preferred's mission as "presenting God and Son, Jesus Christ, to all of Preferred's employees," and its mission statement announced that the company's primary role was "to be a Christian, dedicated provider of quality health care." Preferred's employees were required, as a condition of continued employment, to sign each year a statement that included the commitment that "I have examined myself and I agree that I have respected and actively supported Preferred's Mission and Values during this past year of employment and I agree to respect and actively support Preferred's Mission and Values in the coming year." Employees were evaluated and disciplined in accordance with this statement, and those who violated its precepts were terminated.

Preferred's corporate organizational chart, known as "the wheel," located Jesus at its center, representing the rock upon which Preferred was built, and from this center all company departments radiated as spokes. Steuerwald exhibited the wheel at management meetings, explaining that with Jesus as its foundation, the company would grow and benefit. Preferred customarily gave copies of its mission statement and of the wheel to all job applicants, who were asked how they felt about working for a Christian organization. Those who felt there was little or no room for religion in the workplace were denied employment. The newly employed were fully versed in the basic religious concepts adopted by Steuerwald to guide Preferred in the business world, and they understood the religious roles they were expected to assume as employees of the company.

Preferred offered its employees the opportunity to attend prayer and religious gatherings, referred to as "devotions." Although company officials claimed that attendance was not mandatory, managerial employees generally felt that as role models they were required to attend, and thus they perceived their presence as mandatory. Prayer was also encouraged outside devotions, and prayers were recited before all business meetings.

For many years these circumstances rarely varied, and nearly ten years elapsed before an employee filed a formal complaint with the Equal Employment Opportunity Commission. Subsequently, the EEOC filed legal charges against Preferred on behalf of all its employees.

During the course of the EEOC investigation and subsequent litigation, several employees testified to the details of Preferred's religiously dominated work environment. One of those was Mary Mulder, a staffing coordinator whose job was to prepare schedules for all the home health aides in the company's Indianapolis branch.

Mulder attended Catholic church services with her husband and children but was not herself a Catholic. In fact, her religious convictions were rather vague—she understood a Christian to be one who was kind and honest, and a person was "saved" by believing in God, by being kind to other people, and by taking care of family. She recognized that Steuerwald accepted different religious concepts, believing that to be saved one had to preach the Gospel to others and verbally express one's feeling about religion. On one occasion Steuerwald announced to Mulder that if she wished to be saved, she needed to learn how to preach the word of God to other people, to openly talk about God, and to abandon her sinful way of life.

On another occasion Steuerwald commented to Mulder that she was very open with others about religious matters because she wanted others to have the glory of God in their lives as she did. Mulder rejected Steuerwald's religious views and informed her that she was a very private person, that she kept her religious beliefs to herself, that she was accustomed to praying in private, and that she disliked preaching to others. Steuerwald said that with that kind of attitude, Mulder could not be saved, and since she was not "charismatic" about religion, she could not possibly be walking in the path of God.

When Mulder experienced problems with her work schedules, her supervisor insisted upon praying over Mulder's paperwork. When Mulder asked her to desist from interfering in this manner, her supervisor refused, announcing that this was a common practice at Preferred. In fact, whenever a worker left the employ of the company, Steuerwald or a member of the supervisory staff prayed over the ex-employee's office so as to rid it of the demons left behind by the departing employee.

During the course of an extended meeting that Mulder attended with other employees, each employee shared with the group some personal information concerning his or her spiritual journey. At the end of the day Mulder left the meeting mulling over the fact that all the people who spoke had revealed that they had had at least one religious experience. She had always believed that religious experiences were rare, usually occurring once in a lifetime, and for many persons not at all. Mulder considered it strange that all the speakers had had one or more such experiences, but she nevertheless felt excluded. She began to think of herself as an outcast. Not long after, she grew increasingly more uncomfortable—and sometimes nauseated—whenever a religious matter was discussed in the office.

Mulder grew frustrated with office inefficiencies and disciplinary problems that affected her ability to perform her job tasks. Whenever she raised these concerns with her supervisors, the response focused on religion rather than on a solution to the problem, and thus Mulder grew even more frustrated. Morale in the Indianapolis office was low, and Mulder perceived that many employees were upset and afraid they would lose their jobs if they openly opposed the religious content of their work environment. Matters did not improve when Steuerwald held a meeting with several employees, including Mulder, and told them that several departments were not operating smoothly because their employees were not on the path of God. She advised the group, "You realize that you're all sinners, that you all play a part in this, of being a sinner.... Until you people release your vanity and quit becoming vain people, you're always going to come up with these problems."

Steuerwald left no doubt that she intended to convert Mulder. When she asked Mulder whether she prayed over her work, Mulder responded that she was not raised to pray for material gain as she thought it was selfish to do so. Steuerwald replied, "Your kind are the hardest to break."

The continuous references to religious matters began to undermine Mulder's work performance. During a staff meeting she started to cry, and when she could not stop, she fled the room. She was depressed, and her depression seemed to grow each day. She found herself going home nearly every night in tears. In the end, she resigned, no longer able to tolerate Steuerwald's daily expressions of religious conviction and her campaign to persuade Mulder to adopt those convictions for herself.

Mulder testified in detail to all these matters during the course of the EEOC investigation and the litigation that followed. The EEOC argued before the court that Preferred had violated Title VII by making employment decisions on the basis of religious beliefs that were unacceptable to some employees, thus fostering a hostile work environment. It set out to prove that Steuerwald and other management personnel routinely made their own religious values and preferences the guiding principles of daily work life, that they preached a particular brand of religion as workplace orthodoxy, that they conditioned the work environment on their particular religious beliefs, and that they proselytized their employees to join in their religious preferences.

Preferred's defense to the EEOC charges was centered on its contention that all employees were informed before they joined the company that Preferred was a Christian business enterprise, that attendance at devotions and prayer sessions was not mandatory, and that participation in other religious practices was voluntary. The EEOC countered that while Preferred did not advance a written policy specifically requiring employees to attend devotions and prayer sessions or to commit to the religious beliefs promulgated in its workplace, Steuerwald's expectation that they attend such devotions and prayer sessions and commit to such religious beliefs amounted to a form of coercion. The jury agreed and awarded the seven complainants punitive damages in varying sums. Mary Mulder's punitive damages award was $85,000.[3]

An employer set on proselytizing its employees may succeed in its purposes without adopting the extreme measures utilized by the owners of the Sports and Health Club, by Jake and Helen Townley of the Townley Manufacturing Company, or by Jackie Steuerwald and her company, Preferred Home Health Care. A more reasoned approach, using less intrusive

methods, may elicit a more positive response from workers than those described in the cases discussed in this chapter. As long as an employee does
not object to an employer's efforts at proselytization, the employer may
proceed. Once an objection is asserted, however, the employer must desist.
The employer is always skating on thin ice when it engages in workplace
religious activities, and therefore its management must remain constantly
on guard that it not pass over the line separating activities that are condoned by Title VII from those that are not.

8

Employer Liability for Employee Acts of Religious Harassment

Title VII requires employers to maintain a discrimination-free work environment, a nonhostile environment free of acts of harassment, whether racial, national origin, sexual, or religious. Religious discrimination claims charging an employer with creating and maintaining a hostile work environment are closely allied to claims charging it with acts of harassment. The two types of claims go hand in glove, and both frequently appear in employee proselytization cases. A worker subjected to a coworker's unwelcome attempts at proselytization may call upon the employer to order the coworker to cease all such activities, and if the employer fails to act, the worker may then charge it with maintaining a hostile work environment. Alternatively, he may charge his employer with liability for the coworker's acts of harassment, alleging that despite his complaints, the employer failed to undertake any action to halt the coworker's campaign to persuade fellow workers to adopt his religious beliefs.

The EEOC has failed to adopt a set of regulations specifically defining "harassment" or a "hostile work environment" in religious discrimination cases. The courts, therefore, have had to look elsewhere, and in general have adopted the rules and standards developed in sexual harassment cases. In those cases an employer that encourages or tolerates a work environment replete with forms of harassing conduct that is sufficiently severe or pervasive to alter the terms and conditions of employment of workers subjected to harassment may be held liable for maintaining a hostile work environment or, alternatively, for the acts of harassment perpetrated by its workers. The courts define a sexually hostile work environment as one that is both subjectively and objectively hostile, subjectively hostile if the victim of the harassment finds her workplace to be hostile, and objectively hostile if a reasonable person also perceives it to be so. Whether a work environment is sufficiently hostile or abusive to support a sexual harassment claim is determined by viewing all the circumstances, including

- the frequency of the acts of sexual harassment
- the severity of the offensive conduct
- whether the victim was humiliated by reason of the conduct
- whether the harassment was that of a coworker or a supervisor
- whether other workers joined in the harassment
- whether the harassment was directed at more than one individual
- whether the harassment interfered with the victim's work performance to such extent as to alter the terms and conditions of employment.[1]

In the context of a religious harassment or hostile-work-environment case, the courts have used these standards to determine whether the religious practices of the employer or one or more of its employees constitute acts of unlawful harassment or create a hostile or abusive work environment. These were the standards the court applied when Sherry Kantar sued her employer for religious discrimination, purportedly by maintaining a hostile work environment.

After working for a number of years for the Baldwin Cooke Company as a telemarketer sales representative, Kantar sued the company, alleging that her group leader customarily made derogatory remarks about her religion, often referring to her as a JAP, or Jewish American Princess, inquiring about the "cost" of her Jewish faith, and needling her about leaving work early on Fridays to attend religious services.

During the course of the litigation that ensued, the court was required to determine whether Kantar had been compelled to work in a hostile work environment, and in this regard it applied the test factors generally used in sexual harassment cases. It examined the frequency of the alleged discriminatory conduct, its severity, whether it was humiliating or merely offensive, and whether it interfered with Kantar's work performance. As the court observed, not all workplace conduct that falls within the rubric of harassment necessarily affects the terms and conditions of person's employment. To be actionable, such conduct must be sufficiently severe or pervasive to alter the conditions of employment. Conduct that does not meet this criterion cannot be considered as having created an objectively hostile or abusive workplace.

In support of her claims that she had been subjected to acts of religious harassment and compelled to work in a hostile environment, Kantar relied upon a handful of offensive comments made over an extended period of time. The court rejected her claims, ruling that the comments she identified as having their source in religious bias could not reasonably be regarded either as religious harassment or as evidence of a hostile work environment because they were not severe or pervasive enough to support either claim.[2]

As noted in chapter 6, when an employee engages in acts of workplace proselytization, his employer must attempt to accommodate his religious beliefs and practices while preserving a work environment free of religious discriminatory animus. Ren Laboratories of Florida confronted such a balancing act when one of its supervisors insisted upon exercising his religious rights while at work even when they conflicted with the rights of his subordinate workers.

Kenneth Weiss sued Ren Laboratories under the provisions of Title VII, claiming that it had terminated his employment on account of his religious beliefs. Weiss, a born-again Christian, believed that he was required to share his religious faith with others, including his coworkers, and he showed no hesitancy in practicing that belief even when confronted by coworker resistance to his proselytizing initiatives. As a supervisor, he was responsible for maintaining a harassment-free workplace, and he claimed to have fulfilled that responsibility by refraining from discussing religious matters with workers whenever he was aware that such discussions were offensive to them. The testimony elicited during the course of the trial of his Title VII suit, however, showed otherwise:

- A Ren supervisor testified that Weiss initiated religious discussions with a subordinate female worker that centered on his admonition to her that according to the Bible she was headed for hell because she was a lesbian.

- He verbally attacked another female worker by condemning her dating habits.
- A Muslim worker complained to management that Weiss repeatedly spoke to him of his religious beliefs while condemning the beliefs and practices of others and that he was offended by Weiss's incessant attempts to convert him to Christianity.
- Another female employee testified that Weiss persisted in raising religious matters with her even after she advised him that she found these discussions unwelcome. He told her he was a prophet and that she should alter her lifestyle so as to be right with God. On one occasion he attempted to lay hands on her to cure her headaches.
- Many other employees, offended by Weiss's actions, had complained to management that he was interfering with their work performance.

Weiss was advised by management that he was free to discuss religious matters with coworkers as long as he encountered no objection, but he was barred from initiating or continuing religious discussions with employees who informed him that they did not wish to participate in such conversations. Weiss, however, disregarded those directions and continued to speak of religious matters, even with workers who advised him they were offended by these religiously oriented encounters. Ultimately management warned Weiss that he would be terminated if he persisted in engaging in nonconsensual religious discourse. He persisted and was terminated. He then sued Ren Laboratories.

At the trial Ren Laboratories produced ample evidence in support of its decision to terminate Weiss. His acts of harassment in its workplace were severe, frequent, and directed at a number of workers, including those holding positions subordinate to his. His actions interfered with the work performance of those employees, thus altering the terms and conditions of their employment. Ren Laboratories had not only the right but the legal duty to maintain its workplace free of religious harassment. Weiss's termination was fully justified.[3]

It must be emphasized that Ren Laboratories did not seek to bar all of Weiss's religious activities. Rather, management advised him that he was free to discuss religious matters with those employees who offered no objection. In a sexual harassment case, a female employee cannot reasonably complain about a coworker's sexual advances if her responses to those advances indicate that she welcomed them. In a religious harassment case, religiously oriented conduct will not be condemned unless coworkers make it known that they find such conduct offensive. Weiss was free to engage in his religious practices as long as he did not confront coworker resistance. At the point of resistance, however, he was obligated to cease those activities.

At what point does a work environment become hostile? In most instances, a single incident will not create a hostile working environment, but a pattern of repeated acts of harassing conduct almost always culminates in a hostile and offensive workplace. In a case involving a Jewish worker, one of his coemployees made repeated references to the Holocaust, often in a joking manner. These occurrences in and of themselves did not create a hostile work environment for the Jewish worker, but in the context of other events, they did. Because he was Jewish, his supervisors denied him the opportunity to work overtime. When he was assigned the task of collecting donations to a charity drive, he was subjected to comments about the nature of the assignment "because Jews were supposedly skilled in dealing with money." These types of comments, in combination with the offensive Holocaust jokes, were sufficiently pervasive to create a hostile work environment. Taken together, they disclosed a pattern of workplace conduct that materially interfered with the victim's work performance, thus altering the terms and conditions of his employment.[4]

Once an employee apprises her employer that she has been subjected to acts of religious harassment or that her working environment has turned hostile, her employer is obligated to investigate those charges and, if the circumstances warrant, undertake appropriate remedial action. Employers have utilized a variety of approaches to resolving employee hostile environment and religious harassment charges, and in certain circumstances, they have undertaken several measures before the problem was resolved. That is precisely what occurred in a case involving the Yellow Book company.

Tammy Powell began her employment with Yellow Book as a data-entry processor and later was promoted to financial services representative. In her new position Powell was assigned a work station located adjacent to that occupied by coworker Victoria Kreutz. Soon afterward, Kreutz experienced a religious conversion, became a parishioner of the First Assembly of God Church, and began to speak to Powell about her religious beliefs. Although she was receptive at first, Powell later grew weary of hearing about Kreutz's religious activities, and she asked her to cease speaking of those matters in her presence. But Kreutz persisted, attempting to convince Powell to accept her religious beliefs. When Powell complained to management about the continued proselytizing, Kreutz was directed not to broach religious matters with Powell. Even after management's intervention, Powell continued to complain of Kreutz's religious outspokenness. Management then transferred Kreutz to another cubicle, far distant from Powell's, and again ordered her to end all discussions of religious matters with Powell.

Powell, unhappy with management's handling of the matter, filed a Title VII action against Yellow Book. The trial court later observed that once Yellow Book's management became aware of Kreutz's harassing conduct, it undertook remedial actions reasonably calculated to end it, and it continued to monitor the situation to ensure that any improper conduct by Kreutz did not resume. Moreover, Powell failed to prove that Kreutz's communications about her religion amounted to severe or pervasive harassment or that these discussions altered the terms and conditions of her employment. The court held that Yellow Book's responses to Powell's complaints were prompt and reasonable. The court dismissed her case.[5]

Immediate and forceful responses to hostile environment and harassment claims generally relieve an employer of liability for errant employee behavior. That was the case when Denora Sarin sued the Raytheon Company, alleging that it had failed to take immediate and appropriate action to remedy the harassing actions of two of its employees.

Sarin, a Cambodian Buddhist, had worked for Raytheon as a systems engineer for two and one half years when he was transferred to another project. Within a week of the transfer, fellow worker Alan Goldberg approached Sarin and told him he knew that he was from Cambodia and was a Buddhist and he wanted to know what kind of Buddha he worshiped, "the skinny or the fat one?" About the same time, another worker taunted Sarin but later apologized and never repeated that conduct.

When Goldberg later again asked Sarin which Buddha he worshiped, Sarin informed his supervisor. Two months later Goldberg made some intimidating remarks that Sarin interpreted as a physical threats against his life. He again reported the incident, and in response the supervisors transferred Goldberg to another work station. Nonetheless, Goldberg thereafter frequently appeared at Sarin's place of work to stare at him but refrained from speaking to him. When another worker threatened Sarin with physical violence, he again apprised his supervisors. Both workers were then told they would be subject to severe disciplinary actions if they again harassed Sarin. By that point Sarin was experiencing chest pains and had difficulty eating and sleeping. Upon the recommendation of his doctor, he resigned his employment at Raytheon.

In the litigation that followed, Raytheon argued that it could not be held liable for the actions of its employees because it took immediate and appropriate action as soon as it learned of the harassment. The court agreed that Raytheon should not be held liable because it immediately acted upon learning of each harassing incident. The court observed that "Sarin's supervisors...responded promptly to each incident Sarin brought to their attention, [and] warned offenders that any subsequent discriminatory conduct would constitute grounds for severe discipline." In those circumstances, Raytheon was not liable.[6]

When an employer fails to take action to eradicate harassing conduct from its workplace, it acts at its own peril, for if one of its workers files legal charges complaining about its conduct, it is highly likely that a court will find the employer liable for failing to halt the harassment. That was the case when Spencer Press of Maine failed to heed the pleas of one of its employees that his supervisor was daily harassing him on account of his religious views.

Shortly after Albert Johnson started working in Spencer's custodial department, Steven Halasz was promoted to supervisor of that department. Prior to his employment with Spencer, Johnson had earned a B.S. degree in Bible studies and served as a pastor of a local church. He freely disclosed his religious views to his fellow workers, and although Halasz was aware that Johnson was a religious person, he made extremely inappropriate and lewd comments in Johnson's presence, some of which targeted Johnson's religion. Halasz expressed the opinion that Johnson must be a Catholic as he refrained from extramarital sexual activities. He called Johnson a "religious freak" and told him that he did not want to hear any of his "religious bullshit." On one occasion Halasz presented Johnson with a copy of *Playboy* magazine, and when Johnson declined to view the photographs of nude women, Halasz again commented that Johnson must be Catholic since he grew flustered whenever confronted with a sexual situation. Halasz concluded that Johnson was just too chaste.

On at least six occasions Johnson complained to Spencer's human resources department about his treatment by Halasz, and each time he was advised that nothing could be done about it. His only option was to leave the company. Instead, Johnson requested a transfer to another division in the company, but that request was denied. Subsequently he suffered severe depression and panic attacks and once had to be taken to a hospital by ambulance. At that point he resigned and sued Spencer for religious harassment.

Spencer had no defense to Johnson's claims. Halasz's treatment of Johnson was sufficiently severe and pervasive to alter the terms and conditions of his employment, as it significantly interfered with his work performance. Yet Spencer failed to undertake any action to stop Halasz's harassing conduct. By not acting, Spencer in effect approved of Halasz's behavior and thus became liable for it. A jury awarded Johnson compensatory and punitive damages and both awards were affirmed by the appellate court.[7]

The human resources person assigned to handle Johnson's harassment charges informed him that if she were to pursue his complaint against Halasz, she herself would be fired. This suggests that Spencer, regardless of the circumstances, did not intend to take action to halt the harassing conduct of its employees. It knowingly violated the provisions of Title VII, and thus the damage awards levied against it were well deserved.

Employers have the means to insulate themselves from liability for employee conduct that is clearly harassing, and those means are readily at hand. They merely have to act to halt the harassment.

9

WORKPLACE DISCRIMINATION
AND CERTAIN RELIGIOUS GROUPS

A recent survey disclosed that nearly every religious group in the country has experienced some form of religious bias in the workplace. For example, 77 percent of the Muslim workers responding to the survey reported they were concerned or troubled about the presence of religious bias in their workplaces. Sixty-seven percent of Jewish workers, 56 percent of Buddhist workers, and 70 percent of Christian workers had similar concerns. Seventeen percent of Muslim respondents disclosed that they had personally been subjected to acts of religious bias on the job, while the percentage of the other groups who had experienced workplace religious discrimination ranged from 20 percent of Christian workers to 12 percent of Buddhist workers and 6 percent of Jewish workers.[1]

Each religious group suffers modes of harassment and workplace hostility unique to that group. In this chapter we will examine the acts of discrimination experienced by certain religious groups and the ways in which the courts have responded to their complaints.

Atheists

We examined in chapter 5 the case involving Martha Young, who was required by her employer to attend monthly staff meetings that were preceded by a religious homily and followed by a prayer, both led by a local Baptist minister. Young, an atheist, objected to attending those meetings because of their religious content.[2]

The court that later considered Young's legal claims ruled that her atheistic beliefs were protected by Title VII, and consequently her employer could not require her to attend meetings where she would be compelled to participate in what amounted to a religious ceremony. We are presented here with anomalous circumstances in which a worker holding no religious beliefs is granted the protection of a statute enacted to protect the religious rights of workers. Before becoming overly exercised about this, however, we should consider the following. When men and women deny God, they may be denying a particular conception of God, a conception that may in fact be false, and they may be correct in rejecting it.[3] Thus we should not be too quick to deny the protections of the statute to those who think differently than most do, and that includes atheists.

Support for this position has been offered by believers, no less. One of them, Douglas A. Hicks, an ordained minister of the Presbyterian Church (USA), has observed that atheists hold moral convictions and in their daily lives draw upon their own value systems: "One's atheism need not be stated in negative terms.... Indeed, many persons who do not practice religion or spirituality are eager to state their values in positive terms. They try to share those values...with co-workers and, in some cases, convince co-workers that all people should hold these values."[4]

Thus as far as Title VII is concerned, atheists stand in the same position as believers. They may rely upon the provisions of the statute to protect them from the discriminatory acts of their employers as well as their co-workers, but they are also subjected to the same restrictions on their workplace conduct as believers.

Catholics

Anti-Catholic bias, once prevalent, still surfaces on occasion. Henry Heffernan, a Jesuit priest, was employed as a chaplain by a clinic operated by the National Institutes of Health in Washington, D.C. Heffernan had several disputes with his boss, who frequently displayed an animosity toward Catholics, often joking about priests being pedophiles and averring that he never again would hire a Catholic for the clinic. He targeted Heffernan for special treatment, requiring him to take elementary courses in chaplaincy, even though Heffernan had been a priest and a hospital chaplain for many years. Heffernan, out of concern that Catholic patients were being deprived of sufficient spiritual services, said Mass for patients on his days off. For his efforts, he was suspended and ultimately fired. He then filed a discrimination charge with the EEOC, and after a hearing on the merits of his charge, the EEOC ruled that Heffernan had been discharged because of his religion and ordered his reinstatement.[5]

In that case, the evidence of anti-Catholic bias was clearly present. That is not always the case, as Catholic workers frequently find that evidence supporting their claims of religious bias is in short supply. Paula Skorup worked in the racking department of the Modern Door Corporation. During her employment, the company purchased two machines to automate the racking process, thus initiating the downsizing of the department. The general manager of the company instructed the racking department head to lay off two workers, and Skorup was one of the two selected.

Skorup, a Catholic, later alleged that she would not have been terminated had she been a Baptist, the faith shared by the company's general manager and several other employees. She claimed that Baptist management personnel showed a strong preference for Baptist workers, hiring a disproportionate number of them and providing them with preferential job assignments. But she had little evidence to offer in support of these allegations. In addition, she failed to address a powerful piece of evidence standing in opposition to her position: the department head responsible for selecting her for termination was himself a Catholic. Skorup's religious discrimination claim was dismissed.[6]

As previously noted, religious discrimination claims should not be pursued unless the plaintiff worker possesses evidence strongly supporting the existence of workplace bias. This caveat is especially relevant for workers alleging anti-Catholic bias, as large numbers of Americans now profess the Catholic faith, and a Catholic plaintiff may find that some of the employees she charges with bias are themselves Catholic. Such an occurrence generally ends in defeat for the plaintiff.

Christian Fundamentalists

Several cases examined in previous chapters point up the problems Christian fundamentalists bring to the workplace. In many instances, those professing fundamentalist beliefs leave their employers with no option other than to suppress religious practices devoted to converting fellow employees. Fundamentalists, of course, have the right to pursue their conversion practices as long as the targeted employees express no opposition (and they are not the cause of workplace disruption or interference with normal procedures), but once confronted with dissent or resistance, they must desist from further practices of that nature. Religious discussion in the workplace must always be consensual.

Employers holding fundamentalist beliefs are subject to the same rule. An employer is free to introduce religious issues into its workplace as long as it accommodates employees who do not wish to participate in such practices. Conversely, an employer may not bar all religious discussion in its workplace as a means of ensuring that its employees are not subjected against their will to religious commentary and attempts at conversion.

Jehovah's Witnesses

Jehovah's Witnesses interpret the Bible as commanding all persons, at the risk of God's displeasure, to decline to participate in the pledge of allegiance to any flag or take any oath other than one swearing allegiance to their faith and God. Gregory Lawson, a Jehovah's Witness, was hired by the Washington State Patrol and directed to begin his basic training as a trooper cadet at the patrol's academy in Shelton, Washington. At the time of his hiring he was issued a manual setting forth the patrol's procedures, rules, and regulations; it stated that all cadets were required to assemble twice daily for flag formations, and any cadet deviating from that rule would be subjected to discipline, including termination. In his first two days at the academy, Lawson participated in flag formations and performed the required hand salutes. But he was troubled. He firmly believed that he was barred from saluting the flag of any nation, including that of the United States. But he was equally troubled by another requirement set forth in the manual. Upon the completion of his training, he would be required to take an oath to support the constitutions of the United States as well as the State of Washington. He realized that his Jehovah's Witness beliefs barred him from taking such an oath.

On the third day at the academy, Lawson met with the acting commander and informed him that his religious beliefs prevented him from saluting the flag or taking an oath of allegiance to any governmental authority. He then signed a letter of resignation stating that he was leaving the academy for personal reasons.

Lawson subsequently filed a Title VII suit alleging that the Washington State Patrol had forced his termination by failing to accommodate his religious beliefs. The court rejected his claim, ruling that because he had voluntarily resigned his position, the patrol was not under any compulsion to offer him any accommodation.[7]

The religious convictions of Jehovah's Witnesses have caused workplace problems of another type. In a case examined in chapter 2, a Jehovah's Witness worked for a steel company that fabricated sheet steel for a variety of industrial uses. When he was later transferred to a department that produced turrets for military tanks, he terminated his employment, claiming that his religious convictions as a Jehovah's Witness prevented him from participating in the production of war materials.

He subsequently applied for unemployment compensation benefits. During the course of an administrative hearing conducted to determine his right to such compensation, he testified that he believed contributing to the production of military arms violated the religious beliefs of the Jehovah's Witnesses. But another Jehovah's Witness employee testified that he had no scruples about working in the turret department. The review board then ruled that unemployment benefits were unavailable to the worker on the ground that when he resigned his employment he had made a personal rather than a religious choice.

When the case reached the United States Supreme Court, the Court noted that intrafaith differences are not uncommon among followers of a particular creed, such as that adopted by the Jehovah's Witnesses, and that the judicial process is singularly ill equipped to resolve those differences. The Court then ruled that it was clear that the worker sincerely held the belief that he was barred from involvement with the manufacture of military armaments. He had thus terminated his employment for religious reasons and consequently was entitled to unemployment compensation benefits.[8]

Jews

As apparent from cases examined in previous chapters, anti-Semitism is no stranger to the workplace. But even where it is absent from the workplace, Jews still encounter opposition because of their religion. We will examine both sets of circumstances.

Kenneth Shanoff, a medical school graduate, worked in Chicago as a staff development and training coordinator at the John Madden Mental Health Center, operated by the Illinois Department of Human Services. Sylvia Riperton-Lewis, a manager at the Madden Center, was Shanoff's direct supervisor. Shanoff, who was white and Jewish, alleged that Riperton-Lewis, who was black and not Jewish, had harassed him with remarks directed at his race and religion:

- Riperton-Lewis referred to Shanoff as a "haughty Jew."
- When Shanoff reported these remarks to the director of the Madden Center, Riperton-Lewis told Shanoff that she was determined to keep his "white Jewish ass…down." She repeated this comment on several occasions.
- When he reported to her that his health was failing because she was harassing him, she responded "good."
- She prohibited him from teaching medical students, even though that task was included in his job description. When he complained, she struck out this provision from his job description, remarking that she knew "how to put you Jews in your place."
- She told him that "she knew how to handle white Jewish males, and once and for all time [he] needed to get out of her hair."
- She once said to him, "I hate everything that you are."

Riperton-Lewis continued to direct anti-Semitic remarks at Shanoff, stating that she was tired of his "not knowing his place." After nearly two years of similar remarks, Shanoff, by that time suffering from depression, was forced to take extended sick leave. While on leave, he filed a charge with the EEOC and later a Title VII action, alleging that Riperton-Lewis had discriminated against him on account of his religion and race. After considering the evidence, the court concluded that through her anti-Semitic remarks, made in Shanoff's presence, Riperton-Lewis had clearly expressed her hostility to Shanoff's Jewish faith and his Caucasian race and was motivated to drive him from the Madden Mental Health Center. "She used her supervisory position to bully, intimidate and insult Shanoff because of his race and religion, which is the type of...harassment that is the hallmark of a hostile environment claim."[9]

The work schedules of Jewish workers may interfere with their obligation to attend religious services on the Jewish Sabbath, thus leading to disputes with their employers. Shari Gordon, an Orthodox Jew, applied for a position with MCI Telecommunications Corporation in New York City. Because of her religious beliefs, Gordon was unable to cook, ride in a car, write, carry money, or turn on electricity from sundown Friday until sundown Saturday. During the fall and winter months, she had to leave work on Fridays in sufficient time to be home and prepare her house for the Sabbath before sundown.

Gordon interviewed for the position of staff assistant in the human resources department of MCI's New York City office. MCI offered her the position but advised her that it would be unable to arrange for her to leave work early on Friday afternoons during the fall and winter months. Gordon responded that she could not accept the position unless her work schedule was arranged so that she could meet her Sabbath requirements.

Gordon filed suit against MCI, alleging that it had discriminated against her on account of her religion. MCI countered by asking the court to dismiss her case on the ground that Gordon had rejected its job offer before it had the opportunity to suggest an accommodation to satisfy her Sabbath needs. But the evidence showed that MCI's offer of employment was conditioned on Gordon's presence at work until 5:30 p.m. on every Friday throughout the year. Gordon's proof that MCI had no intention of accommodating her religious needs carried the day.[10]

Mormons

Workers who are not Mormons have at times accused their Mormon supervisors of discriminating against them merely because they were not Mormons. Alexander Shapolia based his Title VII action against his employer on the claim that his Mormon supervisors had undermined his employment status, and that this had led to his discharge. After Shapolia had worked eleven years as an electrician at the Los Alamos National Laboratory, his supervisor, Ray Martin, provided him with a poor performance evaluation. When Shapolia attempted to have the negative evaluation altered or removed, John Whetten, an associate director, agreed with Martin's evaluation and rejected Shapolia's efforts to have it modified. Shapolia was then placed on conditional employment status and transferred to another department. Later he was terminated by another supervisor for failing to meet the conditions of his conditional employment status.

In his Title VII suit that followed, Shapolia alleged that the negative performance evaluation and the ensuing review procedures were tainted by religious discrimination. As a nonpracticing member of the Greek Orthodox Church, he argued that his performance had been rated deficient solely because Martin, a bishop in the Mormon Church, was biased against non-Mormons, and Whetten, as a fellow Mormon, had failed to act impartially in reviewing the evaluation.

Shapolia endeavored to back up his claim that Martin and Whetten discriminated against non-Mormons by describing Mormons as "clannish," but such an assertion possessed no probative value. The mere fact that a Mormon associate director had approved a Mormon supervisor's performance evaluation of a non-Mormon employee was insufficient to prove religious bias. Since Shapolia could offer no independent evidence demonstrating that religious bias played any role in his termination, the court dismissed his claims.[11]

Muslims

A recent study found that American Muslims, along with Buddhists and Hindus, are the least comfortable and the most vulnerable groups in the American workplace.[12] The events of September 11, 2001, accentuated American Muslims' perception that religious prejudice runs rampant throughout every aspect of their lives, including their jobs. After the terrorist attacks, state and federal civil rights agencies were flooded with complaints by Muslims contending that their employers and coworkers openly denigrated Islam. For the seven-month period after the 9/11 attacks, the number of complaints filed with the EEOC by Muslims alleging religious discrimination in the workplace increased by 300 percent.[13] Two years later, the Council on American-Islamic Relations reported more than a thousand incidents of alleged harassment and discriminatory acts perpetrated against Muslims, an increase of 70 percent over the previous year. Most of those incidents occurred in the workplace.[14] In 2005 the council reported that the number of these incidents had increased to nearly two thousand, although those occurring in the workplace appeared to have tapered off.[15]

From an early age, Mohammed Hussein dreamed of becoming an airline pilot, and he devoted his life to attaining that dream. Born and educated in Fiji, he focused his high school studies on science and mathematics to better prepare himself for aviation studies in college. After attaining his undergraduate degree at a university in New Zealand, he attended the Sierra Academy of Aeronautics in Oakland, California, where he later taught for three years as an instructor. In February 2001, he was hired by Trans States Airlines as a pilot.[16] Hussein was a Muslim.

On September 11, 2001, commercial air travel was suspended as a consequence of the terrorist attacks. Two days later, Trans States directed Hussein to fly a plane to the St. Louis airport. After arriving in St. Louis, he rented a room in a nearby hotel. According to Trans States' vice president of flight operations, he received a phone call later that day from an unidentified caller reporting that a pilot in a Trans States uniform had been seen in a hotel bar making comments about the attacks of September 11 and that a bartender had asked him to leave. The caller also stated that he had read the pilot's identification tag and his name was Hussein. After determining from his staff that Trans States employed a pilot named Hussein and that he was based in St. Louis, the vice president of operations ordered Hussein to be terminated.

It was later revealed that the unknown caller was a pilot employed by another airline. While eating dinner at the hotel bar, he had observed a man in a pilot's uniform drinking beer at the bar and watching television. When a replay of the plane hitting the World Trade Center appeared on the screen, the pilot sitting at the bar raised his beer in salute. Hussein later confirmed that he was present at the bar but denied that he made any gestures approving the terrorist attacks, which he believed were "contemptible and horrific."

After his discharge, Hussein filed a charge of discrimination with the EEOC. After investigating the matter, the EEOC determined that Trans States had terminated Hussein on account of his religion in violation of

Title VII, and it brought suit on his behalf against the airline. Replying to these charges, Trans States alleged that it had fired Hussein only because he violated company policy by entering a hotel bar while in uniform. Thus the question that confronted the court was whether Trans States was motivated to terminate Hussein by reason of a discriminatory animus or because he had violated company policy. Unfortunately for Hussein, the EEOC was unable to prove that Trans States had been motivated to act by reason of his religion. The most that the EEOC could offer the court to substantiate the discrimination charge amounted to little more than conjecture. It labeled Trans States' assertion that Hussein had been terminated on the basis of information received in an anonymous telephone call as inherently incredible and argued that it was far more credible to conclude, since the events in question occurred shortly after the September 11 terrorist attacks, that he had been terminated only because he was a Muslim. The court rejected these arguments on the ground that they were based solely on uncorroborated circumstantial evidence, insufficient to support a finding of intentional discrimination. The court then ruled in favor of Trans States, dismissing the suit.[17]

The actual reason for Hussein's termination probably will never be known. Was he discharged because he was observed drinking beer while in uniform, in violation of company policy, or was he terminated because he had an Arab- or Muslim-sounding name and was said to have been seen applauding the terrorist attacks of September 11? Hussein may simply have been in the wrong place at the wrong time, and it was his misfortune that others present at the bar observed him drinking while in uniform. No witnesses, however, surfaced to testify that his employer actually acted out of religious bias.

Over the years a significant number of legal complaints regarding workplace dress codes have been asserted by Muslim women. Alima Delores Reardon, a devout follower of Islam, believed that a Muslim woman whenever present in a public place should cover her entire body except her face and hands. She worked as a substitute and full-time teacher in the Philadelphia school system and while teaching, wore a head scarf covering her head, neck, and bosom and a long, loose dress covering her arms to the wrist. On three separate occasions she reported for substitute teacher duty but was informed by school principals that she could not teach in her religious clothing as it violated state law. This law, commonly referred to as the

Pennsylvania Garb Statute, prohibited public school teachers from wearing "any dress, mark, emblem or insignia indicating...that such teacher is a member or adherent of any religious order, sect, or denomination."[18] On each occasion Reardon was given the opportunity to go home and change her clothing, but each time she refused, and on each occasion she was not allowed to teach. After the third incident Reardon filed a religious discrimination charge with the EEOC. Subsequently, the Justice Department, acting on her behalf, commenced legal action against the Philadelphia Board of Education, alleging that it had violated Title VII by refusing to employ a public school teacher who sought "to wear garb or dress that [constituted] an aspect of her religious observance." Despite the efforts of the Justice Department, the board of education prevailed. It argued that it had no choice but to comply with the garb statute, for if it did not, it faced criminal prosecution. In those circumstances, it could not accommodate Reardon's religious practices without incurring undue hardship. The court agreed and dismissed the case.[19]

Other women have not fared much better. A Muslim woman working as a flight attendant for U.S. Airways began to wear a head scarf, or hijab, after becoming convinced that her faith required her to change to that mode of dress. The airline objected, however, and refused to permit her to serve any longer as a flight attendant. Management explained that in the interest of presenting a neutral face to the public, it prohibited employees in uniform from wearing religious symbols, such as a crucifix or a Star of David. The Muslim flight attendant was not persuaded and insisted upon the continued use of the head scarf. Litigation was avoided only after U.S. Airways agreed to allow her to transfer to another position where she would be engaged in training flight attendants, a job that did not require her to work in the presence of airline passengers.[20]

While Muslim women confront head scarf issues, Muslim men face issues relating to their beards. Faruq Abdul-Aziz and Shakoor Mustafa, members of the Newark, New Jersey, Police Department, were Sunni Muslims who believed they were obligated by their faith and the commands of the Quran to grow their beards. This was not a discretionary matter for them, as the refusal of a Sunni Muslim male to grow a beard constituted a major sin. When police officials questioned Aziz and Mustafa about their failure to comply with department policy that prohibited beards except for medical reasons, they admitted that they were growing their beards solely for religious reasons. Department officials refused to exempt Aziz and Mustafa from the no-beard ban and threatened them with disciplinary action for violating police department policy. Aziz and Mustafa then filed a federal court complaint requesting the court to enjoin the Newark Police Department from enforcing the no-beard policy on the ground that it violated their constitutional right to the free exercise of their religious beliefs.

They argued before the court that the police department's decision to grant a medical but not a religious exemption from the no-beard policy unconstitutionally devalued their religious beliefs. The department countered that if it were to permit police officers to grow beards for religious reasons, its morale and esprit de corps would be undermined. Department officials were unable to explain, however, why the presence of police officers growing beards for medical reasons did not have the same effect. Suggesting that the department's true aim was to conceal religious differences among its officers by obscuring the fact that Aziz and Mustafa held religious beliefs differing from other members of the police force, the court concluded that enforcement of the no-beard policy officials should be enjoined.[21]

Their beards identified Aziz and Mustafa as Muslims, and this apparently established the basis for police department objections. Muslims working in other areas have also confronted resistance from their employers when they demonstrated identity with Islam. Elijah Karriem worked as a security guard in an office building managed and operated by the Oliver T. Carr Company in Washington, D.C. While on duty he wore a pin on his guard uniform that identified him as a Muslim. Karriem's supervisors, at the direction of Carr management, directed him to refrain from wearing the pin, but he refused to comply. Several months later he was dismissed, purportedly for violating company policy.

During the course of the Title VII litigation that ensued, the Carr Company claimed that Karriem's pin identifying himself as a Muslim violated a District of Columbia regulation providing that "no security officer shall wear or carry a metal or metallic appearing badge." The court concluded that the regulation was intended to avoid confusion in the public's eye with the official badge worn by members of the D.C. Police Department. Noting that Karriem's pin bore no resemblance to the police badge, the court inferred that the company had ordered adverse employment action taken against him only because it wished to prevent him from wearing a religious pin while on duty. Title VII proscribes such actions, and thus the court ruled in favor of Karriem.[22]

With the passage of time, employers have grown more sensitive to Muslim religious practices and have undertaken somewhat novel actions to accommodate them. When a veiled Muslim woman arrived for her first day of work at an IBM facility, she was told that she had to have her picture taken for her employee identification badge. She objected on religious grounds to showing her face to the photographer and also to allowing other IBM workers to see a photo of her when they viewed her identification badge.

IBM offered a two-step solution. First, she would be photographed while veiled, and this photo would be used on her identification badge. Second, a female photographer would take her picture unveiled, and this photo would be used on a second badge that she was directed to carry in her purse. If she ever had to show that badge, she would be required to do so only to a female security officer. These terms were acceptable to the Muslim employee, and further problems were avoided.[23]

Procter & Gamble provides rooms for Muslim and other employees to pray. Ford supports programs calling for the installation of sinks designed for the religious washings performed by some Muslim workers. Other employers are revising long-standing policies to accommodate other Muslim religious practices.[24]

Native Americans

Cheryl Campos was hired as a crisis counselor by the Blue Springs Police Department's Youth Outreach Unit in Missouri. At the time, she did not have the advanced psychology or social work degree and a Missouri license required by the job description for the position.

Campos's immediate supervisor was Pamela Petrillo, who advised her that she needed to complete her Ph.D. dissertation and obtain a Missouri counseling license, and she set a deadline for Campos to achieve those goals. She also informed Campos that she would be paid an additional $10,000 per year for participating in group support work and that she would be promoted to team leader within three months and to assistant director three months after that.

At first Campos and Petrillo worked well together, but after Campos informed Petrillo that she observed the tenets of Native American spirituality rather than Christianity, Petrillo began to treat her differently. She grew unfriendly and critical and subsequently implied that Campos might not be a good fit for the job. Petrillo also began to exclude Campos from staff meetings, including those in which the topic of discussion was whether the Youth Outreach Unit should be transformed into a Christian counseling unit.

Trouble continued to brew between the two. Petrillo unfairly criticized Campos for missing deadlines, falsely accused her of making mistakes, and refused to promote her to a team leader position as she had promised. She also told Campos that she was not a good role model and advised her that she should find a good Christian boyfriend who could teach her to be more submissive. Campos was not paid the $10,000 extra compensation she had been promised, and when she complained, Petrillo stated that people "sometimes [have] to give up the things they need most in order to be a good Christian."

In order to complete the work necessary to obtain her Ph.D., Campos began meeting weekly with her dissertation professor, but Petrillo then refused to grant her permission to leave work to attend those meetings. At that point, Campos resigned, citing Petrillo's religious prejudice as the reason for her resignation, and she filed suit against the city of Blue Springs, alleging that Petrillo had committed acts of religious discrimination. After a trial, a jury awarded her over $181,000 in damages.

On the appeal of the jury verdict, the city argued that Campos had failed to present evidence sufficient to establish liability for acts of religious discrimination. The appellate court rejected this argument, ruling that Campos had indeed presented sufficient evidence to support her claim that she was forced to quit her job with the Youth Outreach Unit because she was not a Christian. The court also ruled that Campos had endured months of harassment only because Petrillo wanted to place a Christian in her position.[25]

Petrillo may have discriminated against Campos because she practiced Native American spirituality, or she may have discriminated against her merely because she was not a Christian. In either case Campos lost her job. The jury and the court of appeals made certain that justice prevailed in this case.

Seventh-day Adventists

The Seventh-day Adventist Church teaches its members to observe the Sabbath from sundown Friday to sundown Saturday and to refrain from engaging in secular work during that time; it also holds that repeated violations of the Sabbath observance imperil one's salvation. This teaching has been the source of serious workplace problems for many members of that church.

Paula Hobbie worked for Lawton and Company, a Florida jeweler, first as a trainee and then as assistant manager of a retail jewelry store. After two and one-half years with Lawton, Hobbie informed her supervisor that she was to be baptized into the Seventh-day Adventist Church and that she would no longer be able to work on Saturdays. Hobbie's supervisor rearranged her work schedule so that she no longer had to work from sundown Friday to sundown Saturday, and this arrangement continued until Lawton's general manager learned of it. After meeting with Hobbie and her minister, he informed Hobbie she could either work on Saturdays or submit her resignation. When she refused to take either step, he discharged her.

Hobbie then filed a claim for unemployment compensation with the Florida Department of Labor and Employment Security. Under Florida law, as under the laws of many other states, unemployment compensation benefits are available only to persons who become unemployed through no fault of their own. Lawton contested the payment of any benefits to Hobbie on the ground that she was "disqualified for benefits" because she had been discharged for "misconduct connected with [her] work." The Florida authorities agreed and denied her any benefits.

The case ultimately reached the U.S. Supreme Court, which reversed the Florida ruling. The Court noted that a state may not force a worker to choose between following the precepts of her religion and forfeiting job benefits, such as unemployment compensation, nor may a worker be compelled to abandon her religion's precepts in order to maintain her continued employment.[26]

Hobbie declined to pursue a Title VII claim against Lawton. Had she done so, she more than likely would have prevailed because Lawton's general manager had not attempted to accommodate her religious practices. Lawton would have had great difficulty explaining how its general manager was unable to accommodate Hobbie when her supervisor had done so without encountering any obstacles.

Part II

Religion and the Public-Sector Workplace

10

Religion in the Public-Sector Workplace

Federal, state, and municipal employees are afforded constitutional protections not generally available to employees working in the private sector. The First Amendment states that "Congress shall make no law respecting an establishment of religion or prohibiting the free exercise thereof." Although framed as a limitation on the authority of the federal government, the Fourteenth Amendment makes the limitation applicable to state governmental agencies as well. The purpose of the establishment and free exercise clauses is to prevent the intrusion of the church or the state into the jurisdiction or domain of the other. The justification for the separation between church and state is based on the premise that both religion and government can best work to achieve their aims if each is left free from the other within its respective sphere of activity.

The establishment clause pledges that no single religion will be designated a state religion, and it proscribes government sponsorship, financial support, or active involvement in religious activity. The free exercise clause bars a governmental entity from infringing the exercise of religion by individuals, including those it employs. In that regard, the courts must guard the right of every individual to worship according to the dictates of conscience while requiring the government to maintain a course of neutrality among religions. In this chapter we examine how the courts have applied the establishment and free exercise clauses in resolving conflicts arising in public-sector workplaces. Since constitutional protections are generally available only in the public sector, none of the cases that follow involve employees working for private-sector employers.

All the residents of the village of Kiryas Joel in New York were Hasidic Jews. The United Talmudic Academy, a private religious school, provided education for the Hasidic children residing in the village. In accordance with the tenets of Hasidic religious observance, which under certain circumstances prohibits social interaction between the sexes, the academy maintained separate schools for boys and girls

Under the New York Education Law, the local public school district in which the village was located was required to provide bus services for the academy's Hasidic students. On the day that the bus service was inaugurated, the school district authorities assigned bus driver Patricia Dugan to transport a group of male students to the academy, but when she arrived to collect her riders, they refused to board the bus. The academy later advised school district authorities that because of the religious tenets restricting interaction between the sexes, the male students could not board a bus driven by a woman. The school district then replaced Dugan with a male driver.

Dugan, who had greater seniority than her male replacement, claimed that when the school district replaced her with a driver having less seniority, it violated its collective bargaining agreement with the union representing the bus drivers. The school district justified her removal from that bus route on the ground that since the male students would not board a bus with Dugan as its driver, she "lacked the skill and ability to handle" the route and the children traveling on it. Dugan and the union cried foul, and the litigation began.

The primary issue before the court was whether the deployment of only male drivers on bus routes transporting students to the academy would have the effect of advancing Hasidic beliefs. Did the use of male drivers transform the school district's bus service into a vehicle for promoting the Hasidic belief that boys must refrain from contact with women? The court responded in the affirmative, holding that when the school district provided Hasidic students with male bus drivers, it in effect lent support to a Hasidic religious belief, thus violating the establishment clause.

But the academy pointed out that the court's ruling raised another issue. Would not the school district's failure to provide bus services in a manner consistent with Hasidic religious beliefs violate the free exercise clause since it forced Hasidic adherents to choose between the receipt of a governmental benefit and the observance of those beliefs? The court responded in the negative, observing that although the use of both male and female drivers would infringe upon the Hasidim's right to the free exercise of their religion, the resulting burden on their religious freedom was justifiable because the school district had a compelling interest in providing transportation for all students on an equal basis.[1]

A federal or state employer that restricts discussion of religious topics or the display of religious items in its workplace may be acting in violation of the free exercise clause. The board of supervisors of Polk County in Iowa made the mistake of stepping over the line that separates employment actions that comply with the provisions of the free exercise clause from those that do not.

Polk County employed Isaiah Brown, a born-again Christian, as director of its data processing department, and in that capacity Brown supervised over fifty employees. An internal investigation that examined the workplace religious activities of employees working in the data processing unit revealed that Brown was participating in various religious practices with the workers he supervised:

- On occasion, before the workday began, he allowed employees to say prayers in his office.
- Prayers were often said at departmental meetings.
- In addressing a meeting of employees, Brown affirmed his Christian faith and referred to biblical passages relating to slothfulness and work ethics.
- He kept various religious objects on open display in his office.
- He often instructed a secretary to type Bible study notes for him.

Subsequently the county administrator reprimanded Brown, stating that he lacked judgment: "pertaining to his personal participation in and/or his knowledge of employees participating in activities that could be construed as the direct support of or the promotion of a religious organization or religious activities [while] utilizing the resources of Polk County Government." He directed Brown to cease all activities that could be considered proselytizing and to halt further use of county resources in a way that could be perceived as support for a religious organization. He also instructed Brown to remove all religious objects from his office.

On two later occasions the administrator again reprimanded Brown for failing to exercise proper judgment in participating in various workplace religious activities and also for operating county computers for personal use. He then requested Brown's resignation, and when Brown refused, he fired him. Brown countered by suing the county, alleging that it had violated the constitutional guarantees of free exercise of religion and free speech.

In a case of this nature the plaintiff must show that the governmental action complained of substantially burdened or interfered with his religious activities. Brown had no difficulty in establishing that his religious beliefs played a central role in his life and that he believed God expected him to pray always for the nation and the schools and for solutions to the problems of society. Clearly he found the county administrator's prohibitions on his religious practices to be oppressive and a serious hindrance to the exercise of his religious rights. Did these prohibitions violate his constitutional rights?

The court found the administrator's instructions to be far too broad in that they virtually commanded the removal of religion from the workplace. Polk County possessed the legal right to render its workplace free of any religious activity that tended to harass or intimidate its employees, but instead of confining its prohibition of Brown's religious activities to speech or actions that were harassing or intimidating, it baldly directed Brown to "cease any activities that *could be considered* to be religious proselytizing." That order, the court held, exhibited a hostility toward religion that our Constitution simply prohibits:

> It would seem to require no argument that to forbid speech "that could be considered" religious is not narrowly tailored to the aim of prohibiting harassment, although it is certainly capable of doing that. If Mr. Brown asked someone to attend his church, for instance, we suppose that "could be considered" proselytizing, but its prohibition runs afoul of the Free Exercise Clause.

The court then turned its attention to the county administrator's order directing Brown to remove from his office all items having a religious connotation. These included his Bible, a plaque containing the serenity prayer ("God, grant me the serenity to accept the things I cannot change, the courage to change the things I can, and the wisdom to know the difference"), a second plaque that simply read "God be in my life and in my commitment," and a third plaque that set forth the Lord's Prayer. These items had to go, the administrator instructed, because they might be "offensive" to other employees.

No evidence was offered showing that the presence of these items in Brown's office disrupted the workplace or interfered with the efficient operation of the county's business affairs. Even if some workers were to view their presence as offensive, the county could not legally order their removal because it would then be favoring one side in a religious dispute, a move that would be in violation of the establishment clause. If, however, the offensive character of the display had arisen from apprehension among employees of possible discriminatory treatment by Brown—that he would treat subordinates who did not object to his religious activities more favorably than those who did—the case would have been different. Absent those circumstances, the actions of the county administrator had to be rejected. Thus the court ruled in Brown's favor.[2]

The court's decision could have gone the other way had there been any evidence that county employees were harassed or intimidated by Brown's conduct, but the record in the case was silent in that regard. If coworkers fail to complain about the workplace religious activities of other employees, it is not likely the court will restrict those activities absent evidence of workplace disruption or interference with normal procedures.

We now turn to a case where, despite a worker's allegations of First Amendment violations by his employer, a court approved the employer's actions curtailing the employee's religious practices. Daniel Berry described himself as "an evangelical Christian who holds sincere religious beliefs that require him to share his faith, when appropriate, and to pray with other Christians." Berry worked for the Department of Social Services in Tehama County, California. His duties primarily involved lending assistance to clients of the department who, during the course of their transition from welfare programs, found themselves unemployed or underemployed. Berry's duties frequently required him to conduct interviews of those clients, and over 90 percent of those interviews took place in his office cubicle.

When Berry first assumed his duties, he was advised that department policy did not allow him to discuss religion with clients. At first he abided by that policy, but growing increasingly uncomfortable with its restrictions, which he felt conflicted with his religious beliefs, he requested to be relieved of them. He was instructed, however, to continue to adhere to the department's policy that demanded "absolute avoidance of religious communications" with clients and all other persons contacted in the fulfillment of his duties.

Although department policy barred Berry from speaking about matters of religious concern to his clients, the prohibition did not extend to his co-workers, and so he organized a monthly employee prayer meeting to take place in the department's conference room. The director of the department, however, denied Berry the use of the conference room, informing him that he could conduct his prayer meetings in the break room during lunch hours or outdoors on the department grounds.

Despite instructions to refrain from displaying religious items in his work area, Berry placed a Bible in his cubicle and during the Christmas season hung a sign on his cubicle wall that read, "Happy Birthday Jesus." He was reprimanded for these actions and was instructed to remove the Bible as well as the sign from the view of his clients. Berry complied but then filed a discrimination charge with the EEOC and subsequently commenced legal proceedings in the federal court. He asked the court to declare that the department was required by the First Amendment to allow him to (1) share his religious views with clients where they "initiate the discussion or are open and receptive to such discussions," (2) use the conference room for voluntary prayer group meetings, and (3) display religious objects in his cubicle.

As we observed in the discussion of private-sector workplace religious disputes, an employer opting to resolve workplace issues arising out of acts of proselytization may face lawsuits on two fronts. If the employer fails to halt the proselytization efforts, employees targeted for conversion may sue, claiming religious harassment, and if the employer acts to prohibit the proselytization, the proselytizer may charge the employer with failing to accommodate his religious practices (chapter 6). Public-sector employers confront a comparable situation. If a governmental employer fails to respect the free exercise rights of an employee bent on proselytizing his fellow employees, the proselytizer may file suit alleging violation of the free exercise clause. On the other hand, if the employer acquiesces to the demands of that employee and fails to halt the proselytization, it may then be subjected to suit by its other employees alleging that the employer, by reason of its adoption of the proselytizer's position, endorsed his religious practices, thus violating the establishment clause.

The department argued that if it were to acquiesce to Berry's demands, a client might very well charge it with endorsing his religious beliefs and practices in violation of the establishment clause. Thus to avoid this charge the department was justified in curtailing Berry's workplace religious practices. The court agreed:

> Mr. Berry, of course, is entitled to seek the greatest latitude possible for expressing his religious beliefs at work. The Department, however, must run the gauntlet of either being sued for not respecting an employee's rights under the Free Exercise and Free Speech Clauses of the First Amendment or being sued for violating the Establishment Clause of the First Amendment by appearing to endorse the employee's religious expression....We conclude that...the Department's need to avoid possible violations of the Establishment Clause of the First Amendment outweighs the restriction's curtailment of Mr. Berry's religious speech on the job.[3]

On first reading, the rulings in the *Brown* and *Berry* cases appear to be irreconcilable. Berry's workplace religious activities did not greatly differ from Brown's, and yet Berry was barred from continuing them while Brown was not. One factor, however, distinguishes the two cases. Berry's religious practices impacted the clients he was required to interview, while Brown's affected only his fellow employees. Berry's practices primarily affected persons not employed by the department, persons over whom it had little or no control and limited influence. The department therefore confronted litigation initiated by Berry for not respecting his right under the free exercise clause and lawsuits by its clients alleging violations of the establishment clause by appearing to endorse Berry's religious practices. This factor may have motivated the court to deal more stringently with Berry and led to an outcome different from that experienced by Brown.

Cases requiring resolution of disputes involving the tension between the constitutional principle of the free exercise of religion and that barring governmental involvement in religious matters continually appear on court dockets. One such case involved a school district's attempt to avoid establishment clause violations by restricting the religious expression of one of its teachers while not infringing his free exercise rights.

Dan Marchi was a special education teacher who taught socially and emotionally challenged high school students. After ten years of employment with a northern New York school district, he experienced what he described as a "dramatic conversion to Christianity." Subsequently he shared that experience with his students and modified his teaching program to discuss topics such as forgiveness, reconciliation, and the worship of God. Upon learning of this, the school district's director of special education instructed Marchi to refrain from inserting religious topics into his instructional program. Marchi refused to abide by that directive because, in his view, if he were to comply, it would be detrimental to his students and "violate his conscience before God." At this point he was charged with insubordination and suspended for six months.

As a condition to returning to the classroom, Marchi was compelled to affirm in writing that he would comply with the directive requiring him to refrain from raising religious issues with his students. He was then assigned to teach autistic students having little or no communication skills. Shortly afterward, the father of one of those students sent an audiotape of religious music to the school with a note explaining that this music calmed his son. Marchi responded, "Ryan had a good day today. I thank you and the LORD for the tape; it brings the Spirit of Peace to the classroom.... May God Bless you all richly!" His supervisor criticized Marchi for having communicated with the father in that manner, but no disciplinary action was taken.

Unhappy with the restrictions placed upon his religious practices, Marchi brought suit against the school district, alleging that it had violated his right to the free exercise of his religion. One of the matters the court focused on was the note Marchi had sent to Ryan's father.

An educational institution risks allegations of violation of the establishment clause if a teacher's classroom religious practices give the impression that the institution has endorsed them. Because the school district had a strong interest in avoiding establishment clause violations, it was impelled to proscribe communications between teachers and parents that risked giving the impression that the school endorsed particular religious tenets. But what was the risk in this case? Although references to religion in Marchi's note to Ryan's father were minimal, two references were of concern to the school district officials: (1) that Marchi thanked not only the student's father but also the "LORD," and (2) his assessment that the audiotape was a source of the "Spirit of Peace to the classroom." The court felt that the note's intrusion of religious content into school matters was sufficient to expose the district to establishment clause challenges, and thus it ruled that the restrictions placed on Marchi's religious conduct did not infringe his free exercise rights.[4]

Fearful of these types of lawsuits, educational institutions are particularly concerned about any attempt to introduce religious content into their classrooms. Courts also are sensitive to endeavors by teachers to subject children to religious indoctrination, and thus they commonly express negative views of efforts to introduce any form of instruction having religious content. Although Marchi's transgressions were small, he nevertheless was blocked from pursuing efforts to introduce religion into his classroom.

Another teacher forced her school to confront a different problem. Instead of trying to introduce religion to her students, she wanted to excise certain subjects from the curriculum because they conflicted with her religious beliefs. She informed her principal that her Jehovah's Witness beliefs prohibited her from teaching any subjects involving love of country, the flag, or other patriotic matters. When she persisted in refusing to follow the prescribed curriculum in this regard, she was terminated. When she later sued the board of education, alleging that her right to the free exercise of her religion had been violated, the court dismissed her case, ruling that she did not have a constitutional right to require others to submit to her religious views, thus depriving them of educational opportunities they otherwise would enjoy.[5]

As previously noted, courts have been especially attentive to the protection of the rights of persons who fall into the "captive audience" category. Schoolchildren, of course, fit that description, and concerns for their welfare may, at least in part, have motivated the court's ruling against Dan Marchi. As we have seen, courts rarely express support for employers who thrust religion on their employees, for in many instances those employees also occupy a captive-audience status. But who could be better described as a captive audience than a patient sitting in a dental chair? The patient, more or less trapped in the chair, has no alternative but to listen to the words of the dentist or dental technician while he or she proceeds with the task at hand.

A dental hygienist, working for a dentist in Michigan, regularly described to the patients whose teeth she was cleaning how Christ had changed her life, a religious activity she called "sharing her faith." After several patients complained that the hygienist made them uncomfortable whenever she engaged in that type of conversation, the dentist instructed her to discontinue that practice. He felt he could rightfully expect his hygienist, whose work required patients to be verbally and physically submissive, to minimize patient discomfort, but the hygienist thought otherwise and, in disregard of his instructions, persisted in the practice of sharing her faith. He then discharged her.

After the Michigan Employment Security Commission Board of Review denied her application for unemployment benefits on the ground that she had been guilty of misconduct, the hygienist sued the dentist and the Board of Review, alleging that she had been denied her First Amendment right of free exercise of religion.

First, it should be noted that the hygienist's claim against the dentist had no merit. The First Amendment bars the government from prohibiting the free exercise of religion, and thus a free exercise claim must be based on governmental or state action and does not apply to conduct by a private-sector employer. The Review Board's denial of unemployment benefits, however, constituted state action, and thus the hygienist properly named it as a party defendant to her free exercise claim.

On initial examination, the hygienist's claim for unemployment benefits appears similar to that asserted by a claimant in a case reviewed in chapter 9. While working for a Florida jeweler, Paula Hobbie was baptized into the Seventh-day Adventist Church. When she was later terminated for refusing to work on Saturdays, she filed a claim for unemployment benefits. Initially her claim was denied on the ground that her refusal to work on Saturdays disqualified her for such benefits. The U.S. Supreme Court, however, reversed that ruling, observing that a state may not force a worker to choose between following the precepts of her religion and forfeiting job benefits such as unemployment compensation, nor may it compel her to abandon one of her religion's precepts in order to maintain her continued employment.[6]

Did the dental hygienist, like Paula Hobbie, have a valid claim for unemployment benefits? Hobbie was forced to choose between adhering to her religious convictions and the termination of her employment. The Supreme Court ruled that the denial of unemployment benefits in those circumstances was unconstitutional since it amounted to a forced abandonment of religious convictions. As the Court stated in another case:

> Where the state conditions receipt of an important benefit upon conduct proscribed by a religious faith, or where it denies such a benefit because of conduct mandated by religious belief, thereby putting substantial pressure on an adherent to modify his behavior and to violate his beliefs, a burden upon religion exists. While the compulsion may be indirect, the infringement upon free exercise is nonetheless substantial.[7]

The dental hygienist, unlike Paula Hobbie, was not mandated to act by reason of a religious belief or by any religious precept requiring her to share her faith. Rather, her desire to share her faith was personally motivated. She merely wanted to let others know of her personal fulfillment. She was not put to a choice between adhering to her religious faith and losing her job. Instead, she forfeited unemployment benefits for personal reasons. She chose to discuss her religious beliefs; her faith did not command her to discuss them. Thus her free exercise rights were not violated.[8]

A person's rights under the free exercise and establishment clauses are nicely summed up in a case involving a judge and his bailiff. The judge was Wendell Mayer of the Municipal Court of Marion County in Indiana, and the bailiff was David Kelly, a Jehovah's Witness. Shortly after Kelly assumed his duties in Judge Mayer's courtroom, the judge began to receive unsettling staff reports pertaining to Kelly's behavior as his bailiff. These included (1) proselytizing others with his religious beliefs during working hours, (2) reading his Bible in the courtroom and its public reception area, and (3) reading the Bible and preaching to prisoners in a holding cell waiting to appear before the judge. When Kelly failed to accede to the judge's direction to cease these activities, his role as bailiff came to an end.

Kelly then sued the municipal court, alleging that his constitutional rights had been violated. He maintained that the judge had violated the provisions of the free exercise clause when he prevented him from reading the Bible. But the judge's prohibition was limited to those times when Kelly was in the courtroom and in the court's public areas. This directive may have caused Kelly some inconvenience, but the free exercise clause is not "a guarantee against inconvenience." Rather, it prevents governmental authorities from interfering with the exercise of religious beliefs or practices that are "fundamental to the particular adherent's religious sect." As in the case of the dental hygienist, who could not show that her "share the faith" practices were based on a particular religious belief or precept, Kelly could not prove that his courtroom Bible reading was fundamental to his Jehovah's Witness beliefs.

Kelly also claimed that the judge had showed hostility toward his religion when he refused to allow him to read the Bible in the reception area of the court, even though he permitted other court staff to read newspapers and other materials. The reviewing court noted that the evidence in the case failed to indicate that the judge's objective was to demonstrate his disapproval of any aspect of Kelly's faith or beliefs. The judge's only concern was appearances—how Kelly's behavior would reflect on the court and whether it could be considered a form of religious indoctrination.

The judge took no action indicating disfavor of a particular religious faith. His ban was neutral, in the sense that he directed his entire staff not to engage in devotional activities in the court's public areas, including the holding area for prisoners. He was not motivated to order those restrictions by any desire to disparage any particular religion; rather, they were ordered to make certain that the court retained its character as a place where secular law was administered. He did not want a religious tone present in his courtroom, and Kelly's behavior threatened to compromise the appearance of impartiality of the court. In rejecting Kelly's claim, the court noted,"Because it would have been a clear violation of the doctrine of separation of church and state to use the court as a forum for any form of religious indoctrination...the fact that the Judge imposed the restrictions in question itself evinces no hostility or disapproval of [Kelly's] religion."[9]

The First Amendment also provides government workers who engage in certain religious activities with free speech protections, and thus restrictions on religious speech in the public-sector workplace are severely limited. Government employers may not restrict employee speech merely because of its religious content unless the failure to suppress such speech could reasonably be interpreted as an endorsement of that content, thus constituting a violation of the establishment clause.

In 1997 the Clinton administration issued a document entitled "White House Guidelines on Religious Exercise and Religious Expression in the

Federal Workplace."[10] These guidelines are limited in scope, principally addressing the rights of religious exercise and religious expression of employees who work in parts of the federal workplace where the public is generally not present. They encourage federal agencies to maximize their efforts to accommodate the religious beliefs and practices of their workers while allowing personal religious expression to the greatest extent possible. This expression may be limited, however, where it intrudes upon the rights of other employees or creates the appearance of federal endorsement of the views expressed.

The guidelines generally permit federal employees to

- engage in private religious expression in personal work areas not regularly open to the public;
- keep a Bible or Quran at their desks or work areas and read it during work breaks;
- discuss religious views with other employees;
- wear religious clothing, tokens, or medallions or display religious messages on items of clothing to the same extent that nonreligious messages are allowed;
- invite coworkers to religious services or post bulletins on public boards announcing such services; and
- during nonwork periods, gather with other workers for prayer or religious study in rooms generally free for use on a first-come, first-served basis.

On the other hand, the guidelines generally prohibit federal employees from

- proselytizing when a fellow employee asks that it stop or otherwise demonstrates that such religious expression is unwelcome;
- coercing other employees to participate or refrain from participating in religious services or observances;
- subjecting other employees to any form of religious harassment; and
- imposing their religious beliefs on fellow employees.

Although the guidelines are not applicable to the private-sector workplace, they may be helpful in resolving problems that occur there. Clearly they are consistent with the rules of law established in the cases thus far reviewed in this book.

11

Proselytizing in the Public-Sector Workplace

Public-sector employers may curtail employee discussions of religious subjects if discourse of that nature disrupts the workplace, interferes with normal work procedures, negatively affects employee productivity, or creates circumstances that may give rise to an establishment clause violation. Employer intervention in the attempts by one or more employees to convert coworkers or proselytize customers or clients has become more frequent as members of fundamentalist, evangelical, and other religious groups have become more emboldened in their efforts to persuade coworkers and others to accept their religious beliefs and practices. Conflict may arise between employer and employee when the employee asserts that the conversion of others stands as a basic element of her religious faith, requiring the protection of the First Amendment's free exercise clause, but the employer claims that employee proselytizing must cease because it may give rise to the appearance that the employer supports the employee's religious views, an act that would clearly violate the First Amendment's establishment clause. Who prevails in such conflicts, the employer or the employee?

Franklin Baz, an ordained minister of the Assemblies of God Church, was employed as a chaplain by the Veterans Administration Medical Center in Danville, Illinois, a full-service medical facility serving up to 1,200 patients. During the course of his employment, Baz frequently clashed with the center's administrative staff as well as with his supervisor, the chief of chaplains. Significant differences between Baz and the chief surfaced after Baz was placed in charge of the Sunday evening "sung service." This service, originally intended as a recreational period providing music for the patients as its main attraction, was changed by Baz to a Christian evangelical service. After the chief of chaplains determined that Baz was using the service to proselytize patients, he ordered him to be excluded from further participation in those services.

Baz engaged in other activities that the chief characterized as disruptive and in violation of VA policy. On several occasions, Baz entered the operating amphitheater, without permission, to pray while physicians were conducting complex surgical procedures. On other occasions, rather than extending to his patients assurances of God's forgiveness, he reinforced their feelings of guilt, thus causing them greater anxiety and anguish.

Baz saw himself as an evangelistic, charismatic preacher, called to preach the Gospel to hospital residents. The VA, however, intended his role to be limited to that of a passive listener and cautious counselor. Cognizant of the ever-increasing proliferation of differences separating Baz and the rest of the VA staff, the chief of chaplains terminated his employment. Baz then filed an EEOC discrimination charge and later federal court claims alleging violations of Title VII and of the free exercise and establishment clauses.

The court quickly disposed of Baz's Title VII claim by ruling that the VA could not have accommodated his religious practices without standing aside while he practiced his ministry in a manner the VA categorized as damaging to patients and staff. In the court's view, the VA was not required to take steps of that nature to fulfill its duty to accommodate the religious practices of one of its employees.

The court also rejected Baz's free exercise claims. While agreeing that his employment with the VA could not be conditioned on the surrender of his constitutional rights, the court noted that Baz did not possess the constitutional right to conduct religious services and offer religious counsel in a manner other than that established by his employer. The evidence in the case supported the VA's conclusion that his religious activities were detrimental to the best interests of the patients, and in those circumstances the VA was justified in limiting his religious expression. Thus Baz's free exercise rights were not violated.

Baz also contended that the VA had violated his establishment clause rights when it limited the content of his sermons as well as the manner in which he could pray with patients. But, as the court noted, the VA had to ensure that it did not create establishment clause problems by "unleashing a government-paid chaplain who sees his primary role as proselytizing upon a captive audience of patients." The court then also dismissed Baz's establishment clause claims.[1]

The University of Alabama employed Phillip Bishop as an assistant professor, specializing in teaching exercise physiology to graduate and undergraduate students. Bishop was accustomed to referring to his personal religious beliefs during the course of his lectures; some of those references related to the existence of a creative force underlying human physiology, while others related to his approach to resolving problems experienced by students coping with academic stress. Aware that the expression of his personal beliefs could engender opposition, he strove for a middle ground. On the one hand, he suggested to his students that religious belief was more important than study and learning, but on the other hand, he refrained from praying with his students, reading Bible passages to them, or otherwise introducing religion into their courses of study.

Summing up his personal philosophy of life, Bishop stated that when he died he hoped to leave behind something having greater value than a stack of technical papers. He held that belief in God was crucial to success and happiness and that modeling one's life on Christ's was the wisest approach to life. That belief, he affirmed, colored everything he said and did and led him to organize an after-class meeting in which he lectured on "Evidences of God in Human Physiology." These meetings were generally followed by discussions concerning various aspects of the human body, its complexity of design and operation, and they concluded with the affirmation that man was created by God and was not the by-product of evolution.

Some students complained that through his lectures Bishop was subjecting them to his personal religious beliefs. Fearing that Bishop was involved in proselytizing his students, his supervisor sent him a memorandum critical of his conduct:

> I want to reaffirm our commitment to your right of academic freedom and freedom of religious belief. ...I feel [however] that certain actions on your behalf are unwarranted at a public institution...and should cease. Among those actions that should be discontinued are: (1) the interjection of religious beliefs and/or preferences during instructional time periods, and (2) the optional classes where a "Christian Perspective" of an academic topic is delivered.

This memorandum reflected the First Amendment tightrope on which the university found itself perched. It was required to refrain from unnecessarily restricting the academic freedoms of a faculty member while avoiding establishment and free exercise clause violations.

Bishop complied with the restrictions placed upon him but then filed suit, alleging that the university had violated his first amendment rights. The appellate court that later considered those claims was not persuaded, "even in the remotest sense," that Bishop's free exercise rights were implicated, observing that he had not demonstrated that any aspect of the university's restrictions impeded the practice of his religion. In fact, the restraints imposed by the university were directed not at Bishop's religious practices but at his teaching practices.

If Bishop had provided the court with evidence showing that he was compelled by the teachings of his religious beliefs to share them with others, the court would have been unable to dismiss his free exercise claims as easily as it did. It would have been unable to find that the university's restrictions were directed at his teaching rather than his religious practices, thus giving Bishop's free exercise claim greater credibility.

In contrast, Bishop's establishment clause claim commanded greater attention. The memorandum issued by Bishop's supervisor was in the first instance an attempt to avoid a third-party claim that the university had indicated approval of Bishop's religious practices, thus connecting it to a particular religious viewpoint in violation of the establishment clause. The university feared that any suggestion of faculty proselytization of its students could lead to such a claim. Viewing the facts from the perspective of the university, the court agreed that its actions had been appropriate.

Bishop, however, did not give up. He countered that the university's restrictions themselves constituted establishment of religion violations because they excluded the "Christian perspective." The court did not agree, noting 1) that in limiting Bishop's religious comments, the university did not intend to promote other religions or any particular religious viewpoint, 2) that the restrictions neither advanced nor inhibited religious perceptions, and 3) that they did not involve the university in an excessive entanglement in religious matters but instead sought only to extricate it from religious influence in its secular courses of study.

The court also ruled that the memorandum's restrictions on the after-class meetings did not infringe Bishop's First Amendment rights, since the university possessed the authority to control the curriculum offered in optional or after-class meetings, as it did in its regularly scheduled courses. Bishop had no greater right to introduce religion in those meetings than he did in his regularly scheduled classroom courses. Thus the court dismissed each of Bishop's claims and arguments.[2]

The teaching of evolution often presents a problem for fundamentalist and other believers in the literal interpretation of scripture. John Peloza, a high school biology teacher employed by the Capistrano Unified School District in southern California, initiated litigation against the school district, alleging that he had been compelled to teach his students that evolution is a valid scientific theory rather than a "historical, philosophical and religious belief system." He argued that evolution is one of "two world views on the subject of the origins of life and of the universe," that "creationism," a belief system based on the assumption that a Creator created all life and the entire universe, advances the other worldview. Peloza contended that in forcing him to teach evolution, the school district in effect was requiring him to proselytize his students.

School district officials had their own thoughts on the matter. They reprimanded Peloza for bringing religion into the classroom and directed him to teach evolution, not creationism, and to refrain from any attempts at converting students to Christianity. Peloza alleged that his First Amendment rights were abridged when he was compelled to teach evolution but barred form teaching creationism, and that the school district's interference with his efforts to teach students to differentiate between a philosophical, religious belief system on the one hand and scientific theory on the other violated his constitutional rights.

Evolution, according to Peloza, could not be considered a valid scientific theory since it is based on events occurring in the past and not subject to scientific observation, and thus "evolutionism" is a historical, philosophical, and religious belief system. Therefore, he argued, the actions of school district officials tended to establish a state-supported "religion of evolutionism," requiring all students to adhere to this belief system rather than to creationism.

Peloza ignored the fact that evolution is an established scientific theory, accepted by the vast majority of the world's scientists. Instead, he urged the court to accept his definition, one that, the court noted, could not be found in any dictionary or Supreme Court decision. Rejecting that definition, the court concluded that evolution is not in any sense a religion. It then ruled that the school district's requirement that Peloza teach evolution in his biology classes did not constitute a violation of the establishment clause.[3]

As previously noted, the courts generally have little sympathy for workers who engage in the proselytization of their employer's clients or customers and then plead First Amendment violations when they are directed to cease their proselytizing activities. Jo Ann Knight, a nurse consultant for the Connecticut Department of Public Health, was a born-again Christian who believed she was called to proselytize while working with clients of the department.

Knight supervised the provision of medical services for home health care patients, thus requiring her to interview patients in their homes. On the occasion that became the subject of later litigation, Knight visited the home of a same-sex couple, one of whom was suffering the end stages of AIDS. At one point during the visit, she and the two men began discussing religion. She told them that she "experienced a strong sense of compassion for both men and a leading of the Holy Spirit" to talk to them regarding their salvation. After asking them about their religious beliefs, she told them salvation consisted in "confessing...that Jesus is the Son of God and believing in one's heart that God raised Him from the dead." When one of the men stated that he did not believe he would be punished for his homosexual lifestyle, Knight responded that "although God created us and loves us, He doesn't like the homosexual lifestyle."

Apparently that comment did not sit well with the two men, who subsequently filed complaints with the department, alleging discrimination on the basis of sexual orientation in the provision of state medical services.

Shortly afterward, the department suspended Knight without pay for her "misconduct" in dealing with the homosexual couple. Knight then filed a legal action against the department, contending that she had a legal right pursuant to the First Amendment to discuss her religious beliefs when interviewing patients receiving state aid.

The court denied Knight's claims on the ground that the State of Connecticut had a valid concern in limiting the use of religious speech when its employees dealt with clients of the department. At a minimum, the establishment clause prohibits a governmental entity from appearing to assume a position on a question of religious belief. Knight, as a government employee engaged in providing state-sponsored medical services, was acting as a representative of the state, and any speech on her part carried the state's authority. If the department failed to curtail her religiously oriented speech, it would appear to clients, such as the same-sex couple, that it was lending its approval to her religious views, thus violating the establishment clause.

Knight also charged the department with Title VII violations by reason of its failure to accommodate her religious practices, namely, her desire to employ religious speech in her dealings with clients. The court dismissed this charge, observing that the accommodation she requested was not reasonable, for if the department were to allow her to evangelize while providing medical services to clients, its ability to provide those services in a religion-neutral manner would be jeopardized.[4]

Homophobia is common among members of certain religious groups. A private citizen may be free to preach that homosexuality is sinful, but an employee of a governmental entity must restrict commentary of that sort lest his employer be accused of violating the First Amendment rights of others. The Reverend Eugene Lumpkin placed his employer in such jeopardy when he made comments condemning homosexuality, publicly stating that the homosexual lifestyle was an abomination before God, and since the Bible said homosexuals should be put to death (Lev. 20:13), he was justified in preaching against it. At the time he uttered these statements, Lumpkin was a member of the San Francisco Human Rights Commission. When the mayor later removed Lumpkin from the commission, he stated, "Reverend Lumpkin chose to make his beliefs part of the political process, and in so doing crossed the line from belief...to advocacy. Reverend Lumpkin by failing to disassociate himself from specific biblical passages which may appear to justify stoning persons or groups of persons, implied that he condoned physical harm." The mayor made it clear that in San Francisco a private person, if he wishes, may publicly state his religious beliefs, but a public official may not use his office to proselytize or advocate for specific religious beliefs.

Lumpkin sued the mayor and the city, claiming that his removal from the human rights commission violated his First Amendment rights. The court, in no mood to linger long over the reverend's claims, set forth a number of reasons in support of its decision to dismiss his suit. First, the free exercise clause did not require the city of San Francisco to retain a member of its human rights commission who made statements antithetical to the commission's official charge to eliminate prejudice and encourage private persons as well as groups to promote equal opportunities for all people. Lumpkin's statements condemning homosexuality as a sin and his endorsement of violence against homosexuals were not "simply hostile to the Commission's charge, they [were] at war with it." The First Amendment does not require a governmental organization to continue to employ officials who work at cross-purposes with the policies they are responsible for implementing.

Second, although the First Amendment strictly protects freedom of speech, when a governmental entity acts in the capacity of an employer, it has certain latitude in protecting its operations and policies from subversion by its own personnel. Lumpkin did not leave his First Amendment rights at the door of city hall when he took office as a human rights commissioner, but in certain circumstances those rights could be subordinated to the interests of the city he agreed to serve. The city's interest in eliminating prejudice and discrimination prevailed over Lumpkin's interest in condemning homosexuality. Its interest in having commissioners work to promote its policies far outweighed any commissioner's First Amendment interest in publicly expressing views that subverted those policies.

Third, Lumpkin's establishment clause contentions were without merit. He alleged that the mayor's removal of him from the commission violated the establishment clause since it constituted an endorsement of a particular religious belief, one that interpreted scripture less literally than did Lumpkin's beliefs. But in removing Lumpkin from his post, the mayor stated,

> I have not in the past, nor will I in the future ask that a religious litmus test of beliefs be a part of the appointment process for the San Francisco Commission. When [religious] beliefs are volunteered in a way that negatively

influences the operation of state functions, or suggests a justification for actions that may lead to violence, I believe it crosses the line separating church from state.

The court ruled that because this statement adhered to secular principles, it undermined Lumpkin's claim that his removal promoted a particular religious faith. The court dismissed all of Lumpkin's claims.[5]

Are there any circumstances in which employee proselytization will be allowed in a public-sector workplace? On the basis of the cases examined in this chapter, it appears not, but if the proselytization activities complained of do not unduly disrupt the workplace, the courts may permit them to continue.

Monte Tucker worked as a computer analyst for the California Department of Education. Deeply religious, he regularly gave credit to God for the work he performed. After eleven years on the job, he decided to place the phrase "Servant of the Lord Jesus Christ" or the acronym SOTLJC after his name on the label of the software program he was developing. When his supervisor directed him to cease using the phrase and acronym, Tucker filed suit, asking the court to enjoin the department of education from enforcing his supervisor's directive.

The department maintained that Tucker's use of the phrase and acronym disrupted the workplace and reduced employee efficiency, but it offered little evidence in support of its position. The evidence failed to demonstrate that Tucker was threatening the morale of the department or that he had engaged in any aggressive religious advocacy. Although the court recognized the department's legitimate interest in avoiding claims that it was violating the establishment clause through support of the religious beliefs of one of its employees, that interest, in light of the absence of any workplace disruption or reduction in employee efficiency or complaints of coworkers, was insufficient to support the ban on Tucker's actions.[6]

The circumstances that allow employee proselytization in public-sector workplaces are as narrow as those existing in the private sector. In both sectors, nonaggressive behavior directed at fellow workers (but not at clients and customers) that does not elicit a strong negative response and does not disrupt normal workplace procedures, may be viewed by the courts as acceptable. Short of that, workplace proselytization will almost always be banned.

Part III

EXEMPTIONS TO
DISCRIMINATION LAWS

12

EXEMPTIONS FROM THE DISCRIMINATION LAWS GRANTED TO RELIGIOUS ORGANIZATIONS

First Amendment principles do not allow the federal courts to exercise jurisdiction over the internal affairs of religious organizations, especially over issues pertaining to church governance and matters of faith and doctrine. Since the selection of members of the clergy is central to the internal governance of the church, the courts must refrain from becoming involved or "entangled" in legal disputes emanating from church decisions regarding its personnel who exercise ministerial or pastoral functions.

When the Civil Rights Act of 1964 was enacted, Congress exempted religious organizations from much of Title VII's prohibition against employment discrimination on the basis of religion. The exemption reads:

> [Title VII] shall not apply...to a religious corporation, association, educational institution, or society with respect to the employment of individuals of a particular religion to perform work connected with the carrying on by such corporation, association, educational institution, or society of its activities.[1]

Schools operated by religious organizations were granted their own exemption:

> It shall not be an unlawful employment practice for a school...to hire...em-
> ployees of a particular religion if such school...is, in whole or substantial
> part owned, supported, controlled, or managed by a particular religion...or
> if the curriculum of such school...is directed toward the propagation of a
> particular religion.[2]

Thus Title VII authorizes religious organizations and schools to use religious preferences—preferences that would otherwise be discriminatory—in the employment process. For example, a religious organization may limit its staff to members of a particular religious denomination, and religious schools may impose religious requirements in the hiring of their teachers and other workers.

Although the language of these two sections of Title VII is clear, legal disputes concerning their application have been many. Is the institution in question a religious organization within the meaning of the statute? Is it barred for any reason from relying upon Title VII exemptions? May religious organizations and religiously affiliated schools require their employees to subscribe to a code of conduct demanded by church doctrine? Do the Title VII exemptions allow a school established to teach a specified religious faith to discriminate against an employee of another faith solely because her conduct fails to conform to the mores of the faith taught by the school? These and other questions relating to the application of these exemptions are discussed in this chapter.

If the court rules that the employer is entitled to rely on one of the exemptions, the case is over—the employer wins and the plaintiff employee is barred from proceeding with the case. On the other hand, if the court denies the exemption, the case continues to follow its normal litigation path, but with the exemption no longer looming as a barrier to the litigation of the claims of the Title VII plaintiff. Although the employer has been denied the exemption, it still retains the right to defend against the claims asserted by its employee. Thus for the employer, issues relating to the availability of the exemptions present a win-win situation. Either it is granted the exemption and wins the litigation outright, or it retains the right to contest the employee's case.

Before a court involves itself in issues pertaining to the operations of a religious institution, it must first determine whether it is authorized to examine those issues, since the First Amendment strictly limits judicial review of actions undertaken by religious institutions. That was the procedure followed by the court when a math teacher employed by a Catholic high school in New York sued that institution. In addition to his teaching functions, Guy DeMarco was assigned certain religious duties, including leading his students in prayer and escorting them to Mass. After his fifth year at the school, school officials notified him that he would not be offered a contract for the coming year. DeMarco, claiming that his employment was being terminated because of his age, filed discrimination charges with the EEOC pursuant to the Age Discrimination in Employment Act (ADEA). When he later filed suit, attorneys for the school argued that DeMarco had been dismissed for reasons other than age, that he had neglected to begin his classes with prayer and had failed to attend Mass with his students. They also contended that the court should decline to even consider DeMarco's age discrimination claim because its involvement in such a claim would create a substantial risk that the court would violate the "excessive entanglement prohibition" of the First Amendment's establishment clause. In other words, the school contended that since the court would likely become entangled in its religious affairs if it were to rule on DeMarco's age discrimination claims, it should refrain from adjudicating those claims.

The court first pondered whether there was any merit to the allegation that it was about to become excessively entangled with the affairs of a religious institution. It concluded that an examination and review of DeMarco's discrimination lawsuit would not involve inquiries into the value or truthfulness of religious doctrine or require examination of the internal workings of the school. Given that the religious duties that he allegedly failed to fulfill were easily isolated and defined, the court could focus on whether DeMarco was fired for failure to perform his religious duties without putting into issue the validity or truthfulness of Catholic religious teaching. Thus a ruling on DeMarco's age discrimination claims did not pose a serious risk of violation of the nonentanglement prohibitions of the First Amendment.[3]

In another age discrimination lawsuit, the court concluded that the risk of entanglement in a church's religious affairs was sufficient to require it to retire from the scene. Richard Tomic was employed as the music director and organist at St. Mary's Cathedral in Peoria, Illinois. His duties included assisting at Mass, celebrating various diocesan liturgies, and playing the organ for Masses and other events, including weddings and funerals. In his capacity as music director, he was required to prepare music for all Masses "in consultation with the Rector/Pastor where necessary," and to recruit, train, direct, and rehearse members of the chorus.

A dispute between Tomic and the pastor with regard to the scheduling of Easter music culminated in Tomic's termination. When the church replaced Tomic with a much younger person, he filed an age discrimination claim. The court that considered Tomic's claim began its analysis by commenting that "federal courts are secular agencies...and therefore do not exercise jurisdiction over the internal affairs of religious organizations." At that point, the court looked ahead to how the case would likely unfold if litigation were to proceed. The court noted that undoubtedly the church would oppose Tomic's age claim by arguing that he had been dismissed for a religious reason—his opinion concerning the suitability of particular music for the Easter services—thus propelling the court into a religious dispute over Easter music. Tomic more than likely would argue in return that age, not a controversy over the music, had led to his dismissal. The church then would rebut that argument with evidence pertaining to what had theretofore been accepted as liturgically appropriate music for the Easter services, and at that point Tomic would dispute the church's position. By that time, the trial court would have become deeply involved in resolving a religious dispute. Therefore, Tomic's age discrimination claim could not be adjudicated in the courts.

Distinguishing its ruling from that rendered by the court in the *DeMarco* case, the court pointed out that DeMarco either did or did not lead his students in prayer and attend Mass. "These were simple questions of fact...and could be answered without reference to church doctrine. That is not true with respect to the wisdom or propriety of Tomic's choice of music to play at an Easter Mass."[4]

Little reason exists to quarrel with the rulings in either of these cases. They are readily distinguishable, and both courts, in light of the particular facts at hand, appear to have reached an appropriate and equitable conclusion. But this is not true of all courts, as some judges appear inordinately reluctant to become involved in resolving religious issues. This has led to some bizarre results, as we shall see in chapter 14.

We turn to a case where the denial of a woman's application for a pastoral position raised significant issues regarding the appropriate role of the Title VII exemptions. Carole Rayburn, a member of the Seventh-day Adventist Church, held a Master of Divinity degree and a Ph.D. in psychology. She applied to an administrative body within the church for a position as an associate in pastoral care and at about the same time also applied for a vacancy on the pastoral staff of the Sligo Seventh-day Adventist Church, one of the denomination's largest churches. When she was denied both positions, she filed charges with the EEOC alleging that the church had discriminated against her because of her sex as well as on account of her association with African Americans and membership in black-oriented religious organizations.

The appellate court that examined the charges she levied against the church observed that the application of Title VII in a matter of this nature raised serious constitutional issues. While Title VII grants religious institutions a narrow exemption—that they may base hiring decisions upon religious preferences—it does not confer upon them a licence to make those decisions on the basis of race, sex, or national origin. The exemption applies only to one particular reason for an employment decision—that based on religious preference.

In determining whether the church could rightfully rely upon the Title VII exemption to defeat Rayburn's sex and race charges, the court focused on the doctrine of the separation of church and state:

> Each person's right to believe as he wishes and to practice that belief according to the dictates of his conscience, so long as he does not violate the personal rights of others, is fundamental to our system.... This basic freedom is guaranteed not only to individuals but also to churches in their collective capacities which must have power to decide for themselves, free from interference, matters of church governance as well as those of faith and doctrine.... Ecclesiastical decisions are generally inviolate; civil courts are bound to accept the decisions...of a religious organization...on matters of discipline, faith, internal organization, or ecclesiastical rule.

The court ruled that if the court were to subject the church's decisions regarding its employees to Title VII scrutiny, its decision would give rise to concerns of "excessive government entanglement" with the internal affairs of that institution, an act prohibited by the establishment clause. The court thus declined to examine the church's decision not to hire Rayburn and instead dismissed her claims.

The court noted in passing that churches are not above the law. The employment decisions of a religious organization are subject to Title VII scrutiny where they do not involve the church's spiritual functions. Even though the Title VII exemptions generally do not apply to cases involving claims of sex and race discrimination, the court was constrained, in light of the particular facts encountered in this case, from adjudicating Rayburn's charges.[5]

Rulings such as that announced in the *Rayburn* case have led worker plaintiffs to adopt extreme measures in attempts to evade the Title VII exemptions. On occasion, employees have tried to circumvent these exemptions by arguing that the employer is barred from asserting them because it is not a religious organization. That was the route taken by John Killinger after his employer curtailed his teaching activities. Killinger was a professor, author, and preacher employed by Samford University located in Birmingham, Alabama. As a result of a bequest, Samford received a substantial sum to establish a divinity school, and Killinger served that school as Distinguished Professor of Religion and Culture and also taught religion and English to Samford undergraduates.

Killinger and the dean of the divinity school held opposing theological views, and when Killinger questioned the fundamentalist theology advanced by the dean, he was removed from the divinity school faculty and barred from further association with that part of the university. While he continued to teach undergraduate students, Killinger asserted a Title VII claim against the university alleging religious discrimination.

He contended that the Title VII exemptions did not bar his claims because Samford was a secular, not a religious, institution. But Samford presented the court with evidence showing that it had been founded as a theological institution by the Alabama Baptist State Convention, and while it had recently amended its charter to remove the convention's power to elect the school's board of trustees, its trustees were still required to be Baptists. It received over $4,000,000 a year from the convention, its largest source of funding, and it was a member of the Association of Baptist Colleges and Schools, which limited membership to Baptist educational institutions. Samford also relied upon its charter, which specified that its main purpose was "the promotion of the Christian Religion throughout the world by maintaining and operating...institutions dedicated to the development of Christian character." It noted that all Samford students were required to attend chapel and directed the court's attention to its student handbook, which described Samford's purpose as fostering "Christianity through the development of Christian character, scholastic attainment, and a sense of personal responsibility." After reviewing this evidence, the court concluded that Samford was doubtlessly a religious educational institution.

Killinger was not allowed to teach at the divinity school because his religious beliefs differed from those of the dean, the person selected to lead the faculty at the school. Since the Title VII exemptions allow a religious institution to employ only persons whose beliefs are consistent with the institution's, the exemptions protected Samford in this case.[6]

Even though religious institutions are free to base their employment decisions on religious preferences, the courts have continuously made clear that they may not base those decisions on an employee's race, national origin, or sex. The Fremont Christian School ignored that distinction and paid the price. The school, located in Fremont, California, and wholly owned by the Assembly of God Church, provided instruction for children enrolled in the preschool years through grade twelve. Although a person employed by the school was not required to be a member of the Assembly of God Church, she had to be a member in good standing of an evangelical church and also subscribe to certain tenets of faith, including that (1) the Bible was to be taken literally, (2) while the sexes are equal in dignity before God, their respective roles differ, and (3) in all marriages, the husband is the head of the household.

The school provided its employees with health insurance, but this benefit was available only to heads of households, thus rendering women ineligible. Ruth Frost, a teacher married to a man not employed by the school, charged the school with sex discrimination on the ground that it gave health insurance coverage to its married male employees but not to its married female employees. When the school claimed the protection of the Title VII exemptions, the court reminded it that religious institutions are not immune from liability under Title VII for discrimination based on sex, and that was precisely what Frost had alleged.

Fremont then turned to the First Amendment, arguing that Title VII did not apply to its employment policy of supplying health insurance benefits solely to heads of households because that policy was grounded in religious belief and therefore shielded by the free exercise clause of the Constitution. To determine whether the application of Title VII in this instance would violate that clause, the court had to consider the weight of Title VII's impact on Fremont and the exercise of its religious beliefs. Was that impact sufficient to require the court to exempt Fremont from liability for its alleged acts of sex discrimination? The court turned to a statement previously made by the head of the Fremont Assembly of God Church: "The Church, believing as it does, in the God-given dignity and the special role of women, could not, without sin, treat women according to unfair distinctions." This statement, the court ruled, clearly demonstrated that actions taken to prevent sex discrimination in the school would have no significant impact on its religious beliefs.

But the school authorities advanced another argument, claiming that any Title VII relief ordered by the court would violate the establishment clause because excessive governmental entanglement with church affairs would surely ensue. To determine the likelihood of excessive entanglement, courts examine three factors, specified by the U.S. Supreme Court case in an earlier case: 1) the character and purpose of the institution involved, 2) the nature of the intrusion into its religious affairs, and 3) the resulting relationship between the government and the religious authority.[7] The court proceeded to analyze each factor separately.

1. *Character and purpose of the school.* Fremont contended that it had been formed and existed as an integral part of the religious mission of the Assembly of God Church, and thus the role of a Fremont teacher was that of a minister. If that description of the teacher's role were accurate, the entanglement implications would be significant. But the court refused to adopt Fremont's characterization of the role of its teachers, pointing out that since they did not serve as intermediaries between the church and its congregation, they clearly did not function as ministers.
2. *Nature of the intrusion.* The intrusion at issue was a prospective court injunction requiring the school to comply with Title VII. The court recognized that such an injunction would necessitate an ongoing scrutiny of the school's operations. Moreover, a Title VII action is potentially a lengthy proceeding. But because scrutiny of these operations would involve only the school's employment practices, not its spiritual functions, the intrusion was not barred.

3. *Resulting relationship between government and the school.* The relationship between the government—in this case, the court—and the school in this Title VII litigation would be limited in scope and effect. It threatened no greater entanglement than governmental enforcement of other statutory provisions regulating employee compensation at religious institutions.

The court, having determined that excessive entanglement was not likely to ensue, ruled that the school, in opposing Ruth Frost's sex discrimination claims, was barred from relying upon the Title VII and First Amendment exemptions.[8]

Thus far we have seen that religious institutions in certain limited circumstances are shielded from Title VII's prohibitions against employment discrimination. They may employ only individuals who accept the religious faith proclaimed by that institution, and thus a Catholic school may hire Catholics in preference to non-Catholics. But does the Title VII exemption allow a Catholic school to discriminate against a non-Catholic employee because her conduct fails to conform to Catholic principles?

Susan Little, a Protestant, was employed as a teacher in a Catholic elementary school located in the Pittsburgh diocese. School authorities refrained from giving her any responsibilities for teaching religion, but she nonetheless attended Catholic ceremonies with her students and participated in teachers' programs designed to strengthen their ability to impart Catholic values to their students. Included in the terms of her contract with the school was a provision stating that the failure of a teacher to perform in accordance with the terms and conditions of the teachers' handbook would be considered a cause for termination. One of the handbook's provisions, referred to as the "Cardinal's Clause," read as follows:

> One example of termination for just cause is a violation of what is understood to be the Cardinal's Clause [which] requires the dismissal of the teacher for serious public immorality, public scandal or public rejection of the official teachings, doctrine or laws of the Catholic Church. Examples of the violation of this clause would be the entry by a teacher into a marriage...not recognized by the Catholic Church.

When first hired, Little was married, but she later divorced. Subsequently she married a man who had been baptized in the Catholic Church but was no longer a practicing participant in any religion. The Catholic

Church considers that all baptized Catholics remain Catholics for life, but it recognizes the legitimacy of a marriage of a Catholic performed by a member of another denomination, provided the parties have not been previously married. Thus, in the eyes of the Catholic Church, before Little and her second husband married each other, she should have first applied for and obtained an annulment of her first marriage.

At the end of the school year following Little's second marriage, school authorities refused to renew her contract, purportedly because she had remarried without pursuing the proper canonical process to obtain validation of her second marriage. Little then filed a religious discrimination charge against the school.

The court that subsequently considered Little's discrimination claim noted that Congress obviously intended Title VII to free individual workers from religious prejudice, and Susan Little had every right to expect her Catholic school employer to respect her rights as an individual to freely exercise her religious beliefs and practices. But Congress also intended to explicitly exempt religious organizations from the proscriptions of Title VII so as to allow them to create and maintain communities composed solely of individuals faithful to their doctrinal practices. The court, clearly of a mind to broadly interpret the Title VII exemption, ruled in favor of the school:

> It does not violate Title VII's prohibition of religious discrimination for a parochial school to discharge a Catholic or a non-Catholic teacher who has publicly engaged in conduct regarded by the school as inconsistent with its religious principles. We therefore hold that the exemptions to Title VII cover [the school's] decision not to rehire Little because of her remarriage.[9]

In cases of this sort, courts more readily apply the exemptions where the employee's conduct flagrantly undermines her employer's religious principles. Such a case involved an elementary school teacher employed as a music teacher by a Catholic school in Tiffin, Ohio. Connie Gosche signed a teaching contract affirming that she believed in the work of the Catholic Church and that by word and example she would reflect its values. After renewing the contract on a year-to-year basis for several years, Gosche and her husband divorced, and not long after, she became sexually involved with the father of three children enrolled in the Tiffin Catholic schools.

After a marriage of fifteen years, Little's paramour then left his wife. When parents and grandparents of children in these schools complained about Gosche's affair, the local pastor, who held authority over the schools, determined that Gosche was subject to dismissal for having violated her obligation to reflect, by word and example, the values of the Catholic Church. Gosche then sued her school, claiming sex discrimination.

The court observed that school authorities obviously regarded Gosche's sexual conduct as relevant to her employment, and it was not about to second-guess them:

> This court...must defer to the [school's] determination of what is relevant to the job, particularly where, as here, federal law expressly permits religious corporations to discriminate on the basis of religion with respect to the employment of individuals of a particular religion to perform work connected with...its activities.[10]

The court then dismissed all of Gosche's legal claims.

Not every school claiming to be a religious educational institution is entitled to rely upon the Title VII exemption, and in certain instances, even schools having close ties to organized religion may be denied the exemption. Before a court will affirm a school's entitlement to the exemption, it will examine carefully all significant religious and secular characteristics of the institution to determine whether its purpose and character are primarily religious.

Bernice Bishop was a member of the Hawaiian royal family and, at the time of her death in 1884, was the largest landowner in Hawaii. In her will she directed the bulk of her estate to be placed in a charitable trust for the purpose of erecting and maintaining in the Hawaiian Islands two schools, one for boys and the other for girls, to be known as the Kamehameha Schools. Her will specified that the teachers of each of those schools "shall forever be persons of the Protestant religion."

Over a century later, Carole Edgerton, who was not Protestant, applied for a substitute teacher position in the Kamehameha Schools. When she was later informed that her application would not be considered because of the "Protestant-only" requirement, Edgerton complained to the EEOC, which then filed religious discrimination charges against the schools on her behalf. The schools conceded that Bishop's will required them to discriminate in favor of Protestant teacher applicants but that the Title VII exemptions insulated them from liability to non-Protestant applicants for teacher positions.

The court found several factors that conflicted with the schools' contention that the exemptions should be applied:

- The schools had never been controlled by a religious organization, nor had they ever been affiliated with a denomination of Protestants.
- The purpose and emphasis of the schools had shifted over the years from providing religious instruction to equipping students with ethical principles that would enable them to make their own moral judgments.
- The schools had never required teachers to maintain active membership in a Protestant church.
- School authorities did not consider the religious affiliation of prospective students. In fact, fewer than one-third of the students were Protestants.
- Although the schools required limited religious instruction, no effort was made to instruct students in Protestant doctrine, and the school officials explicitly disavowed any effort to convert non-Protestant students.

In summary, the religious characteristics of the two schools were nearly nonexistent, consisting of minimal religious instruction of students, who for the most part were not Protestant, and taught by teachers who were, at best, nominally Protestant. The Title VII exemptions, however, are applicable only to schools that are "in whole or substantial part owned, supported, controlled, or managed by a particular religious corporation...or if the curriculum of such school...is directed toward the propagation of a particular religion."[11] The Kamehameha Schools did not fit that description. Thus the court concluded that they were essentially secular institutions and that the Title VII exemption were inapplicable with regard to the claims made by the EEOC on Edgerton's behalf.[12]

In addition to schools, business organizations affiliated with a church or religious institution may on occasion claim the exemption. The *Christian Science Monitor,* a highly regarded secular newspaper, claimed the exemption when Mark Feldstein sued it for religious discrimination.

The *Monitor* is published by the Publishing Society, an organ of the Christian Science Church. Both the society and the *Monitor* were established by Mary Baker Eddy, the founder of the church. The deed of trust of the Publishing Society declares its purpose as "more effectually promoting and extending the religion of Christian Science," and according to the church's bylaws, it is the "privilege and duty" of every member to subscribe to periodicals published by the church, including the *Monitor.* The board of trustees is directed to conduct the business of the society "on a strictly Christian basis, for the promotion of the interests of Christian Science." It was beyond dispute that the church was intimately involved in the management and day-to-day operations and financial affairs of the *Monitor.*

Feldstein, intent on pursuing a career in journalism, inquired at the offices of the *Monitor* about a possible job opening on its news reporting staff. He was directed to the church's personnel department, where he was advised that the newspaper hired only Christian Scientists except in that rare circumstance where no qualified member of the church was available, and that since he was not a member, he had little chance of being hired. Nonetheless, Feldstein submitted his application for employment.

The application used throughout the church contained several questions relating to the applicant's religious practices:

- Are you a member of the Mother Church or branch church?
- Are you free from the use of liquor, tobacco, drugs, and medicine?
- Do you subscribe to the Christian Science periodicals?
- Are you a daily student of the lesson-sermon?
- Have you ever been or are you now affiliated with any other church or religion?

The applicant was also required to submit references from two members of the Christian Science Church, which were to include comments on the applicant's character and his practice of the Christian Science religion.

One month after Feldstein submitted his application, he was notified that it had been rejected because he was not a member of the Christian Science Church. Feldstein then commenced Title VII religious discrimination litigation against the church, the Publishing Society, and the *Monitor.*

Although the court recognized that the *Monitor* held itself out as an objective and unbiased reporter of world news, it could not ignore the close relationship between the church, the Publishing Society, and the *Monitor,* as well as the newspaper's declared purpose to promulgate the tenets of Christian Science. Even with its established reputation in the secular world, the *Monitor* was itself a religious activity conducted by a religious organization. As such, it was entitled to apply a religious affiliation requirement to candidates for employment. The court dismissed Feldstein's Title VII suit.[13]

Unlike the Kamehameha Schools, the *Christian Science Monitor* was closely tied to religion and church, and its secular activities neither weakened nor detracted from that association. It was owned, supported, controlled, and managed by the Christian Science Church, and its purposes were directed toward the propagation of the teachings of that particular religious faith. It was exempt from Title VII's religious discrimination proscriptions.

Title VII provides for still another exemption from its provisions barring discrimination based on religion. The "bona fide occupational qualification" (the BFOQ exemption) provides, "It shall not be an unlawful employment practice for an employer to hire employees...on the basis of [their] religion...where religion...is a bona fide occupational qualification reasonably necessary to the normal operation of that particular business or enterprise."[14]

This exemption, as with the others previously discussed, has been the subject of frequent interpretation by the courts. May a nonsectarian employer make religion a bona fide occupational qualification for employment? Does this exemption apply when religion is only an incidental aspect of the job in question?

The Society of Jesus, commonly known as Jesuits, is a religious order of the Catholic Church. Composed primarily of priests, the order has for many years been engaged in education in the United States, establishing and maintaining twenty-eight universities throughout the country. One of those, Loyola University of Chicago, has a long Jesuit tradition dating from 1909.

Jerrold Pime, who was Jewish, held a part-time lecturer position in Loyola's philosophy department. He expressed interest in a tenure-track position but was advised that he would not be considered for any of the vacant three tenure-track positions in the department. He then resigned and filed religious discrimination charges against the university.

At the time, seven of thirty-one tenure-track positions in the philosophy department were held by Jesuits, and each of the three positions about to be filled had formerly been held by a Jesuit. The department chairman decided that Jesuits should be assigned to all three positions, reasoning that the philosophy department, as a segment of a university with a long Jesuit tradition, required an adequate Jesuit presence. Because of that tradition, philosophy held a place of special significance in the education of Loyola students, and the chairman believed it was necessary to acknowledge that tradition by maintaining a strong Jesuit influence. Faculty members of the philosophy department agreed, and they subsequently voted to fill each of the three positions with a professionally competent Jesuit philosopher.

There was no hint of invidious action against Pime on account of his religion; the faculty resolution merely excluded every non-Jesuit from consideration, whether of the Catholic or any other faith. In defending against Pime's religious discrimination charge, the university argued that membership in the Jesuit order was a bona fide occupational qualification for each of the three philosophy department positions. The court agreed:

> It appears to be significant to the educational tradition and character of the institution that students be assured a degree of contact with teachers who have received the training and accepted the obligations which are essential to membership in the Society of Jesus. It requires more to be a Jesuit than just adherence to the Catholic faith, and it seems wholly reasonable to believe that the educational experience at Loyola would be different if Jesuit presence were not maintained.

The court ruled that being a Jesuit was a legitimate requirement of those selected to fill the three vacancies. This was a bona fide occupational qualification for each position. As stated by one of the judges on the appellate court that reviewed the case, Pime was rejected not because he was a Jew or a non-Catholic but only because he was not a Jesuit. Every person of every faith faced that same hurdle. The court dismissed Pime's discrimination suit.[15]

All employees of the Valley Christian School in California were required to be "born-again believers, living a consistent and practical Christian life." All were required to sign a statement of faith committing themselves to the church's mission of instilling fundamentalist Christian values and pledging themselves to living a fundamentalist lifestyle that emulated the life of Christ.

When the school librarian gave birth to a child out of wedlock, the school terminated her for entering into an "adulterous relationship." When she later filed discrimination charges against the school, school authorities alleged that since the librarian served as a role model for the students, her moral character was a bona fide occupational qualification for her position, thus exempting the school from liability. Questioning the validity of this argument, the court noted that whether the librarian's moral life was central to her job as a librarian was very much in dispute. The defense of bona fide occupational qualification must be narrowly focused—the duties of the employee in question must reflect the occupational qualification alleged. The court was unable to conclude that this was the case here, and it rejected application of the exemption and allowed the librarian to proceed with her discrimination lawsuit.[16]

Courts often confront difficult decisions in this area of the law. Disputes involving sincere parties, each advancing significant issues of public concern, weigh heavily upon the judges called to rule on these disputes. Those were the circumstances that a Massachusetts state court judge faced when the Jewish Community Center of Greater Boston refused to continue the employment of Francis Piatti because he was not Jewish. The worker felt he was the victim of religious discrimination, but the community center, whose mission was to impart Jewish values and culture to Jewish children, believed it essential to its purposes to employ only practicing Jews.

As a student at Boston College, Piatti studied Hebrew in connection with his courses in theology, archeology, and liturgical music, and he later became acquainted with Jewish customs and cultural sensitivities as a result of his employment with the Jewish Community Center. The center, a charitable, nonprofit organization, provided services to local Jewish residents, and though some of its services and programs had a Jewish component, they were all open to the general public. The center employed both Jews and non-Jews.

Initially the center hired Piatti to serve as the youth director at a facility it sponsored, and he continued to work in that capacity for six years. During his tenure, the facility's youth program served approximately one hundred children, ranging from preschool to high school age. Piatti's responsibilities included planning both religious and secular activities, operating a kosher kitchen, supervising part-time instructors, purchasing supplies, and designing as well as publishing various community center publications.

In the sixth year of Piatti's employment the center experienced serious financial difficulties. In an attempt to resolve the issue, its board voted to eliminate or reduce many of its programs and place greater emphasis on the programs that served the Jewish community. One of the programs eliminated was the youth program directed by Piatti, and he was then terminated. At about the same time the board created a new part-time position to oversee an after-school program having a much greater emphasis on Jewish identity and Jewish education. Piatti applied for that position but was rejected in favor of a Jewish candidate.

The community center admitted that Piatti had been rejected for the new position because he was not Jewish and was thus not considered qualified—he did not have a Jewish background or perspective that he could share with the center's membership. Piatti then filed discrimination charges, alleging he had not been hired for the part-time position because of religious discrimination.

The center's defense was based upon its assertion that Judaism was a bona fide occupational qualification for the part-time position. But Piatti argued that the after-school position was not directly religious in nature, that it did not require the director of that program to partake in any religious activities, and that the director needed only knowledge of Jewish customs and traditions. His argument struck at the heart of the matter. Was an intellectual knowledge of Judaism sufficient for the task, or was a personal belief in Judaism required to fulfill the responsibilities of the position? After examining the facts of the case in great detail, the court ruled that non-Jews would be unable to perform the duties of the after-school program director since "being a believing, practicing Jew [constituted] a bona fide occupational qualification" for that position. The court awarded judgment for the community center.[17]

The Supreme Court has referred to the BFOQ defense as "an extremely narrow exception to the general prohibition of discrimination."[18] In some cases, however, the applicability of the defense to the facts at hand is obviously appropriate, and in those circumstances the courts have shown little hesitancy in applying that narrow exception. Such was the case when Wade Kern filed a religious discrimination case against Dynalectron Corporation.

Kern entered into a contract of employment with Dynalectron to perform duties as a helicopter pilot. The company had contracted to provide helicopter pilots to work in Saudi Arabia. The work consisted of flying helicopters over crowds of Muslims making pilgrimage along Muhammad's path to Mecca. The purpose of the flights was twofold: to protect against violent outbreaks and assist in fighting fires that occurred among the travelers when they cooked their meals. The pilots had to be Muslims, as Islamic law prohibits non-Muslims from entering the holy areas of Mecca under penalty of death. Accordingly, Dynalectron required its helicopter pilots to become Muslims before undertaking duties in Mecca.

Kern was a Baptist but agreed to convert to Islam. Dynalectron arranged an indoctrination course in which he was taught the basics of the Islamic faith. He later changed his mind and advised Dynalectron that he would not convert. The company then declined to permit him to assume helicopter pilot duties in Saudi Arabia.

When Kern filed suit alleging religious discrimination, Dynalectron asserted the defense of bona fide occupational qualification—conversion to Islam was a requirement for the Mecca helicopter jobs since non-Muslims flying into Mecca, if apprehended, would be beheaded. The company argued that if it ignored the ban against non-Muslims entering the holy areas, the essence of its business would be undermined by the beheading of its non-Muslim pilots. The court agreed that the BFOQ defense was dispositive:

> There can be no question but that non-Muslim pilots stationed in [Saudi Arabia] are not safe as compared to Muslim pilots. Therefore, Dynalectron's discrimination against non-Muslims in general, and Wade Kern specifically, is not unlawful since to hire Muslims exclusively for this job is a bona fide occupational qualification reasonably necessary to the normal operation of that particular business.... Notwithstanding the religious discrimination in this case, the court holds that the BFOQ exception is properly applicable.[19]

In addition to the Title VII exemptions examined in this chapter, an employer is also exempt from the proscriptions of Title VII with respect to one other group of employees—its clergy. That exemption will be examined in the following chapter.

13

THE MINISTERIAL EXCEPTION

The cases reviewed in the previous chapter as well as those examined in this one disclose sharp clashes between interests of the highest order—the interest of government to eradicate discrimination from the workplace versus the right of the church to manage its own affairs without governmental interference. In these cases the free exercise clause comes into play when the government encroaches upon the church's management of its internal affairs because a religious organization possesses the right to decide for itself, free of governmental interference, matters of church governance. In that regard, the right to select members of the clergy falls wholly within the domain of the church.

Historically the courts have held that church decisions relating to the selection of clergy are exempt from the proscriptions of Title VII and the Age Discrimination in Employment Act (ADEA). The courts are barred from adjudicating claims under those statutes when advanced by members of the clergy against the religious organizations employing them. This exception is referred to as the "ministerial exemption" or "ministerial exception." It has been applied not only to members of the clergy but also to employees who fulfill the functional equivalent of a minister's duties. More specifically, the ministerial exception comes into play when an employee whose position is central to the spiritual and pastoral mission of a religious institution asserts a discrimination claim against that institution.

When a member of the clergy or a lay employee exercising pastoral or spiritual functions alleges a discrimination claim against the religious organization that employs him, the courts are constitutionally barred from adjudicating that claim. They may not interfere with decisions made by a religious organization on matters of faith, employee discipline, ecclesiastical law, and other matters involving the internal governance of the organization. This rule of law has in most cases strengthened the wall separating church and state but in other cases has led to bizarre and often unjust outcomes (chapter 14).

Early in the history of Title VII, the courts assumed that the ministerial exception would need to be broadly applied if the wall separating church and state were to be preserved. In a 1972 case, a federal appellate court ruled:

> Though that "wall of separation" between permissible and impermissible intrusion of the State into matters of religion may blur, or become indistinct, or vary, it does and must remain high and impregnable. Only in rare instances where a "compelling state interest"... is shown can a court uphold state action which imposes even an "incidental burden" on the free exercise of religion. In this highly sensitive constitutional area "only the gravest abuses, endangering paramount interests give occasion for permissible limitation."[1]

Having set the stage for a broad application of the ministerial exception, the court wasted little effort in justifying the use of the exception in the case pending before it. In that case Billie McClure brought suit under Title VII claiming that her former employer, the Salvation Army, had discriminated against her on account of her gender. It was apparent from the opening paragraph of the court's decision that McClure was headed for defeat: "The Salvation Army is a church and Mrs. Billie B. McClure is one of its ordained Ministers." Once it is determined that the parties to a Title VII litigation are a church and an ordained minister, the court will refuse to adjudicate the dispute.

Under what circumstances will the exception apply where the employee-claimant is not an ordained minister? To what extent must the job functions of a lay employee involve the exercise of pastoral or spiritual duties for the exception to apply? What job functions fall within the sphere of the pastoral and spiritual? We turn to cases that have considered these issues.

Sister Elizabeth McDonough charged the Catholic University of America with sex discrimination in violation of Title VII. After her profession of vows to the Dominican order, Sister McDonough taught mathematics, science, and religion in high schools in Connecticut and later in Ohio. Subsequently, her superior suggested that she pursue a degree in canon law, a field of study that the Catholic Church had only recently made available to women. She then enrolled in the School of Religious Studies at Catholic University, later transferring to the university's Department of Canon Law. After the university awarded her a doctorate in canon law, she applied for a position in the department and became the first woman to be admitted to its faculty with a tenure-track appointment.

In due course McDonough applied for tenure, but after a lengthy process the university denied her application. While recognizing her contributions to canon law, it maintained that these failed to counterbalance her marginal performance in teaching and submissions to scholarly publications. McDonough responded by filing a sex discrimination claim against the university. In opposing that claim, the school argued that McDonough's primary role in the Department of Canon Law had been the functional equivalent of a minister, and thus the free exercise clause precluded judicial review of the decision to deny her tenure.

The court began its review of the case by summarizing previous judicial rulings relating to the scope and application of the ministerial exception. It noted that the Supreme Court had recognized that government action may unlawfully burden the free exercise of religion in two respects: (1) by interfering with a believer's ability to observe the commands and practices of his or her faith and (2) by encroaching on the ability of a church to manage its internal affairs. With respect to the second, the Supreme Court had shown a particular reluctance to interfere with a religious organization's selection of its clergy, and other courts had ruled that the free exercise clause exempted the process of selecting clergy from the proscriptions of Title VII and other antidiscrimination statutes. Thus it was clear that courts were precluded from adjudicating employment discrimination suits initiated by ministers against the religious institutions that employed them. But it also was clear that the courts had not restricted the application of the ministerial exception to members of the clergy. Rather, they had applied it also to a religious organization's lay employees "whose primary duties consist of teaching, spreading the faith, church governance, supervision of a religious order, or supervision or participation in religious ritual and worship"[2] when their positions were essential to the spiritual and pastoral mission of the church. Thus the court in the *McDonough* case had to determine whether her position in the Department of Canon Law fell within the ministerial exception. Did her primary duties consist of teaching and spreading the faith, and were they central to the spiritual and pastoral mission of Catholic University?

Sister McDonough was a member of an ecclesiastical faculty whose stated mission was to "foster and teach sacred doctrine and disciplines related to it." As a member of that faculty she was entrusted (1) with instructing students in the laws that governed the church's sacramental life and (2) with defining the rights and duties of its faithful and the responsibilities of their pastors. It could not be reasonably denied that the role of this faculty was vital to the spiritual and pastoral mission of the Catholic Church. Because McDonough's employment in the Department of Canon Law clearly met the ministerial function test, the court dismissed her claims on the basis of the free exercise clause.[3]

The judge who decided the case next to be reviewed introduced his written opinion with the following statement: "This case presents a very interesting question and that is whether or not federal judges should decide who is eligible to teach in the theology department of a religious university—in this case, Marquette University, which is run by the Jesuits of the Roman Catholic Church." By framing the issue in that fashion, the judge left little doubt about the direction he would take in deciding the case. The application of ministerial exception was about to be affirmed.

Marquette University offers both graduate and undergraduate degrees to approximately ten thousand students enrolled at its sixty-eight-acre campus in Milwaukee. Marquette officials informed the court that the university's basic goals and principles could be best summarized as follows:

> Marquette's primary reason for being is a shared conviction on the part of its sponsors...that their Catholic belief has dimensions pertinent to and

salutary for higher education, and that those dimensions can best be cele-
brated in distinctly Catholic institutions. In other words, a Catholic university is one of the innumerable witnesses Catholics may give of their faith.
It surely is that a part of Catholic belief is the necessity of conforming life
to faith, i.e., to be integral. For some the life to be made whole is the life of
higher education and Catholic universities are an expression of this drive to
integrity.

The university's bylaws provide that its affairs are to be conducted under
the auspices of the Society of Jesus. Eight of the twenty-nine-member board
of trustees are required to be Jesuits, and the bylaws give the Jesuits, if they
vote as a unit, the power to block any action they do not approve of. Early
on, the trustees adopted an affirmative action plan reserving to the university the right to grant a preference to the employment of Jesuits. That
preference, along with a disinclination to hire females, was central to the
sex discrimination claim filed by Marjorie Maguire against the university.

On six occasions, extending over several years, Maguire unsuccessfully
applied for an associate professor position in Marquette's theology department. Approximately one-half of the department members were Jesuits,
and only one of the full-time positions was held by a woman. Maguire
claimed that although she was Catholic and qualified for each position she
applied for, Marquette refused to hire her because of her gender and her
views on abortion. The university responded that if even if her academic
record had been competitive with that of other applicants, her applications
would have been rejected because of her hostility to the teachings of the
Catholic Church and the goals and mission of the university.

The court did not long agonize over its decision. For the most part, the
underlying facts were undisputed, and the law to be applied was clear. The
only point in contention was Maguire's Catholicity. The university claimed
she was hostile to the Catholic Church, while Maguire rejected that claim.
If the court had been willing to delve into the university's hiring decisions
relating to the theology department, it would have been required to determine whether Maguire was or was not a Catholic. The court declined
to make that determination. "That question is one the First Amendment
leaves to theology departments and church officials, not federal judges."

If the court had granted Maguire the relief she sought—placement on
the theology department faculty—it would in effect have forced on the

university the court's understanding of what it means to be a Catholic, and such a ruling would clearly have interfered with the right of the members of the theology department to freely exercise their religion. "The court can no more rule that [Maguire] is not a Catholic than it could find that members of the hiring committee are Catholic."

Unquestionably the government has a significant interest in eradicating sex discrimination from the workplace, but, as the Supreme Court has made clear, the First Amendment recognizes a religious organization's right to exercise religious faith free of governmental interference, even when an individual's right not to be discriminated against remains unaddressed. In this case the ministerial exception required the court to block Maguire's efforts to pursue her sex discrimination charges against the university. The court was satisfied that if it failed to enforce the exception, it would be guilty of violating the free exercise clause, impermissibly entangling the government with the university's religious affairs.[4]

Leaving the world of academia, we turn to the world of public relations. Gloria Alicea-Hernandez claimed that her former employer, the Catholic Diocese of Chicago, had discriminated against her on the basis of her national origin and gender. She worked for the diocese as its Hispanic communications manager, a position requiring her to perform a number of tasks—to compose media releases for the Hispanic community, to develop a working arrangement with local Hispanics aimed at promoting church activities, and to compose articles for church publications. She encountered difficulties in fulfilling these duties because of what she considered poor office conditions. When she attempted to rectify those conditions, she was opposed by her superiors, denied the resources necessary to perform her functions, and excluded from management meetings. Ultimately she resigned, and the diocese replaced her with a less qualified male and paid him a higher salary. Alicea-Hernandez then filed sex and national origin discrimination charges against the diocese. The question for the court was whether her position as Hispanic communications manager could be classified as functionally equivalent to a position held by a member of the clergy.

Alicea-Hernandez served in part as a press secretary, and in that capacity she was responsible for conveying the message of her employer, often serving as the primary communications link to the general populace. Her role was critical in disseminating the church's message to the Hispanic community, and in fact she served as the church's liaison with that community.

In that capacity, she served a role that was functionally equivalent to that of a minister or member of the clergy, and thus her Title VII claims were barred by the First Amendment.[5]

Alicea-Hernandez's employment role clearly was not that of a minister, but her role placed her close to the center of the Church's mission. Thus the court did not hesitate to extend the ministerial exception to cover her position as a communications manager.

We have yet to review a case where a court declined to apply the ministerial exception. Are there any such cases? The Southwestern Baptist Theological Seminary was owned and operated by the Southern Baptist Convention, an association of Southern Baptist churches. The seminary's mission was "to provide theological education, with the Bible as the center of the curriculum for God-called men and women to meet the need for trained leadership in the work of the churches." The degrees it offered were limited to those relating to theology, religious education, and church music.

The seminary's employees fell into three groups—faculty, administrative staff, and support personnel. Members of the faculty and the administrative staff were considered ministers and were hired, assigned, promoted, tenured, evaluated, and terminated on religious criteria. Support personnel were not considered ministers but nevertheless performed some religious and educational functions.

A conflict arose between the seminary and the Equal Employment Opportunity Commission when the seminary refused to file reports required by the EEOC. Pursuant to the authority granted it by Congress, the EEOC had promulgated regulations that required private institutions of higher education to biennially file a Higher Education Staff Information Report EEO-6. This report called for detailed data relating to each employee's job description, length of employment contract, salary bracket, gender, race, and national origin. When the seminary refused to file the EEO-6 report, the EEOC initiated legal action asking the court to compel the filing.

The seminary defended its refusal to file on the ground that the application of EEOC regulations to any aspect of the employment relationship between the seminary and its employees would lead to excessive governmental entanglement with religion and would infringe its rights under the free exercise clause. That position would have carried the day if all its employees had either been ministers or served ministerial functions, but the EEOC questioned the seminary's grouping of all its employees under the ministerial umbrella.

Surely members of the faculty belonged under that umbrella. Decisions regarding faculty were largely made according to religious criteria, as the level of personal religious commitment of faculty members was considered of greater significance than their devotion to the Baptist Church or their academic abilities. They modeled the ministerial role for their students.

Some members of the administrative staff served the seminary in a capacity similar to that of the faculty. The president and executive vice president, the chaplain, the deans of men and women, and other personnel who supervised faculty were considered ministers since they, without question, served ministerial functions, thus entitling them to stand next to the faculty. But that could not be said of administrators whose functions related exclusively to the seminary's finance, maintenance, and other non-academic departments. They were not charged with ministerial functions and thus could not be considered ministers or members of the clergy any more than could the support personnel. Ruling in favor of the EEOC, the court stated that when churches and religious organizations expand their operations beyond the functions traditionally held essential to the propagation of their beliefs and practices, those employed to perform services traditionally thought of as nonreligious may not be considered ministers.[6] Imprecise as this definition is, it is the best that our study has yet offered.

Occasionally an employer has asserted the ministerial exception in defense of a Title VII or age discrimination claim when the employee-claimant performs services that may only be described as nonreligious. A chef for a Catholic monastery was met with the ministerial exception defense when he charged the monastery with age discrimination. The court dismissed the monastery's assertion of the exception, noting that there was little risk that the adjudication of the chef's age discrimination claim would lead to excessive governmental entanglement in the monastery's religious affairs or call into question the monks' religious tenets. "Culinary demands, not church doctrine, will be the subject of scrutiny."

The court also dismissed the monastery's claim that application of the ADEA would violate its rights guaranteed by the free exercise clause. The ADEA is a neutral law of general applicability to employers and does not target or discriminate against any religious organization in any way. Thus the monastery's free exercise rights remained intact.[7]

Sidney Weissman served as the temple administrator for the Congregation Shaare Emeth, a Reform Jewish temple located in Missouri. At the time, the temple's congregation was one of the largest in the country, with a membership of approximately two thousand families. Weissman was responsible for logistical support of temple activities, including the supervision of administrative, clerical, maintenance, and custodial personnel, and in addition he was charged with managing the temple's property and equipment and maintaining its financial records.

As he was not a member of the clergy, Weissman played no role in decisions relating to spiritual matters. His job description, however, required him to maintain an affirmative attitude toward Jewish life and an understanding of the temple's purposes, ideals, and goals, and in this regard, he was required to promote a positive image of the temple among its members and the general public.

After Weissman had served as administrator for four years, the temple's executive committee called for his termination, citing a general dissatisfaction with his performance. He was sixty-three years old at the time and was replaced with a thirty-seven-year-old. Weissman sued the temple for age discrimination. The temple asked the court to dismiss Weissman's age claim on the ground that application of the ADEA to employment decisions regarding temple matters raised serious constitutional issues. The court affirmed previous judicial opinion that in certain cases the relationship between an employer and employee may be so pervasively religious that it would be impossible to engage in an age discriminatory inquiry without serious risk of offending the First Amendment, but was this one of those cases?

Fulfilling the requirement that he maintain an affirmative attitude toward Judaism and promote a positive image of the temple's purpose, ideals, and goals was Weissman's only duty that could be said to have a religious component. Nearly all his other responsibilities were wholly secular in nature. The mere fact that an employee has some religious duties does not shield a religious employer from a discrimination claim. The court held that in this case the enforcement of ADEA proscriptions against age discrimination would be insufficient to impose a significant risk of infringement of the temple's First Amendment rights.[8]

We have now passed from an employee who performed no religious functions (the chef) to one who performed a few (the temple administrator).

In the case of the chef, it is difficult to conceive of a convincing argument demonstrating that he functioned as clergy, thus entitling his employer to assert the ministerial exception to defeat his discrimination claims. In the case of the temple administrator, a convincing argument is at least conceivable. Although the court was not convinced, if it had viewed the administrator's religious-based responsibilities in a more positive light, it might have reached a different conclusion. The perception of the court turned the tide in one direction rather than the other. In order to develop our own perspective on the matter, we need to review one more case.

John Bollard claimed that while he was a novice in training to become a Jesuit priest, he was sexually harassed by superiors at two Jesuit schools. He alleged that they had sent him pornographic materials, made unwelcome sexual advances, and engaged him in inappropriate sexual discussions. Although he reported the harassment to Jesuit officials, they took no corrective action. Bollard claimed that the harassing conduct was so severe that he was forced to leave the Jesuit order before taking his vows. When he sued, the primary issue before the court was whether the ministerial exception precluded him from pursuing his claim.

Evidence in support of the application of the ministerial exception, however, was lacking. Rather than offering a religious justification for the alleged acts of harassment, the Jesuits condemned all types of harassment as inconsistent with their religious values and beliefs. Their disavowal of the harassment assured the court that application of Title VII to Bollard's charges would have no significant impact on their religious beliefs or doctrines. Thus there was no danger that the court would be thrust into an untenable position of being required to pass on questions of religious faith or doctrine.

The central issue in the case related to Bollard's charge that the Jesuit authorities had failed to intervene to halt the sexual harassment. In denying the application of the ministerial exception—thus allowing the case to proceed—the court would not be required to intrude upon church autonomy in any greater degree than if it allowed a suit against a church for negligent supervision of a minister charged with inappropriate sexual behavior with a parishioner.

Ultimately the court would have to determine whether Bollard had been victimized by acts of sexual harassment sufficiently severe or pervasive to be actionable under Title VII. As the trial proceeded, the Jesuits would undoubtedly assert that they had exercised reasonable care to prevent and correct the harassing conduct that Bollard alleged had occurred and that he had failed to take advantage of opportunities offered to him to avoid the harassment. Nothing in the character of that defense would require an evaluation of religious doctrine or religious practices followed by the Jesuit order. Instead, the judicial inquiry would involve secular judgments concerning the nature and severity of the harassment and the measures undertaken by the Jesuits to stop it. Since the limited nature of this inquiry would prevent a broad-based intrusion into sensitive religious matters, the court concluded that the ministerial exception was inapplicable, thus allowing Bollard to proceed with his case.[9]

We will have occasion to visit the Bollard case again in the next chapter.

14

QUESTIONABLE APPLICATIONS
OF THE MINISTERIAL EXCEPTION

The *New York Times* article was headlined "Where Faith Abides, Employees Have Few Rights." The article began with the story of a nun, a
member of a Catholic religious order in Toledo, who was dismissed from
her order after being diagnosed with breast cancer. The nun subsequently
sued the religious order, claiming that it had violated the Americans With
Disabilities Act (ADA) when it dismissed her solely because of her physical
condition. Her lawsuit did not long survive because the court ruled that
the ministerial exception required the judiciary to remove itself from the
case.[1] The nun lost her home (the convent), her occupation and vocation
(that of a contemplative nun), and her health insurance.

The nun's name was Mary Rosati.[2] In middle age she had joined the
Contemplative Order of the Sisters of the Visitation of Toledo Ohio, a religious order affiliated with the Catholic Church. Members of the Sisters of
the Visitation are contemplative nuns, living lives of prayer and contem-
plation. They lead a cloistered life, rarely leaving their convent.

The affairs of the order are regulated by the mother superior with her council, composed of several other nuns living in the convent. A candidate for the order enters the convent as a postulant. The postulancy, lasting from six to twelve months, is a time of transition from the secular life to life in the cloister. After that period the postulant may be admitted to the novitiate, a period of initiation into the evangelical life of the order and the church. At the end of the novitiate, generally lasting two years, the novice is admitted to a status referred to as "temporary profession," normally lasting three years, and at the end of that time she may take her perpetual vows, thus becoming a permanent member of the order.

When Rosati joined the convent, she passed a physical examination and was enrolled in the Toledo diocese's employee health insurance program. After fulfilling the requirements of the postulancy, she passed to the novice stage of her preparation for taking her permanent vows. Until that point, no concerns had been expressed by any of the sisters regarding her vocation as a contemplative nun.

A year and a half after entering the convent, Rosati discovered a lump in her breast. She was examined by Dr. Candilee Butler, a Toledo surgeon specializing in the diagnosis and treatment of breast cancer. After a series of tests, including a biopsy, Butler determined that Rosati had a slow-growing form of breast cancer. She asked Rosati to schedule an appointment at her office to discuss the treatment options available to her. Accompanied by Sister Jane Frances, the mother superior of the convent, and Sister Mary Bernard, an assistant to the mother superior who served as Rosati's immediate superior, Rosati met with Dr. Butler, who explained that further tests would be necessary—bone scan, chest examination, and liver and other tests—but the best treatment option appeared to be surgery to remove the lump, followed by six weeks of daily radiation therapy. At that point the mother superior stated, "We will discuss this at home." Rosati then asked the mother superior if she had her permission to schedule the next appointment in the process recommended by Dr. Butler. When the mother superior failed to respond, the doctor asked her directly whether Rosati could proceed to the next step in the process. This time she did respond: "We will have to let her go. I don't think we can take care of her."

Stunned and in a state of near panic, Rosati could hardly comprehend what had just occurred. Dr. Butler immediately asked the mother superior to reevaluate her position, that she take into account that Rosati was about to begin long-term treatment for a life-threatening illness. If she were to be dismissed from the order, she would lose her health insurance and it would be extremely difficult for her to obtain new coverage. Again the mother superior failed to respond. The three sisters then left without scheduling the next step in the treatment of Rosati's cancerous condition.

Later that day, after their return to the convent, Sister Mary Bernard took Rosati aside and said to her, "Maybe God is trying to tell you something. Perhaps you don't have a vocation [as a nun]." This was the first time since she had entered the convent that anyone had even hinted at the possibility that Rosati did not have a vocation to the religious life.

The following day Sister Mary Bernard reversed course, stating that the question of Rosati's vocation was not then an issue, that the convent's council would be voting on that matter sometime in the future, but that in her opinion it would be ridiculous to dismiss Rosati from the convent. She added that the sisters would walk Rosati through her illness and recovery process. Rosati was relieved.

Her relief was short-lived. As she pursued the treatment process recommended by Dr. Butler, she began to experience other physical problems, the most serious of which was numbness in her arms and neck, a condition apparently unrelated to her cancer. Ultimately it was determined that she would require neurosurgery for a herniated disc in her neck. Shortly after this new health issue was revealed, Sister Mary Bernard commented to Rosati that in light of all these health issues, "Don't you think God is trying to tell you something?"

Some months later, Sister Mary Bernard advised Rosati that although she had always acted properly during her life at the convent, the council had nevertheless voted to dismiss her from the order. She believed that with all her health problems, Rosati would be better off outside the convent. Among the other issues Rosati had to confront following her dismissal from the order was the loss of her health insurance coverage.

After recovering from the shock of what she had experienced at the Sisters of the Visitation convent, Rosati turned to the law, asking the court to award her damages for the humiliation, loss of self-esteem, and severe emotional distress she had suffered as a consequence of her dismissal from the convent, a dismissal she claimed had occurred only because of her health issues. In the complaint she filed with the court, Rosati alleged that the Sisters of the Visitation had dismissed her because of her health problems, thus violating the ADA, a federal statute that bars an employer from rendering workplace decisions, such as termination of employment, based on an employee's state of health.[3]

The attorneys for the order immediately asked the court to dismiss Rosati's claim, contending that the free exercise clause of the First Amendment protects the power of a religious organization to decide for itself, free from state interference, all matters of internal management, particularly in the selection of their religious personnel. In other words, they claimed that the ministerial exception barred Rosati's ADA claim.

The Sisters of the Visitation informed the court that they had concluded that Rosati was not suited for their way of life and thus was not an appropriate candidate for permanent membership in their religious order. Because she would be unable to take her permanent vows, Rosati had to leave the convent. Their attorneys argued that if the court were to second-guess the sisters' decision, it would be guilty of committing an act of impermissible interference with the internal ecclesiastical affairs of a church organization in violation of the free exercise clause.[4]

Rosati's attorneys, arguing in opposition to the contention that the ministerial exception required dismissal of her ADA claim, relied heavily on the decision in the *Bollard* case (chapter 13). John Bollard had alleged that while he was a novice in training to become a Jesuit priest, he was sexually harassed by his superiors. When Bollard later sued the Jesuits, the primary issue before the court was whether the ministerial exception precluded him from pursuing his claim. But evidence in the case showed that the Jesuits condemned all types of harassment as inconsistent with their religious beliefs and values, and thus there was no danger that if the court allowed Bollard's suit to proceed, it would be required to pass on questions of religious faith and doctrine.

The *Bollard* case did not concern a religious organization's choice of clergy. Rather, the court had to determine whether the Jesuit authorities had intervened to halt the sexual harassment. If it allowed the case to proceed, it would not need to intrude upon church autonomy in deciding that issue. Rosati's attorneys argued that her case was similar. The Sisters of the Visitation could not conceivably take the position that they supported acts in violation of the ADA or that the proscriptions of that statute were inconsistent with their beliefs and values. If Rosati's suit were allowed to proceed, there was no danger that the court would need to immerse itself in questions of religious faith or doctrine or intrude upon the order's autonomy.

Rosati's attorneys also argued that the sisters were using the ministerial exception simply to shield themselves from liability under the statute. The sisters did not deny that the decision to exclude Rosati from the convent had been made because of her disabilities; they simply stated that she was not suitable for their way of life. But that statement appeared inconsistent with earlier comments made by Sister Mary Bernard that Rosati's health problems, not her suitability for the religious life, raised questions concerning her future with the order. It also appeared to be inconsistent with the fact that prior to the occurrence of Rosati's health issues her vocation to the contemplative life had not been questioned.

Her attorneys also maintained that the court should not apply the ministerial exception merely because the individual in question served in a minister-equivalent role, that the ministerial exception should not be applied automatically but rather on a case-by-case basis. That is what the *Bollard* court ordered and that is what the court in this case should also do.[5]

The attorneys for the sisters were quick to point out that Bollard had not been asked to leave the Jesuit order. On the contrary, the Jesuits had encouraged him to pursue his vocation to the priesthood while remaining in the order. Thus the court in that case did not need to involve itself in issues relating to the selection of religious personnel. In contrast, the sisters' decision not to allow Rosati to remain in the convent had been made in the course of a selection process instituted to choose those who would remain as permanent members of the order. If the court were to permit Rosati to litigate her ADA claim, it would of necessity involve itself in that selection process. Thus the sisters' attorneys concluded,

> [W]hen a case—like the present case—involves a [religious organization's] selection or rejection of ministerial personnel, the First Amendment bars inquiry regardless of the motivation attributed to the decision maker. There is no need to determine whether... religious doctrine is involved in the decision making process in order to gain the protection of the First Amendment. In fact, to start down that road would ultimately require the court (or a jury) to decide the contours of the [sisters'] religious doctrine in order to determine whether the rationale proffered was grounded on that doctrine. This the First Amendment forbids.[6]

In the end the court adopted that reasoning. The *Bollard* decision turned on the fact that the principal issue in the case did not involve the ministerial selection process. In the *Rosati* case, in contrast, the sisters' determination that Rosati was unsuitable for permanent membership in the order emanated from a selection process utilized to determine their membership, and that decision fell within the ministerial exception.[7]

The problem with this ruling is obvious. A religious organization may cut off judicial inquiry into its motives in terminating one of its members merely by misrepresenting the facts. If it can categorize an employment decision as one made with respect to the selection of its religious personnel, the judicial process must be halted. If the sisters were to falsely state the basis for their decision to force Rosati out of the convent, they could block any further inquiry by the court.

The position taken by the sisters was open to serious doubt. Prior to the appearance of her health issues, Rosati's vocation to the religious life had never been questioned. It was only after those problems arose that her vocation became an object of discussion. When Sister Mary Bernard informed Rosati that the council had voted to remove her from the convent, she reported that the council members were of the opinion that with all her health problems Rosati would be better off living outside the order. She did not say that Rosati was unsuitable for the religious life. She did not denigrate her vocation as a nun. She referenced only health problems as the reason for asking Rosati to leave. Thus it appears that the sisters were not engaged in making a decision regarding the selection of religious personnel. Rather, the evidence tended to show that they made an employment decision that terminated an employee for reasons of health. In those circumstances, a strong argument may be made in support of Rosati's position that the ministerial exception should not have been applied.

The response the sisters would have made to such an argument is predictable. Before they could have relied upon the ministerial exception, they would have been required to demonstrate a religious justification for their decision to dismiss Rosati. This process, however, would have required the court to involve itself in the religious affairs of the convent—was Rosati asked to leave because she was unsuited to the religious life or because of her health problems? That was an inquiry the court could not make without violating the free exercise clause. It was an ecclesiastical issue regarding church governance and administration, beyond the reach of the court because the First Amendment bars governmental intervention in religious matters of this nature

Strictly adhering to the law as it has developed in this area, the court appears to have made the correct decision in dismissing Rosati's claims. But did justice prevail? When the underlying facts of a case cry out for further investigation, should that investigation always be halted in its tracks? Should a religious organization be allowed to avoid the application of federal discrimination laws by misstating the basis for an employment action taken against one of its employees? Is not the enforcement of those discrimination laws of such great importance as to allow a court, in limited circumstances, to determine whether a religious organization is using the ministerial exception for invalid purposes? Should laws requiring employers to desist from acts of workplace discrimination always fall victim to demands that religious organizations be free to hire and discharge religious personnel without governmental interference?

Three years after the *Rosati* case was decided, another court wrestled with these questions. Gannon University, a Catholic institution located in Erie, Pennsylvania, appointed Lynette Petruska its first female chaplain. In addition to fulfilling her religious responsibilities, Petruska served on the university president's staff as the cochair of the Catholic Identity Task Force and also as a member of the Sexual Harassment Committee. Several months after Petruska's appointment, a female employee of the university accused its president of sexual harassment. According to allegations Petruska later made, she was instrumental in bringing that claim to the attention of the local bishop. When the bishop ordered university officials to undertake steps that appeared to attempt to cover up the president's misconduct, Petruska strenuously objected, and subsequently the president resigned. As a member of the Sexual Harassment Committee, Petruska later participated in the preparation of a report critical of the university's discrimination and harassment policies. When university officials asked Petruska and other committee members to modify the report, they refused.

After a new president was installed, he notified Petruska that he had ordered a partial restructuring of the university's administrative personnel and was reassigning some of her responsibilities and removing her from the president's staff. Henceforth she would report to a male member of the university who had formerly served in the chaplain post. Sensing that this restructuring and demotion were about to end in her termination, Petruska resigned as chaplain and then commenced litigation against the university, claiming sex discrimination in violation of Title VII.[8]

At the outset of the litigation the court observed that the judiciary has long struggled to balance the government's vital interest in promoting a discrimination-free workplace and the constitutional rights of a religious institution to be free of excessive state interference. In balancing those interests, the courts have traditionally applied the ministerial exception, which exempts religious organizations from Title VII suits brought by employees charged with ministerial duties. The question put to the court was whether the exception should be applied to the facts at hand thus barring Petruska's sex discrimination claim.

The court answered in the negative, reasoning as follows. Petruska alleged she had been demoted because she was a woman. When a religious organization demotes a woman on the basis of sex, it may be acting according to religious belief, and in such a case, its actions would be immune from a Title VII lawsuit. But the institution might also demote a woman because the persons making that decision are simply sexist. In that case, religious belief would play no role in the decision.

Petruska alleged that she had been demoted because of a discriminatory animus against women, an animus that was not condoned by Catholic belief or doctrine. Thus the court asked itself, may an employee with ministerial duties bring a Title VII claim against a religious institution when the employment decision in issue is not one grounded in faith, doctrine, or internal regulation? The court concluded in the affirmative:

> The Constitution protects religious exercise and we decline to turn the Free Exercise Clause into a license for the free exercise of discrimination unmoored from religious principle. We therefore conclude that under the Free Exercise Clause the ministerial exception will not bar Title VII claims by ministerial employees when an employment decision is not motivated by religious belief, religious doctrine, or church regulation.[9]

The *Petruska* case was decided by a three-judge panel. The opinion, above referred to and quoted, was written by Judge Edward R. Becker, who died a few days after the decision was formally issued by the court. After his death, the university asked the court to reconsider Judge Becker's decision, and the court agreed, ordering the case to be considered anew by a newly appointed three-judge panel. This time the tide turned against Petruska.

The new panel of judges started its review of the case from a different perspective. Whether the ministerial exception should be applied in this case depended upon the resolution of one question—would the court's decision on Petruska's Title VII claims limit the right of Gannon University (clearly a religious institution) to select the people it wanted to perform particular spiritual functions? In stating the issue in those terms, the court could arrive at only one conclusion. It thus reaffirmed previous court rulings that, regardless of the motivation of the religious institution, the ministerial exception applies to claims involving its selection of those who perform spiritual functions.

Petruska alleged that the university had retaliated against her because of her opposition to the positions assumed by the university in dealing with sexual harassment claims asserted against its president. She contended that it had discriminated against her, solely because of her gender, by demoting her, thus forcing her to resign her position as chaplain. Her discrimination and retaliation claims were based in part on the university's decision to restructure its administrative staff, a decision that Petruska argued was merely a pretext for sex discrimination.

The court rejected her characterization of this decision, ruling that the university was merely engaged in selecting those persons it wanted to perform spiritual functions. Accordingly, the court concluded, the application of Title VII to the decision to restructure would violate the free exercise clause, and thus Petruska's claims must be dismissed:

> The First Amendment protects a [religious organization's] right to decide matters of faith and to declare its doctrine free from state interference. A [religious organization's] ability to select who will perform particular spiritual functions is a necessary corollary to this right. The function of Petruska's position as University Chaplain was ministerial in nature, and therefore her Title VII...Claims—each of which turns on the propriety of Gannon's personnel decisions—must be dismissed.[10]

For the short period of time between Judge Becker's decision and the later decision of the second panel, Title VII complainants had some hope that the courts would consider their claims when an employment decision of a religious organization was not motivated by religious belief, religious doctrine, or church regulation. The decision of the reconstituted court dashed those hopes, returning the law to that announced in the *Rosati* case. Like Rosati, Petruska was deprived of her day in court because of a questionable application of the ministerial exception.

Age discrimination complainants who have confronted the ministerial exception have not fared any better than Title VII complainants. After John Paul Hankins was ordained by the United Methodist Church, he served as a member of its clergy for forty-one years. When he reached the age of seventy, he was forced into retirement, as prescribed by the Methodist Book of Discipline. When he filed age discrimination charges against his bishop and the Methodist Church, he contended that the Book of Discipline contained matters both sectarian and ecclesiastical in nature, that the mandatory retirement sections of the book were secular, uncontrolled by any religious considerations, and thus the ministerial exception did not bar his age claim from being litigated in the federal courts. The lower court that considered the issue disagreed with Hankins and dismissed his complaint on the ground that the discrimination laws, including the ADEA, cannot govern a church's employment relationships with its ministers without violating the free exercise clause. Hankins appealed this decision to the appellate court.

The appellate court agreed with Hankins that in his case the lower court had misapplied the ministerial exception, but it then asserted a new hurdle to block his path. It stated that whether a minister may sue his religious employer depends not upon the ministerial exception but rather upon the Religious Freedom Restoration Act, a federal law providing that the government may not substantially burden the exercise of religion unless it can demonstrate that the application of the burden is (1) in furtherance of a compelling governmental interest and (2) the least restrictive means of furthering that interest.[11] The appellate court then remanded the case to the lower court, directing it to apply that statute to the facts at hand.[12]

Reverend Hankins expressed little hope that his age discrimination claim would fare any better the second time around. He believed, however, that because he had questioned the validity of the mandatory retirement rule, the church would eventually realize its unfairness. "I don't need to win the case. I feel the movement of history at work here. Ideas find their feet, and start to work."[13]

It is too late for the "movement of history" to be of any assistance to Rosati or Petruska. Any hope they may have had for attaining justice has come and passed.

Part IV

ACCOMMODATING WORKER RELIGIOUS PRACTICES

15

General Principles
of Accommodation

Reference has been made throughout this work to the employer's duty to reasonably accommodate the religious observances and practices of its employees. We now examine what that precisely means.

As enacted in 1964, Title VII failed to specifically provide for accommodation, but in the EEOC's first promulgated guidelines, employers were directed to accommodate the "reasonable religious needs" of their employees "where such accommodation can be made without serious inconvenience to the conduct of [their] business." One year later, the EEOC revised its guidelines to provide that accommodation is required whenever it "can be made without undue hardship on the conduct of the employer's business."[1] Six years later, in 1972, Congress added a provision for accommodation to Title VII itself. The newly added language, awkward in construction, reflected the EEOC guidelines:

> The term "religion" includes all aspects of religious observance and practice, as well as belief, unless an employer demonstrates that he is unable to

reasonably accommodate to an employee's or prospective employee's religious observance or practice without undue hardship on the conduct of the employer's business.[2]

Unfortunately, in amending the statute, Congress failed to specifically define the terms "reasonable accommodation" and "undue hardship." There the matter stood until 1977, when the Supreme Court agreed to consider the case of *Trans World Airlines, Inc. (TWA) v. Hardison.*[3]

TWA operated a large maintenance and overhaul base in Kansas City, Missouri. Larry Hardison worked as a clerk in the stores department at the base. Because of its essential role in the Kansas City operation, the stores department operated twenty-four hours a day, 365 days a year, and whenever a position in that department was not filled because of illness or other absence, an employee from another department or a supervisor was assigned to cover that job, even when work in other areas of the base would suffer. Like all employees at the base, Hardison was subject to a seniority system provided by the terms of a collective bargaining agreement TWA had with the International Association of Machinists and Aerospace Workers.

Approximately one year after the commencement of his employment with TWA, Hardison became immersed in the study of the teachings of the Worldwide Church of God. One of its tenets required Sabbath observance by abstention from work from sunset on Friday to sunset on Saturday. When Hardison informed the manager of the stores department of his newly acquired religious convictions regarding observance of the Sabbath, the manager authorized a change in shift to allow him to meet his Sabbath requirements. Shortly thereafter, Hardison asked for and was granted a transfer to a day-shift position. After the transfer, he was assigned to work on a Saturday as a substitute for an employee on vacation. Lacking sufficient seniority to avoid the Saturday assignment, he asked the union to waive the seniority provisions set out in the collective bargaining agreement so that another worker could be assigned to that position, but the union refused on the ground that were it to agree to a waiver, it would in effect be undermining the contractual rights of other employees.

In an attempt to avoid future Saturday assignments, Hardison proposed an accommodation, that his workweek be limited to four days. TWA rejected that proposal because Hardison's job was essential, and on weekends he was the only person on his shift to perform it. To leave the position vacant would have impaired supply-shop functions that were critical to airline operations. To fill Hardison's position with a supervisor or an employee from a different area would have undermanned another plant operation. And to employ someone not regularly assigned to work Saturdays would have required TWA to pay premium wages.

When TWA and Hardison could not agree upon any course of action that would relieve him of working on Saturdays, Hardison simply refused to report for work on Saturdays. TWA discharged him on grounds of insubordination for refusing to work during his designated shift. Hardison then claimed that his discharge constituted religious discrimination in violation of Title VII.

When the case reached the Supreme Court, the Court first noted that TWA had made significant efforts to accommodate Hardison's religious needs, conducting several meetings with him in attempts to find a solution to his Sabbath problem. In addition, it had made efforts to find him another job and had authorized a union steward to search for workers to swap shifts with him.

Hardison argued, however, that TWA should have done more. He insisted that Title VII provisions obliging an employer to accommodate the religious observances of its workers took precedence over both the collective bargaining contract and the seniority rights of TWA's other employees. But the Court disagreed. The duty to accommodate did not require TWA to take steps inconsistent with the terms of its agreement with the union, and an established seniority system need not give way to the accommodation of a worker's religious observances:

> The foundation of Hardison's claim is that TWA...engaged in religious discrimination...when [it] failed to arrange for him to have Saturdays off. It would be anomalous to conclude that by "reasonable accommodation" Congress meant that an employer must deny the shift and job preference of some employees, as well as deprive them of their contractual rights, in order to accommodate or prefer the religious needs of others, and we conclude that Title VII does not require an employer to go that far.

The court also rejected Hardison's contentions that TWA should have permitted him to work a four-day week or replace him with supervisory personnel or workers from another department, as both alternatives would involve costs to TWA, in the form of either lost efficiency or higher wages. The court concluded that to require TWA to bear more than a "de minimis cost" in order to give Hardison Saturdays off was an "undue hardship."

Justices Marshall and Brennan dissented from the decision on the ground that from that point onward the courts need not grant even the most minor accommodation to religious observers to enable them to follow their religious beliefs and practices. Justice Marshall concluded that despite Congress's enactment of Title VII, one of this country's "pillars of strength—our hospitality to religious diversity—has been seriously eroded."[4] We will look to the cases that follow to determine whether Justice Marshall was correct in that assessment.

After the Supreme Court's decision in the *Hardison* case, the EEOC revised its guidelines in some areas, including the following.

Reasonable accommodation. A refusal to accommodate is justified only when an employer can demonstrate that an undue hardship will result from all available forms of accommodation. The assumption that many employees with the same religious practices as the person being accommodated may also need accommodation is not evidence of undue hardship. Some alternatives for accommodating religious practices may disadvantage the person accommodated with respect to employment opportunities, such as compensation. Therefore, when there is more than one means of accommodation, the employer must offer the alternative with the fewest disadvantages.

Undue hardship. An employer may assert undue hardship to justify a refusal to accommodate only if it can demonstrate that the accommodation would require more than a de minimis cost. The EEOC will determine what constitutes "more than a de minimis cost" by giving due regard to the identifiable costs in relation to the size and operating costs of the employer and the number of individuals who require the accommodation.[5]

The *Hardison* decision, the EEOC guidelines, and the cases that follow call for both the employer and the employee to fulfill certain responsibilities when engaged in the process of finding an appropriate accommodation. The employer is solely responsible for initiating a good-faith discussion to determine whether the employee's religious beliefs and practices can be accommodated, while the employee is required to make a good-faith attempt to satisfy her needs through the means offered by her employer. In endeavoring to work out a solution, the employer and the worker have a duty to cooperate with each other.

If an employer is to adequately perform its obligation to accommodate the religious observances of its employees, it had better understand fully what that obligation entails. Consolidated Freightways hired Corine Proctor as a payroll clerk and later assigned her to various other positions, including that of data input clerk and balancing clerk. During her employment Proctor became a member of the Seventh-day Adventist Church and began to observe the Sabbath from Friday sundown to Saturday sundown. Prior to that time, she had occasionally been required to work on Saturdays. On the first such occasion after joining her new church, she notified her supervisors that her religious beliefs now precluded her from working on Saturdays. When she failed to appear at work on the designated Saturday, she was placed on five-day suspension. But Consolidated's manager of labor relations then directed Proctor's supervisors to accommodate her religious beliefs by not requiring her to work on Saturdays, and over the next three years, other employees were substituted for her when Saturday work was necessary.

After seven years on the job, Proctor bid for a balancing clerk position. She was asked to sign a statement acknowledging that if given the job she would be required to work Saturdays. Even though she refused to sign the statement, Consolidated awarded her the position. For the next several months, the company was able to honor Proctor's request not to work on Saturdays by arranging for volunteers to work on those days instead. This state of affairs came to an end when Proctor's supervisor insisted that she work, as others did, on certain Saturdays. When she failed to appear for work on the first of these days, she was suspended for three days without pay. When these circumstances occurred again the following week, she was terminated.

Proctor filed a grievance, but an arbitrator ruled against her, finding that she had caused her own problem by requesting and then accepting a job that obligated her to work Saturdays. She then filed discrimination charges against Consolidated, alleging that after her assignment to the balancing clerk position, it had failed to accommodate her religious practices. The company's defense was in large part based on the efforts it had made to accommodate Proctor in her position as a data input clerk. But the court held that Consolidated's obligation to accommodate continued after she left the data input clerk position and assumed the duties of the balancing clerk position, even though at the time she applied for that job she was fully aware that Saturday work would be necessary:

> It is clear that Consolidated had an obligation to initiate good faith efforts to accommodate Proctor's religious beliefs after she assumed her new position as a balancing clerk. [Title VII] makes it an unfair labor practice to refuse to hire an individual because of her religion. A refusal to hire Proctor because she was unable to work on Saturdays would have been a violation of Title VII in absence of good faith efforts to accommodate her religious beliefs. The fact that Proctor applied for a position which she knew required Saturday work thus does not exempt Consolidated from its statutory duty to initiate a good faith effort to accommodate her in that position.[6]

Despite the fact that Consolidated could point to a long history of having accommodated Proctor when she held a data input clerk's position, its obligation did not end when she changed positions.

While an employer is obligated to attempt to accommodate an employee's religious beliefs and practices, an employee is obligated to cooperate with the employer in finding a reasonable accommodation. This responsibility on the part of the employee frequently becomes a subject of contention. The subject arose during the course of litigation involving an employer's refusal to hire a worker because of his prior use of drugs in a religious ceremony.

Wilbur Toledo applied for a position as a truck driver for Nobel-Sysco, a supplier of food equipment to restaurants in several western states, including New Mexico. The position would have required him to drive over mountainous roads and work without day-to-day supervision. It was Nobel-Sysco's policy not to hire applicants who had used illegal drugs during the two years preceding their job applications. During the course of his application interview, Toledo disclosed that he was a member of the Native American Church, and that he had used peyote as part of a church ceremony in the previous six months. Although the religious use of peyote was legal, Nobel-Sysco rejected Toledo's application on the ground that hiring a known user of peyote would expose the company to liability if Toledo were to be involved in an accident while driving for the company.

The Native American Church combines elements of Christianity with traditional Native American beliefs, including a belief in the use of peyote as a most sacred church practice. Believers consider peyote a deity, a healer, a teacher, and a way of communicating with God. Church members may request a peyote ceremony for healing purposes or other special occasions. The ceremony generally is conducted in the late evening and consists of a series of rituals and prayers, culminating in the ingestion of peyote. Toledo testified he normally felt the effects of the peyote for approximately four hours, but experts agreed that a person ingesting peyote at one of these ceremonies should not drive a truck for at least twenty-four hours. It was undisputed that Toledo abstained from the use of peyote outside the ceremonies conducted by the Native American Church.

After Nobel-Sysco rejected his application, Toledo filed religious discrimination charges against the company. At that point, Nobel-Sysco offered to settle the charges levied against it by agreeing to hire Toledo if he agreed (1) to give the company one week's notice before participating in a peyote ceremony and (2) to take off one day after each ceremony. Toledo rejected the offer and proceeded to file a Title VII lawsuit against the company.

The court had to decide two issues: (1) whether Nobel-Sysco's offer of settlement constituted an attempt at reasonable accommodation, and (2) whether it could have accommodated Toledo without incurring undue hardship. On the first issue, Nobel-Sysco maintained that Toledo, in adopting an intractable bargaining position, breached his duty to cooperate with the company's accommodation efforts. But the court held that a settlement offer cannot stand as an attempt at accommodation. When the company rejected Toledo's application solely on account of his religious practices and without any attempt to accommodate him (assuming it could have done so without undue hardship), it committed an illegal act. Its later advanced offer of settlement, therefore, could not be viewed as an attempt at accommodation, and thus Toledo was not obligated to respond to it. The statutory burden to accommodate rests with the employer, and the employee's duty to make a good-faith attempt to satisfy his religious needs through the means offered by the employer does not come into play until the employer satisfies its obligation under the statute. Because the accommodation offer came after the initial unlawful refusal to hire, the court concluded that

Toledo did not breach his duty to cooperate with Nobel-Sysco in reaching a reasonable accommodation.

With regard to the question of undue hardship, the court ruled that the risks of increased liability created by hiring Toledo were too speculative to qualify as undue hardship. Requiring him to take a day off after each ceremony would virtually have eliminated the risk that the influence of peyote would cause an accident, and thus Nobel-Sysco failed to show that it could not have accommodated Toledo's religious practices without incurring undue hardship. The company's refusal to hire him therefore constituted a violation of Title VII's prohibition against employment discrimination based on religion.[7]

Elizabeth Anderson, a believer and follower of the Christian Methodist Episcopal faith, was accustomed to expressing her faith by concluding her conversations and correspondence with the phrase "Have a Blessed Day." After working for over three years for U.S.F. Logistics, she was promoted to office coordinator, a position in which she acted as liaison between U.S.F. and its customers and vendors. In her new position Anderson continued to use the phrase "Have a Blessed Day" with coworkers and customers, but her use of the phrase drew a complaint from an employee working for Microsoft, U.S.F.'s largest customer. In response to the complaint, U.S.F. instructed Anderson to cease using the phrase on all documents sent to Microsoft. Anderson refused to obey and continued to use the phrase in her e-mails directed to Microsoft. When Microsoft again complained, Anderson's supervisor instructed her to refrain from using the phrase in all her daily interactions with Microsoft. Anderson then notified her supervisor that the "Have a Blessed Day" phrase constituted an essential aspect of her religious practices. She offered, as an accommodation, to cease the use of that phrase with all persons her supervisor identified as offended by it. Her supervisor did not respond.

Anderson's persistence in using the phrase culminated in a reprimand and notification that continued use would be considered grounds for termination. U.S.F. then issued a policy statement to its employees requiring them to refrain from using "religious, personal, or political statements" in their closing remarks in verbal or written communications with customers and fellow employees. Despite the policy statement, U.S.F. permitted Anderson to continue the use of the phrase with her coworkers.

She then stopped using the phrase with Microsoft personnel. Approximately four months later, however, she sent an e-mail to Microsoft with the phrase in all capitals and set off with quotation remarks—"HAVE A BLESSED DAY." Again she was reprimanded, but Anderson was not one to acquiesce without a fight. She filed legal action against U.S.F., alleging that it had violated Title VII by reason of its repeated failures to accommodate an essential element of her religious practices. The court ruled, however, that U.S.F. had reasonably accommodated Anderson by allowing her to freely use the phrase with her coworkers while restricting its use with the company's primary customer. Despite this reasonable accommodation, she had refused to be moved, declining to compromise in any respect. The court ruled against her.[8]

Workers are not placed under any burden to propose specific forms of accommodation. They are obligated, nonetheless, to cooperate with measures proposed by their employers. Where an employee fails to cooperate with her employer's attempts at reasonable accommodation, the court may find her responsible for the failure to achieve such an accommodation. The search for reasonable accommodation requires bilateral cooperation, a joint effort to find an acceptable accommodation of the worker's religious needs without unduly upsetting the employer's business practices. Although the statutory burden to accommodate rests squarely with the employer, the employee is nonetheless charged with a correlative duty to attempt to satisfy her religious needs through the means offered by her employer. Compromise is nearly always an element of a successful search for a reasonable accommodation.[9]

Nine years after the *TWA v. Hardison* case, the Supreme Court again had an occasion to consider a case presenting accommodation issues. It involved a high school teacher, Ronald Philbrook, who taught business and typing classes in Ansonia, Connecticut. While teaching in the Ansonia high school classrooms, Philbrook joined the Worldwide Church of God. The tenets of the church obliged members to refrain from work on designated holy days, causing Philbrook to miss six school days each year. The school board's collective bargaining agreement with its teachers provided for three days of annual leave for the observance of mandatory religious holidays. It also provided for three days of personal leave, but this leave could not be used for religious purposes. That left Philbrook in a position where he was forced to take unauthorized leave to cover three of his church's six holy days. On each of those occasions his pay was reduced accordingly.

After following this agenda for a number of years, Philbrook decided to change it. Instead of taking unauthorized leave on the three holy days, he scheduled medical visits on those days. When this proved unsatisfactory, he asked the school board to adopt one of two alternatives. His preferred alternative would have allowed him to use three days of personal leave for religious observance, effectively giving him six days of annual leave for the observance of mandatory religious holidays. Alternatively, he offered to pay the cost of a substitute teacher if he were paid for the three additional days of leave. The school board rejected both proposals.

Philbrook then filed suit against the school board, charging it with violations of Title VII by reason of its refusal to permit use of personal leave for religious observance. After Philbrook lost in the trial court but later won on appeal, the case moved to the Supreme Court, where the Court was called on to answer the following question: Is an employer obliged to accept its employee's preferred proposal for accommodation if that accommodation does not cause undue hardship in the conduct of its business? The Court responded in the negative—nothing in Title VII requires an employer to choose any particular reasonable accommodation. *Any* reasonable accommodation is sufficient to satisfy the employer's obligation. Where an employer has already reasonably accommodated an employee's religious practices, as it did in this case, it need do nothing more. Thus the school board was not obligated to show that alternative accommodations suggested by Philbrook would result in undue hardship because hardship becomes an issue only when the employer claims that it is unable to offer any reasonable accommodation without incurring such hardship. The school board did not act improperly in rejecting Philbrook's suggestions for alternative means of accommodation.[10]

As one commentator noted, both the *Hardison* and the *Philbrook* rulings present serious difficulties for an employee seeking an accommodation of his or her religious practices. "The message sent by the [Supreme Court] is that the 'reasonable accommodation' standard mandated by Title VII need not be all that accommodating." Despite the presence of more accommodating alternatives, an employer may fulfill its statutory duty by offering a far less extensive accommodation.[11] Another commentator put it more starkly: "After these cases, the religiously observant employee in the secular corporation is left with very little [Title VII] protection for religious practices and observances."[12]

Despite the Supreme Court opinions in the *Hardison* and *Philbrook* cases, the lower courts continue to view the employer's duty of accommodation less restrictively. A good example of how far a court will extend the employer's responsibility to formulate an appropriate accommodation appears in a case involving a coal miner.

Pyro Mining Company operated a coal mine in Kentucky, employing over 1,000 underground workers and 150 surface workers. Danny Smith worked as an underground mechanic. As a member of a local Baptist Church, Smith held the offices of treasurer and trustee and served as a Sunday School teacher. Church doctrine precluded all officers and teachers of the church from working on Sundays, and Smith personally believed it morally wrong, in the absence of a life-threatening situation, to work on Sundays.

During the first year of his employment, Smith was not required to work on any Sunday. But then Pyro Mining instituted a new work schedule that required each worker to work approximately twenty-six Sundays per year. A worker who objected to working on Sundays was authorized to trade shifts with a worker who did not object. Smith decided that it was morally wrong of him to ask another worker to swap shifts with him since, in effect, he would be inducing that person to sin by working on Sunday. On the first Sunday that Smith was scheduled to work, he advised his supervisor that because of his religious convictions he would be unable to appear at the mine on that day. When he did not arrive at the mine as scheduled, he was sanctioned and charged with an unauthorized absence. On the next Sunday that he was scheduled to work, he was again sanctioned for his absence. After his third unauthorized absence, Pyro Mining terminated him in accordance with its long-standing policy.

On the day of his termination, Smith appealed his discharge, suggesting to the mine superintendent that he be allowed to work additional days without overtime pay to make up for Sunday absences. Alternatively, he proposed a transfer to a surface job that did not require Sunday work. Both requests were rejected. Smith then filed suit, alleging that Pyro Mining had violated the religious discrimination provisions of Title VII by discharging him on account of his religious beliefs.

The company alleged that Smith's refusal to solicit a replacement constituted a failure on his part to cooperate with efforts to accommodate him. As the courts have repeatedly made clear, although the burden is on the employer to accommodate the employee's religious needs, the employee must make some effort to cooperate with the employer's attempt to accommodate. Where an employee refuses to engage in any effort to accommodate his own beliefs or refuses to cooperate with his employer's endeavor to reach a reasonable accommodation, he may render it impossible to find one. But the cooperation that Pyro Mining suggested—that Smith himself arrange for a shift swap—was an act that he considered sinful. If he had had no religious qualms about asking others to work on Sunday, then the company's proposed accommodation would have been reasonable. But that was not the case. Where an employee sincerely believes that working on Sunday is morally wrong and that it is sinful to induce another to work in his place, a proposed accommodation that forces the employee to seek his own replacement is not reasonable.

Since the accommodation proposed by mining company officials was unreasonable, Pyro Mining should have made further attempts at accommodating Smith. It would not have constituted an undue hardship for the company to arrange a shift swap. In fact, before instituting the new work schedule, Pyro Mining had had a long-existing policy of informing its employees of the need of a worker for a shift trade, and it took an active role in contacting employees willing to participate in shift trades. Moreover, the company had in place a mechanism for soliciting replacements. It could have accommodated Smith simply by placing a notice in its monthly newspaper or on its bulletin boards that a replacement was needed for him on a designated Sunday. No undue hardship was involved. Thus the court ruled in favor of Smith.[13]

As will become apparent in the next chapter, the federal district courts and the circuit courts of appeal have been more inclined than the Supreme Court to search out the truth lying beneath facades erected by some employers to obscure their opposition to involvement in the accommodation process. But at the same time, these courts rarely exhibit empathy for workers who refuse to compromise and thus block efforts to accommodate their religious needs.

History shows that Justice Marshall correctly assessed the negative results of the role played by the Supreme Court in accommodating worker religious beliefs and practices but that he failed to anticipate the corrective role the lower courts would later play.

16

ACCOMMODATION IN PRACTICE

Having established the general principles of accommodation, we now examine the day-to-day application of those principles by the courts. That has not been an easy matter for our judges.

Truck driver David Virts worked for Consolidated Freightways at its facility in Nashville. Consolidated's dispatchers assigned truck runs in accordance with the seniority provisions of the company's collective bargaining agreement with the International Brotherhood of Teamsters. Virts had been working for Consolidated for nearly ten years when one evening, upon arriving at the truck terminal to begin an overnight run, he discovered that the dispatcher had assigned a woman as his codriver on the run. Virts informed the dispatcher that because of his religious convictions, he could not accept an assignment with a female driver. He explained that traveling with a woman would violate the beliefs he had adopted when he became a born-again Christian. He believed that the Bible commanded Christians to avoid appearances of evil, and if people were to see him on an overnight truck run with a woman, they would wonder whether he was engaged in sinful activity. In addition, such a situation could lead to his own lustful thoughts and sexual temptation.

The dispatcher arranged for the female driver to swap assignments with a male driver on another run, and Virts proceeded on his assigned run. He was later advised that the swap in run assignments had violated the collective bargaining agreement and that the next time he was paired with a female driver, he would have to accept the assignment and proceed with the run as directed. The company made it clear to him that it would not again violate the collective bargaining agreement in order to accommodate his religious convictions.

Approximately a year and a half later, Virts again found himself paired with a female driver on an overnight run. When he objected on the basis of his religious convictions, the dispatcher informed him that he was required to make the run, and if he refused, he would be deemed to have voluntarily resigned. Virts did not drive.

A few days later, the terminal manager scheduled a meeting with Virts and union representatives. Virts, accompanied by his pastor, detailed the religious beliefs underlying his refusal to drive with females and the reasons why he should not again be assigned a truck run paired with a female driver. A few days later Virts learned that he was no longer employed by Consolidated Freightways.

Virts sued the company for religious discrimination and then offered four proposals for accommodation. Each proposal, as the court noted, would have required Consolidated to violate the seniority provisions of its collective bargaining agreement with the Teamsters as well as the contractual rights of other drivers, thereby causing it undue hardship. The very fact that Virts was unable to offer an accommodation that did not violate the terms of the collective bargaining agreement supported Consolidated's position that an accommodation of Virts's religious beliefs was not possible.[1]

If a court finds that an employee unjustifiably refused to cooperate with his employer in locating an acceptable religious accommodation, the court will most likely reject the employee's claim. An unwillingness to pursue an acceptable accommodation undermines the cooperative approach Congress intended to foster in resolving issues of this type. Yvonne Shelton learned this the hard way.

Shelton worked as a staff nurse in the Labor and Delivery Department of the University of Medicine and Dentistry of New Jersey. Employees of that department performed routine vaginal and cesarean-section deliveries. They did not perform elective abortions but on occasion were required to perform emergency procedures that resulted in the termination of a pregnancy. As part of their responsibilities, nurses working in that department were obligated to assist in such emergencies.

Shelton, a member of a Pentecostal church, was forbidden by her beliefs from participating in any medical procedure that directly or indirectly resulted in the ending of a life. Of course, that included abortion. When possible, the hospital allowed Shelton to trade assignments with other nurses rather than participate in emergency procedures involving what she considered to be abortions. But trading assignments was not always a viable alternative.

In two incidents, Shelton's religious beliefs clashed with the emergency treatment of patients with life-threatening conditions. In the first, she refused to participate in the treatment of a pregnant patient, suffering from a ruptured membrane, because the hospital planned to induce labor by giving the patient oxytocin. After the incident, Shelton's supervisor asked her to provide a note from her pastor specifying her religious beliefs. Instead, Shelton submitted her own note: "Before the foundations of the earth, God called me to be Holy. For this cause I must be obedient to the word of God. From his own mouth he said 'Thou shalt not kill.' Therefore, regardless of the situation, I will not participate directly or indirectly in ending a life."

In the second incident, Shelton refused to participate in the treatment of a patient standing in a pool of blood who was diagnosed with placenta previa. The situation was life-threatening and the attending physician ordered an emergency cesarean-section delivery. Because this procedure would terminate the pregnancy, Shelton refused to assist or participate in the delivery. This refusal required the hospital to locate another nurse before the attending physician could begin the procedure, thus causing a delay of thirty minutes.

Two months later, after hospital officials had closely reviewed the details of the two incidents, they determined that Shelton's refusal to assist at these emergency procedures had risked patient safety. Because of her refusal to assist in "medical procedures necessary to save the life of the mother and/or child," the hospital removed her from the labor and delivery department. Instead of terminating her, however, it offered her a lateral transfer to a staff nurse position in the newborn intensive care unit, and if she found that assignment unsatisfactory, invited her to contact the human resources department to help her identify other available nursing positions.

Shelton contacted the newborn ICU and later claimed she had been told that "extremely compromised" infants who were not expected to survive were "set aside" and allowed to die. She declined to contact the human resources department to investigate other available positions.

The hospital then gave Shelton thirty days to either accept the newborn ICU position or apply for another nursing position. Shelton did neither. Instead, she wrote to her supervisor: "The ultimatum given me ... doesn't align with the response I am [allowed by God] to submit. The decision is not ours to make but the Lord's. The Living God is in control of that which concerns my life and job. 'Many are the plans in a man's heart but it's God's plan/purpose that will prevail.'" Shelton was then terminated.

Shelton sued, claiming violations of Title VII. The primary issue before the court was whether the hospital had reasonably accommodated Shelton by offering her a transfer to the newborn ICU. She argued that the offer was not reasonable because in that position she would again be asked to undertake religiously untenable nursing actions. The hospital responded with testimony showing that severely compromised infants were not denied medical treatment, were not taken off life support, and were not denied nourishment. Shelton had no evidence to counter that testimony and thus was unable to support her position that she would confront religious conflicts if assigned to that department.

The court then turned to the hospital's suggestion that Shelton confer with its human resources department about other available nursing positions. Once that proposal had been placed on the table, she was obligated to determine whether it was reasonable. This she failed to do, even though, as she later admitted, nursing positions to which she could have transferred were open at the time. She claimed that her duty to cooperate in finding an accommodation never arose because any transfer would have required her to give up eight years of specialized training and would have compelled her to undertake extensive retraining for a new position. Again, the evidence failed to support her contentions. Some retraining would have been necessary, but it would not have been burdensome, and there was no evidence she would have lost pay or benefits by transferring to a new position. In short, Shelton's failure to cooperate with the hospital in searching for a reasonable accommodation was unjustified. By failing to cooperate, she undermined the cooperative approach to resolving religious accommodation issues. The court dismissed her lawsuit against the hospital.[2]

A Title VII claimant must be prepared to support each of her claims with admissible evidence establishing the truth of the matters asserted. This cannot be overly emphasized. A claim that the employee knows cannot be established should be abandoned because a claim that remains unproven undermines the entire case. Shelton claimed that a nurse in the newborn ICU had told her that extremely compromised infants who were not expected to survive were set aside and allowed to die, but she could not recall the name of that nurse. She was testifying to hearsay statements, not admissible to establish the fact that infants were actually treated in that manner. When she advised the court that she could not remember the nurse's name, her credibility was destroyed. That was her first mistake, one having deadly consequences for her case.

Mistake number two occurred in connection with Shelton's assertion that a transfer to any other nursing position would have made it necessary for her to undertake a course of retraining for the new position. Again, she made a factual assertion she was unprepared to support with admissible evidence. When testimony given in support of the hospital showed that any required retraining would not have been burdensome and that she would not have suffered any diminution in pay or benefits in consequence of making the transfer, the weakness of her case became apparent.

It was clear to the court that Shelton did not have the slightest intention of cooperating with the hospital in searching out a reasonable accommodation. A noncooperative stance generally ends in defeat. Allegations that are not supported by the evidence always end in defeat.

Another situation that nearly always concludes with the dismissal of the claimant's case is one in which all modes of accommodation either undermine the rights of coworkers or cause work-related problems for them. After earning a master's degree in marriage and family counseling, Sandra Bruff began working for the North Mississippi Medical Center as a counselor in its Employee Assistance Program (EAP). Bruff was one of three EAP counselors, one of whom acted as the program's supervisor. Counseling sessions were held during and after regular business hours in two Mississippi cities, requiring a counselor to travel to a given location for each scheduled session.

Bruff counseled a woman, identified as Jane Doe, who after several sessions informed Bruff that she was a homosexual and needed help in improving her relationship with her female partner. Bruff declined, advising Doe that homosexual behavior conflicted with her religious beliefs, but she offered to continue her counseling services on matters unrelated to homosexuality. Instead of appearing at her next counseling session, Doe lodged a complaint with the medical center, alleging that Bruff's response to her request for counseling was discriminatory. Bruff then wrote to the medical center requesting that she be excused from counseling homosexuals and other persons living in sexual relationships outside marriage.

The medical center management met several times to determine whether Bruff's request could be accommodated by shifting responsibilities among the three EAP counselors, but eventually it was determined that such an accommodation was not feasible. Management personnel reminded Bruff that persons counseled by EAP counselors were treated for a wide variety of psychiatric and clinical issues, and specific patient care issues could not be identified in advance. They also noted that her request to exclude from her care those patients who presented specified issues would create an uneven distribution of the patient workload, and thus the logistics of accommodating her religious views would cause an undue hardship on the medical center staff. Moreover, her request not to treat some patient issues while continuing to treat others raised serious ethical concerns. When Bruff was offered a transfer to a section of the medical center that performed pastoral and Christian counseling, she demurred on the ground that the head of that section held religious views more liberal than hers and that he likely would not tolerate her conservative perspective. Since no other accommodation was possible, Bruff was terminated.

Bruff sued the medical center, alleging Title VII violations. Although she prevailed in the trial court, an appellate court reversed that decision and dismissed her case on the ground that the center could not accommodate her without materially increasing the workloads of the other EAP counselors. Her request that the center refer all patients desiring to be counseled on matters that conflicted with her religious principles would require the other two counselors to care for those patients in addition to their own, thus substantially increasing their responsibilities.

Voluntarily accommodating the preferences of other counselors was the accepted practice among the EAP counselors. One counselor, for example,

preferred not to counsel young children, and she requested not to be assigned those cases. Bruff and the other counselor agreed to assume that
responsibility whenever possible, but when neither of them was available,
the first counselor proceeded with the assignment despite her aversion to
the task. Bruff's request for an accommodation was not similarly flexible.
Rather, she claimed that Title VII commanded the medical center to excuse her at all times from counseling homosexuals and other persons living
in sexual relationships outside marriage. Given the small size of the EAP
counseling staff, the area covered by the program, and the nature of the
psychological counseling required by their patients, the court ruled that
any accommodation of Bruff's religious beliefs would involve more than a
de minimis cost to the medical center:

> Requiring one or both counselors to assume a disproportionate workload
> or to travel involuntarily with Bruff to sessions to be available in case a
> problematic subject area came up, is an undue hardship as a matter of law.
> Requiring the center to schedule counselors for sessions or additional coun-
> seling sessions to cover areas Bruff declined to address, would clearly in-
> volve more than a de minimis cost.[3]

In another case, a court refused to order an employer to compel one of
its employees to switch from a daytime to a nighttime shift so as to accommodate another employee's Sabbath observance.[4] Where the employer is
able to accommodate a worker's religious beliefs only by undertaking an
action that adversely affects one or more other employees, the courts most
often rule that such an action involves more than a de minimis cost to the
employer, thus constituting an undue hardship.

Precisely what is a de minimis cost? When does an employer's cost
constitute an undue hardship? In determining whether a cost is more
than de minimis, EEOC guidelines provide that the cost of the accommodation should be considered in relation to the size of the employer,
its operating costs, and the number of employees who will need such an
accommodation.[5]

These issues were confronted by a federal district court when Volkswagen of America dismissed Angeline Protos because she refused to work on
her Sabbath. Hired by Volkswagen to work on its assembly line, Protos was
assigned to the trim department as an assembler. Her task was to connect

four color-coded wires to four connectors and to attach a ground screw. Initially her work schedule did not conflict with her religious principles, but three months after she was hired, Volkswagen announced new work schedules that included mandatory overtime work on a significant number of Saturdays. Protos's church prohibited her from working on Saturdays, and her failure to observe the Sabbath commitments constituted grounds for excommunication. She duly advised her supervisor that she would be unable to comply with the demands of the new work schedule, and when she persisted upon not working on Saturdays, Volkswagen discharged her.

After Protos sued Volkswagen, alleging religious discrimination, the principal issue presented to the trial court was the degree of hardship that would have been imposed on Volkswagen if it had accommodated her request to be relieved of Saturday work. The court ruled that Volkswagen had suffered no economic loss because of her absence on the Saturdays in question because the "efficiency, production, quality, and morale" of the trim department remained intact. The court concluded that Volkswagen could have accommodated Protos without undue hardship and at no cost, not even a de minimis cost. Unsatisfied with this outcome, Volkswagen appealed the trial court's decision.

In reviewing the case, the appellate court considered the evidence showing that Volkswagen regularly maintained a crew of roving absentee relief operators to be deployed as substitutes for absent employees. Since the requirements of Protos's job were easily learned by an absentee relief operator, the efficiency of the assembly line did not suffer by reason of her absence. The appellate court affirmed the lower court's ruling in favor of Protos.[6]

An employer may argue that if it were to accommodate the religious beliefs of one of its workers, other workers would seek a similar accommodation, thus multiplying the costs of accommodation. The difficulty with this argument is that more often than not it is based on speculation. An employer offers the argument unsupported by sufficient evidence that other workers would be interested in attaining a similar accommodation. The Watertown School District in South Dakota made that mistake in defending against discrimination claims asserted by one of its teachers.

Orley Wangsness was hired by the school district as its junior high school industrial arts teacher. He taught five classes daily involving approximately 125 students. As a member of the Worldwide Church of God, he was required by one of its tenets to attend a religious festival known as the Feast of Tabernacles, an event observed each fall over a period of seven days at several places around the world, including locations in the United States. Wangsness submitted a written request to the principal of the junior high school for a one-week leave of absence to attend the Feast of Tabernacles in Missouri, but his request was denied, first by the principal, then by the superintendent of schools, and finally by the board of education. Wangsness was warned that if he attended the festival, he would be discharged. He attended anyway and was fired.

When he filed a Title VII action against the school district, it proffered a defense described by the courts as the "multiplier" effect. It maintained that if it had approved Wangsness's request for a leave of absence, it would have set a precedent, which would have led to requests by other teachers for other types of absences, thus seriously affecting the discipline of the school system. As the court noted, references to future hardships, wholly speculative in nature, were irrelevant. Because the school district had failed to make any attempt at accommodation and had not established that it had suffered undue hardship, the court ruled in favor of Wangsness.[7]

If an employer intends to assert undue hardship as the reason for its failure to accommodate a worker's religious practices, it had better have at hand detailed evidence of the hardship it claims to have suffered. Otherwise, the court will surely rule against it. That fate befell a Chicago beauty salon.

Lyudmila Tomilina and Alina Glukhovsky were employed by the Ilona of Hungary beauty salon, Tomilina as a manicurist and Glukhovsky as a skin care specialist. Both were Jewish, and both asked to be excused from work on the Saturday that Yom Kippur was observed. Their requests were refused. When neither appeared for work on Yom Kippur, both were fired.

At the trial of the ensuing religious discrimination case, Ilona maintained that its decision to refuse the requested day off was based not on a failure to accommodate but on legitimate business concerns. Ilona emphasized that its salon could not afford to operate with less than a full complement of service personnel on Saturdays, the busiest day of the week in the beauty industry. Maximizing revenues was a matter of some concern for Ilona's owners because the salon had been operating at a loss for several years.

Ilona's owners testified in detail that they had denied the requests for the day off because they anticipated a loss of revenue if Tomilina and Glukhovsky were absent on the Saturday in question. But the salon's financial records did not show a significant correlation between the number of manicurists and skin specialists on duty on a given day and the revenues produced on that day. In fact, those records disclosed that the salon at times generated even greater revenue with a reduced staff than it did with a full complement of manicurists and skin specialists. After reviewing this evidence, the court concluded that Ilona would not have suffered undue hardship had it accommodated Tomilina's and Glukovsky's religious requests.[8]

The foregoing review of cases allows us to formulate some general rules applicable to the resolution of accommodation issues:

1. A worker's discrimination suit will almost certainly fail if it is shown that he refused to cooperate with his employer in its efforts to find a suitable accommodation of his religious beliefs and practices. In those circumstances courts nearly always side with the employer.

2. When an employer establishes the nonavailability of any appropriate form of accommodation, the courts have no alternative but to rule in its favor.

3. The courts will not order an accommodation of a claimant's religious practices if that accommodation adversely affects coworkers.

4. The courts reject all accommodations that require the employer to violate the terms of a collective bargaining agreement.

5. An employer pleading undue hardship must support its position with actual—not speculative—evidence of the hardship.

6. An employer's reliance upon unsubstantiated predictions of requests for accommodation by other employees is generally considered by the courts to be speculative and thus must be rejected.

7. Employer allegations of losses of revenue occasioned by acts of accommodation will be rejected if the losses are not confirmed by the employer's financial records.

If the parties to an accommodation lawsuit keep these principles in mind, their differences are likely to be quickly resolved.

17

Accommodation in
Out-of-the-Ordinary
Circumstances

Over the years, as workers have placed greater reliance on the rights and protections established by Title VII, employers have grown much more aware of their legal responsibilities to accommodate the religious beliefs and practices of their employees, and as a consequence, the circumstances in which accommodation arises as an issue have greatly expanded.

Kimberly Cloutier had been working in the deli department at Costco's West Springfield, Massachusetts, store for several months when Costco revised its dress code to prohibit food handlers from wearing jewelry. Cloutier, averse to surrendering her right to wear jewelry, requested a transfer to a position where such restrictions did not apply.

At the time, she did not attribute her insistence upon wearing jewelry to a religious belief. Over the ensuing two years she engaged in several forms of body modification, including facial piercing and cutting, and although these modifications were meaningful to her, they apparently were not based on any form of religious belief.

Costco then again revised its dress code. All employees in all departments were prohibited from wearing any form of facial jewelry other than earrings. At the time, Cloutier favored eyebrow piercings. When instructed to comply with the new directive, she informed her supervisor that she was a member of the Church of Body Modification and that her eyebrow piercings were based on the teachings of her church. She refused to remove them.

Established two years before this incident, the Church of Body Modification had approximately one thousand members, all of whom participated in such practices as piercing, tattooing, branding, cutting, and body manipulation. Its mission statement established that its members were to endeavor "to grow as individuals through body modification and its teachings," to "promote growth in mind, body and spirit," and to be "confident role models in learning, teaching, and displaying body modification."

Although church tenets did not require body modifications to be visible at all times, Cloutier interpreted the mission statement's call to members to be "confident role models" as requiring her to exhibit them, thus precluding her from removing or covering her eyebrow piercings. Cloutier told her supervisor she could not accede to the demands of the dress code, but she agreed to meet with the store manager to try to work out a compromise. Subsequently she offered to cover the piercings with flesh-colored Band-Aids, but the store manager rejected that solution. In the end, she was told to remove the piercings or leave the store. She left.

Soon afterward Costco terminated her, but it nevertheless continued discussions aimed at finding an appropriate accommodation. Both parties reversed their original positions. Costco offered to allow Cloutier to return to work provided she wear a Band-Aid over the piercings, precisely the proposal she had first made while discussing possible compromises. But this time she rejected that proposal, now expressing the belief that any covering of her piercings would constitute a violation of her religious convictions. She claimed that the only acceptable accommodation would be for Costco to excuse her from the obligations of the dress code, thus allowing her to wear facial jewelry while at work. Costco responded that an accommodation of that sort would interfere with its ability to maintain a professional appearance in its store, thereby creating an undue hardship.

Cloutier at this point was not proposing any type of accommodation. As we have seen, the obligation to search for a reasonable accommodation extends in both directions. While Costco proposed an accommodation that balanced its interest in presenting a professional appearance with Cloutier's religious beliefs, Cloutier simply proposed that Costco refrain from applying the dress code to her. Costco had a legitimate interest in presenting a workforce that was reasonably professional in appearance. As its dress code stated, "Appearance and perception play a key role in member service. Our goal is to be dressed in professional attire that is appropriate to our business at all times.... All Costco employees must practice good grooming and personal hygiene to convey a neat, clean and professional appearance." Clearly, exemption from the dress code would have thwarted the company's business goals.

Costco made a business determination that facial piercings detracted from the professional image it was attempting to cultivate. In Cloutier it faced an employee who would accept no accommodation short of an exemption from its dress code. Because such an exemption would adversely affect the professional appearance of its workforce and, consequently, its public image, it constituted an undue hardship for Costco. When the parties to the dispute turned to litigation, the court ruled in Costco's favor.[1]

Cloutier maintained that her insistence on displaying her eyebrow piercings was based on a sincerely held religious belief. That was questionable. What constitutes a legitimate religious belief is an issue difficult for the courts to resolve, and more often than not, they will undertake measures to avoid ruling on that issue (see chapter 2). That is precisely what the court did in this case. Using a "cart before the horse" approach, it noted that it was clear that Costco was unable to accommodate Cloutier's religious beliefs without incurring undue hardship. Thus the court was compelled to rule in the company's favor, hence obviating any need to "delve into [the] thorny question" relating to the legitimacy of Cloutier's religious beliefs. In the cases that follow, the courts also assumed the sincerity of the claimant's religiously held views without becoming involved in that thorny question.

Charan Singh Kalsi's religious discrimination lawsuit against his former employer, the New York City Transit Authority, placed in issue two conflicting interests—Kalsi's personal religious beliefs and the transit authority's work safety policies. Kalsi was a member of the Sikh religion, which required him to wear a turban at all times other than when he was sleeping or bathing. Kalsi believed, therefore, that this tenet of his faith prohibited him from wearing a hard hat, even though his position with the transit authority required him to wear one.

The transit authority had hired Kalsi as one of its car inspectors, who work in subway maintenance shops, performing repairs to electrical and mechanical subway car equipment. Much of their work is performed in pits situated below floor-level tracks in the authority's maintenance shops. The pits allow an inspector, working in a stooped position, to inspect and repair the equipment attached to the underside of the cars. In the cramped space in which they work, various parts of the subway car intrude, all of which are made of metal and often have sharp edges. Many of the tasks performed by car inspectors, whether undertaken below, alongside, or inside subway cars, subject them to the risk of head injury. For example, when he is working in the pits, an inspector's head may come into contact with exposed high-voltage wiring, and thus he needs protection against electric shock and even electrocution.

At the time of Kalsi's hiring, the transit authority had in place a hard-hat policy intended to minimize injuries caused by the many hazards daily encountered by its car inspectors. When Kalsi refused to wear a hard hat over his turban, the authority initially considered an accommodation of his religious beliefs that would place him in an inspector position that would not require him to wear a hard hat, but such an accommodation ran afoul of the seniority provisions of its collective bargaining agreement. Any other accommodation would have compromised workplace safety, and the authority ultimately concluded that it could not accommodate Kalsi's religious beliefs without incurring undue hardship and that his termination was necessary.

Kalsi filed suit, alleging Title VII violations. In analyzing the problems his religious beliefs presented to the transit authority, the court noted that if the authority had accommodated Kalsi by allowing him to work without a hard hat, the potential for injury would have extended not only to him but to other car inspectors as well. If his turban were to catch fire while he was working in a pit, for example, he might not be the only worker burned since the fire could well spread to others. If he were electrocuted, other inspectors working close by could also be subjected to electric shock. Others might suffer injury in rescuing him from the effects of accidents caused by his not wearing a hard hat. An accommodation that required the transit authority to bear such risks clearly imposed an undue hardship on it. The court dismissed Kalsi's Title VII claims.[2]

George Daniels was no more successful than Kimberly Cloutier and Charan Kalsi in convincing his employer to alter its policies affecting religiously oriented dress. Daniels, a police officer of thirteen years' standing in Arlington, Texas, wore, as a symbol of his evangelical Christianity, a gold cross on his shirt while working in a plainclothes person's position. When he was transferred to a uniformed position, he wore the cross on his uniform, and this brought him into conflict with Arlington Police Department policy that barred police officers from wearing religious pins on their uniforms. When the police chief ordered Daniels to remove the pin, he refused on the ground that his religious beliefs required him to wear the cross at all times. Subsequently, department officials made three offers of accommodation: (1) that Daniels wear a religious ring or a bracelet in lieu of the cross, (2) that he wear the cross under his uniform shirt, or (3) that he transfer to a nonuniform position. Daniels did not deign to respond to the offers of accommodation and continued to wear the cross on his uniform. Ultimately, the police department fired him for insubordination. Daniels then filed Title VII claims against the department.

Few persons would seriously argue that a police officer should be allowed to openly display religious symbols on his uniform. If Daniels continued to insist upon displaying the cross, the Arlington Police Department clearly could not reasonably accommodate his religious needs without incurring undue hardship. The court therefore had no alternative but to rule in the department's favor. Alluding to Daniels's failure to fulfill his responsibility to cooperate in searching out a reasonable accommodation, the court noted that his Title VII claims were also subject to dismissal on those grounds.[3]

Some workers are prohibited by their religious beliefs from associating with labor unions, others are prohibited from paying union dues, and still others are barred from both. Robert Roesser, an electrical engineer with a Ph.D., worked for the University of Detroit as an assistant professor of electrical engineering. The university, a private institution affiliated with the Jesuits, was party to a collective bargaining agreement with a local union affiliated with two large labor unions, the Michigan Education Association (MEA) and the National Education Association (NEA). Nearly all of the dues collected by the local union were passed on to the two larger unions. The collective bargaining agreement required all employees covered by its terms to either join the union or, as a condition of employment, pay to the union a service fee equal in amount to the union dues. At first, when Roesser began teaching at the university, he refrained from joining the union but authorized the deduction of the service fee from his pay-check. Later, after learning that the NEA and the MEA had campaigned to protect the right of women to choose abortion, a position inconsistent with his religious convictions, he withdrew the authorization to deduct the service fee.

Roesser advised the union that the fee requirement conflicted with re-ligious beliefs that barred him from associating with or financially sup-porting any organization promoting abortion. "I may not pay money to the union to support... pro-abortion activities nor may I associate with the union because of these activities." Accordingly, he refused any longer to authorize the payment of the service fee to the union but as a compromise, offered to pay an amount equal to the fee to a charitable organization. The union rejected his proposal. Instead, it offered to reduce the fee by an amount proportionate to the percentage of the MEA budget that was connected with abortion issues, but Roesser rejected that proposal. Con-cluding that the union had offered him a reasonable accommodation of his religious beliefs, the university terminated his employment.

At that point, the EEOC intervened in the matter, filing suit against the university and the local union on behalf of Roesser. The EEOC alleged that the university and the union had engaged in unlawful employment practices in violation of Title VII by terminating Roesser's employment because of his religious beliefs. The federal district court ruled against the EEOC and Roesser, but they then appealed to the court of appeals. The ap-pellate court began its analysis of the issues in contention by stating a basic premise: "A private employer must make reasonable accommodations to the religious needs of employees but need not make accommodations that pose an undue hardship.... Title VII entitles employees only to a reason-able accommodation, not an absolute one." Any reasonable accommoda-tion is sufficient to meet the requirements of Title VII, but in this case, the proffered accommodation related to only one of the two religious beliefs requiring accommodation. The proposal was directed at accommodat-ing Roesser's belief that he could not contribute money to an organization that supported abortion, but it ignored that aspect of his beliefs that pro-hibited him from associating with such an organization. Thus it failed to accommodate all aspects of his religious beliefs and in that sense was not reasonable. The court of appeals thus ruled that

[t]he duty to accommodate cannot be defined without reference to the specific religious belief at issue. Here, the employer was confronted with two religious objections, one of which was completely ignored. Accordingly, this cause must be remanded [to the district court] for a determination as to whether Roesser's entire religious belief may be reasonably accommodated short of undue hardship.

The appellate court suggested that on remand the district court consider as a solution to the matter a proposal that apparently had at one time been discussed by Roesser and the local union. Though Roesser's religious beliefs constrained him from associating with the MEA and NEA, it did not appear that he harbored any objections to associating with the local union, which had not taken a position on abortion. Would it not be a reasonable accommodation for Roesser to pay the service fee to the local union to be used solely for local collective bargaining purposes?[4]

In a similar case, a Catholic worker who objected to paying dues to his union because of its positions on abortion and the death penalty requested that he be permitted to donate the dues to a charity rather than to an organization with which he was religiously and morally at odds. The union opposed his request but offered to reduce his payments by an amount equivalent to that portion of the dues normally allocated to the support of the positions opposed by the worker.

The court that ruled on the case noted that there were two objections to the union's proposal, one relating to support for the particular issues the worker objected to—abortion and the death penalty—and the other concerning the organization that supported those issues. Reducing the amount of the dues addressed the first issue but not the second. Only by redirecting the dues in their entirety would the worker's religious objections be wholly satisfied. Allowing him to pay to a charity an amount equivalent to his union dues satisfied those objections.[5]

The guidelines issued by the Equal Employment Opportunity Commission align with the rulings in these two cases:

Some collective bargaining agreements include a provision that each employee must join the labor organization or [in the alternative pay it] a sum equal to dues. When an employee's religious practices do not permit compliance with such provision, the labor organization should accommodate the employee by not requiring the employee to join the organization and by permitting him or her to donate a sum equivalent to dues to a charitable organization.[6]

Congress has also gotten into the act, amending the National Labor Relations Act to specifically provide for alternatives to paying union dues by workers holding religious convictions that oppose union activities:

> Any employee who is a member of and adheres to established and traditional tenets or teachings of a bona fide religion, body, or sect which has historically held conscientious objections to joining or financially supporting labor organizations shall not be required to join or financially support any labor organization as a condition of employment; except that such employee may be required ... in lieu of periodic dues ... to pay sums equal to such dues to a nonreligious, non-labor organization charitable fund.[7]

Between the National Labor Relations Act and judicial and EEOC interpretations of Title VII, it now appears well settled that the way out for workers with religious convictions that oppose labor unions is to pay to charitable institutions what other workers pay to their union as dues.

Part V

RETALIATION AND OTHER ISSUES

18

Religious Discrimination and Retaliation

The reactions of employers to charges of employment discrimination—whether religious, race, sex, national origin, age, or disability—do not differ greatly from their reactions to allegations of fraud or criminal activity. Employers are all too prone to strike back at any worker who even utters the words "discrimination." Once a supervisor or company official is accused of committing discriminatory acts, he may make life extremely difficult for his accuser. The victim of discrimination then also becomes a victim of retaliation.

The law provides protection from acts of employer retaliation when workers are engaged in exercising the rights granted them by Title VII. When Congress enacted that title, it decreed it unlawful for an employer to retaliate against a worker who charges it with a discriminatory policy or practice or who participates in a legal or administrative proceeding relating to the company's employment policies or practices. Once a worker has engaged in a protected activity, defined as

- an action opposing an act of discrimination, such as the filing of a charge of discrimination, or
- testifying on behalf of a fellow worker who has asserted a claim of discrimination, or
- participating in an investigation of alleged discriminatory conduct,

the employer is barred from retaliating against that worker on account of her participation in that protected activity. More specifically, Title VII provides,

> It shall be an unlawful employment practice for an employer to [retaliate] against any of his employees or applicants for employment...because [he or she] has opposed...an unlawful practice...or...has made a charge, testified, assisted, or participated in any manner in an investigation, proceeding, or hearing under this sub-chapter.[1]

An employer who ignores its legal duty to refrain from retaliatory acts subjects itself to liability for damages suffered by the worker as a consequence of those acts. Charges alleging retaliation in violation of Title VII precepts, filed annually with the Equal Employment Opportunity Commission, steadily increased between 1997 and 2009. Over 30 percent of all Title VII complaints filed with the EEOC in 2009 charged employers with acts of retaliation.[2] This steady rise in the filings of retaliation charges reflects an increased tendency on the part of employers to react negatively and irresponsibly to charges of discriminatory conduct. It reflects as well an increased willingness on the part of workers to call their employers to task for acts of retaliatory conduct.

A retaliation claim consists of four components, each of which must be established by the claimant:

1. The worker participated in a protected activity.
2. At the time, the worker was performing his or her job functions in accordance with the employer's legitimate expectations.
3. Subsequently the worker was subjected to an adverse employment action.
4. A causal connection existed between the worker's participation in the protected activity and the adverse action.

The cases that follow in this chapter center on issues that typically arise in religious discrimination cases when workers also charge their employers with retaliatory conduct. These issues commonly appear in cases where the worker has charged the employer with religious harassment or some other form of flagrant discriminatory conduct; they rarely appear in cases where accommodation issues predominate.

Cynthia Firestine sued her employer, Parkview Health System, under Title VII, charging the company with having retaliated against her for complaining about religious discrimination occurring at its work sites. Firestine worked as an administrative secretary in the medical/oncology/ nursing department under the direction of Janette Bowers, her immediate supervisor. Firestine was a Catholic; Bowers was a lesbian. Although Firestine's Catholic faith led her to disapprove of Bowers's lifestyle, she informed Bowers that her religious views would not affect her friendship with her. Their friendship, however, fell apart after Bowers conducted Firestine's performance evaluation. Although she increased Firestine's numerical performance rating, she inserted comments in the evaluation form that Firestine viewed as harsh and inaccurate. Fearing that comments of that nature would adversely affect her future advancement in the company, Firestine informed Parkview's employee relations department that the only reason she could discern for the harsh comments was that Bowers knew that Firestine, as a Catholic, did not approve of Bowers's homosexual lifestyle.

On several occasions both employees discussed the matter with personnel in the employee relations department and ultimately they decided that Firestine should transfer to another position in the company. But when Firestine discovered that no comparable jobs were available, since all jobs proposed to her were lower-level positions, she chose to search for work with another employer. She then filed suit against Parkview charging it with retaliatory conduct.

The court first had to determine whether Firestine had satisfied the four components of her retaliation claim.

1. Did she participate in a protected activity? Yes. She engaged in a protected activity at the time she apprised the employee relations department that her supervisor had conducted a false performance evaluation after she had made it known that she disapproved of the supervisor's homosexual lifestyle. To satisfy this component of a retaliation claim, Firestine had to establish that she reasonably believed in good faith that Bowers had committed a discriminatory act. Only a groundless claim, based on factual assertions that no reasonable person could possibly believe, would fail to pass that test.

2. At the time, was Firestine performing her job functions in accordance with Parkview's legitimate expectations? Since Bowers had increased Firestine's numerical performance evaluation, Parkview could not reasonably dispute Firestine's assertion that she was adequately performing her job functions.

3. Was Firestine subjected to an adverse employment action? Parkview's removal of Firestine from her job, followed by an offer of a transfer to a job inferior to her former position, constituted a materially adverse employment action.

4. Was there a causal connection between Firestine's participation in the protected activity and the adverse employment action? Yes. A causal connection existed between Firestine's report to the employee relations department and her removal from her position.

The court concluded that Firestine had easily satisfied the four components of her retaliation case.[3]

At times a claimant's discrimination claim ends with defeat but an accompanying retaliation claim with success—the court dismisses the discrimination claim but rules in favor of the retaliation claim. If a worker has not been discriminated against, how is it possible that he was retaliated against? We examine Sanford Hertz's discrimination and retaliation claims for an answer to that question.

Hertz, who was Jewish, accused his supervisor, who was not Jewish, of making anti-Semitic comments in his presence. When Hertz informed the supervisor that he intended to bring legal action against him and their employer, the supervisor fired him. Hertz proceeded to file suit, alleging that his supervisor had engaged in religious discrimination and that when he protested the discriminatory conduct, the supervisor had retaliated against him by terminating his employment. The case was tried before a jury, which ruled against Hertz on the discrimination claim but in his favor on the retaliation charge. In approving the jury's verdict, the appellate court noted that Hertz did not need to convince the jury that his supervisor actually discriminated against him; he was required only to show that when he engaged in a protected activity, he had a reasonable good-faith belief that the supervisor's behavior was discriminatory.

When Hertz complained that his supervisor had made anti-Semitic remarks, he was engaging in a protected activity, thus laying the groundwork for the first of the four components of a retaliation claim. He easily established the second component because his job performance was never

in issue, and thus he had no difficulty showing the jury that he had performed in accordance with his employer's expectations. The third element
of proof, requiring Hertz to demonstrate that he had suffered an adverse
employment action after participating in a protected activity, was easily
established. Retaliatory adverse employment actions come in varied forms:
termination, refusal to promote, demotion, disadvantageous transfer, refusal to grant a merited or scheduled pay increase, or issuance of an unwarranted adverse performance evaluation. Almost all courts have ruled
that any materially adverse change in a worker's terms and conditions of
employment may provide the basis for a retaliation charge. Termination,
however, appears to be the preferred retaliatory act, and that also was the
action selected by Hertz's supervisor.

Hertz also provided evidence to support the fourth element of proof—
demonstrating a causal relationship between his charge against his supervisor and his subsequent termination—by offering evidence that his
termination had followed immediately upon his claim that his supervisor had committed discriminatory acts. The causal connection between a
worker's participation in a protected activity and the employer's adverse
employment action may in some instances, as in this case, be shown by
demonstrating to the court or jury that a relatively short period of time
elapsed between the employee's involvement in a protected activity and
the employer's action. The closeness in time of the two events raises the
inference that there must have been a connection between them.

Causality may also be demonstrated through the introduction of other
forms of indirect evidence. A sudden change from positive to negative
in an employer's attitude toward a worker may be sufficient to prove
the connection. It may also be established by showing that the employer
at different times gave inconsistent reasons for acting adversely to the
worker's interests. Then again, a pattern of employer conduct, such
as continuous harassment of the worker, may prove adequate for the
purpose.

Even though Hertz was unable to convince the jury that he had been a
victim of religious discrimination, his retaliation claim remained viable if
he could persuade the jury that he truly believed his supervisor had acted
in a discriminatory manner. In the course of establishing the four components of his retaliation claim, Hertz also convinced the jury that he possessed a good-faith belief that he had been subjected to acts of religious

discrimination. The jury decided the retaliation charge in his favor, and the appellate court later confirmed the jury's verdict.[4]

Allegations of anti-Semitism also were central to a religious discrimination and retaliation case initiated by a police officer of the Suffolk County Police Department in New York. Howard Mandell, who retired after thirty years on the force with the rank of deputy inspector, asserted that throughout his career with the police department he had confronted a pro-Catholic and a pro-Irish bias. Mandell was Jewish. He contended that anti-Semitism had long been a part of the police department's culture, that he had continuously been the target of anti-Semitic remarks and taunting, and that he had been subjected to insulting and demeaning conduct by fellow police officers.

Early in his police career as a young lieutenant, Mandell had testified before the Suffolk County legislature's Public Safety Committee that racism and anti-Semitism were systemic in the police department. Subsequently he was expelled from the Suffolk County Patrolmen's Benevolent Association for having expressed this view.

Several years later Mandell was interviewed by a local newspaper concerning the problems that arise when a nearly 100 percent white police force operates in predominantly African American communities, some of which existed in Suffolk County. During the course of the interview, he disclosed that the Suffolk County Police Department had experienced difficulty in recruiting African Americans because black communities often viewed police officers as oppressors. In some instances, because of the racist attitudes of certain officers, Mandell had been compelled to remove them from these communities, reassigning them to predominantly white areas. Police department officials were not pleased when the details of the interview appeared in the newspaper.

After Mandell had served the police department for twenty-eight years, a new police commissioner, John Gallagher, was appointed. Soon afterward, Mandell accused Gallagher, who was Irish-Catholic, of promoting a pro-Catholic mentality in the department. At official functions, Gallagher was accustomed to making statements such as "We are all good Christians" and "We can all work well together because we all went to good Christian schools, were taught by the Christian Brothers, and learned good Christian values."

Gallagher declined to promote Mandell to the rank of inspector, instead promoting a Catholic officer to that position. After Mandell was passed over for the fourth time, he complained to Gallagher about discrimination in the department. Not long after, Gallagher demoted him to a subordinate position.

Rabbi Jeffrey Wartenberg, a Suffolk County police chaplain, supported Mandell's discrimination charges. During Wartenberg's twenty years with the department he had heard many Jewish officers complain about the disparaging remarks directed at their religion, and he was well aware that department officials nearly always favored Catholics for promotion. On the basis of his personal experience, he concluded that anti-Semitism was a way of life within the department and that as a consequence the careers of Jewish officers were adversely affected.

Ultimately Mandell filed suit against the police department, alleging that adverse actions had been taken against him because of his religion and in retaliation for his testimony before Suffolk County's Public Safety Committee and also on account of his newspaper interview. Subsequently, attorneys for the police department sought to have the court dismiss Mandell's case on the ground that he was incapable of submitting evidence sufficient to support his legal claims.

The court did not long linger over that issue, ruling that the evidence of anti-Jewish discriminatory animus was more than sufficient to support Mandell's allegations of religious discrimination. Gallagher's several speeches to members of the department were replete with references to Catholic values and education, and one could infer from statements of that sort that he viewed Catholicism as a necessary background for a good police officer and that he considered non-Catholic officers to be lacking in that regard. Evidence indicating that the department leadership knowingly tolerated anti-Semitic attitudes and conduct supported assertions that Gallagher's decisions not to promote Mandell and instead transfer him to a subordinate position were motivated by a discriminatory bias.

Turning to Mandell's retaliation charge, the court considered the police department's argument that Mandell had failed to establish a causal connection between his public criticism of the department and its decisions not to promote him. As previously noted, causation may be established either indirectly by showing that the claimant's participation in a protected activity was followed by employment decisions adversely affecting him or by direct testimony of a retaliatory animus. Mandell chose to rely upon the latter.

He testified that after his public statements critical of the department and his subsequent expulsion from the Suffolk County Patrolmen's Benevolent Association, a memo was placed in his personnel file stating that he had "branded the entire department as racist and anti-Semitic," and that this "attitude should be taken into account when placing him in any future assignment." Unquestionably this memo impacted Mandell's career opportunities in the ensuing years. The court concluded, therefore, that he had submitted proof adequate to show causation in support of his retaliation charge.[5]

The refusal to promote is a popular form of employer retaliation, but as earlier noted, there are many others. A disadvantageous transfer, an assignment of onerous work tasks, and an unwarranted adverse performance evaluation are some of the forms of retaliation used against workers as punishment for engaging in protected activities. Some courts have also ruled that even acts that do not adversely affect the worker's economic status, such as unwarranted reprimands, long-term surveillance of the worker in question, or workplace harassment, may qualify as retaliatory acts.

The various ways in which retaliatory conduct may return to haunt an employer are well illustrated in a case, litigated in a New York federal district court, involving allegations of age and sex discrimination. Laws barring retaliation in age and sex discrimination cases and those proscribing it in religious discrimination cases are in all major respects identical. This case discloses the difficulties employers create for themselves when they engage in retaliatory conduct, whether the underlying discriminatory charge be sex, age, or religion. The proceedings in this case also bring to light the pitfalls employers confront in defending against charges of retaliation, regardless of the merit of the underlying allegations of discrimination, and disclose the difficulties generated by unreasonable reactions to a worker's charge of discriminatory conduct.

The case is discussed at some length in my book *Age Discrimination in the American Workplace: Old at a Young Age.*[6] Because this case was ultimately settled pursuant to terms that bar the parties to the suit, as well as their attorneys, from discussing its details, fictitious names are used in the narrative that follows.

I doubt that I have ever had a more difficult client than Barbara Jones. She was overly critical of everyone and everything, including me and my handling of her case. She was obstinate, intransigent, and uncompromising, and consequently, nearly all our meetings and discussions about her case ended in anger and frustration on my part. On many occasions, I pleaded with her to find another lawyer. Although she made the effort, she was unsuccessful in persuading any other lawyer to assume responsibility for her case. She later advised, "You are stuck with me; better make the best of it."

Jones first came to my office convinced she was about to be fired, and not long afterward she indeed was terminated. We then filed suit against her former employer, alleging age and sex discrimination. During her last few months on the job, Jones felt that both age and sex bias had warped and perverted her employer's decisions affecting her status as an employee. Initially I evaluated her case as rather weak, but sufficient evidence was on hand to justify proceeding with it, at least through the initial stages of the litigation. If we were unable to develop more compelling evidence of either age or sex discrimination, we would be confronted with the prospect of withdrawing the case or suffering a court-ordered dismissal. As we proceeded to gather evidence in support of the claims and to prepare generally for the forthcoming trial, the likelihood of proving either type of discrimination grew increasingly problematic. But in addition to age and sex discrimination, we had charged Jones's employer with retaliation, alleging that her supervisor had deliberately undermined her status with the company after she filed discrimination charges with the EEOC. As we proceeded to develop the case, we collected evidence strongly supporting the retaliation charge.

Of course, charging an employer with retaliation is one thing, and proving it is another. We were well aware that we had the burden of proving a causal connection between her participation in a protected activity and the retaliatory actions taken by her employer. A sudden change in an employer's attitude toward the worker often provides the necessary connection. Similarly, a pattern of employer conduct, such as continuous harassment of the worker, may also prove adequate for that purpose. Both occurrences were present in this case.

Jones's employer argued that her termination had occurred not as a result of any discriminatory conduct on its part but rather because of interpersonal problems Jones had with her coworkers and supervisors. She was described as generally uncooperative, insubordinate, overly opinionated, and argumentative and was portrayed as creating such a disruptive force in the office that her termination was required. My own experience with Jones readily led me to conclude that this description might not have been wholly unjustified and that many of her problems might have been of her own making and not the result of discriminatory acts committed by her employer. Apparently a host of her former coworkers were prepared to testify on their employer's behalf and against her at the forthcoming trial. Since her claims of age and sex discrimination were not developing as we had hoped, we decided to shift gears and focus our efforts on proving the retaliation charge.

Unlike most workers who have been subjected to discriminatory conduct, Jones filed a discrimination charge with the EEOC *before, not after,* her employment was terminated. Many workers delay the filing of a charge until after they have been fired, but that often proves to be a mistake. Understandably, a worker still on the job has no desire to alienate her employer with the filing of a discrimination charge, as the employer will nearly always react negatively in those circumstances. Thus the charge itself may precipitate additional discriminatory and adverse actions against the worker. But on occasion, the filing of a charge generates positive results for the worker. The filing of Jones's charge prior to her termination had been an astute move, and she was about to reap its benefits.

Two weeks after Jones filed age and sex charges with the EEOC, she suffered the first in a series of adverse actions directed against her by her employer. The layout of the office in which she and other employees worked consisted of two parallel rows of cubicles. Each cubicle was just large enough for a desk and chair, and the cubicle walls were little more than waist high, thus affording little privacy for any of the workers. Until that time, the assignment of cubicles had been done, not on the basis of any preconceived plan, but randomly. Jones's supervisor occupied one of the front cubicles, and Jones was in one in the rear. Now the seating arrangement was changed. Her supervisor moved to a rear cubicle, and he assigned Jones to a cubicle located immediately in front of his. This change enabled him to monitor her daily activities. As the company's most senior worker, Jones was humiliated in the presence of coworkers when her supervisor daily peered over her shoulder and recorded her every move.

It was apparent that after she filed the EEOC charge, her employer had decided to fire her, and the change in seating arrangement had been undertaken primarily to facilitate the gathering of evidence to support her forthcoming discharge.

After scrutinizing her work for nearly two months, Jones's supervisor issued her a warning notice, citing three incidents of "improper conduct demonstrating a lack of responsibility." All three incidents were based upon false premises, as Jones was later able to demonstrate.

Not long afterward, her supervisor conducted Jones's annual performance evaluation, and he rated her performance as "marginal." He manipulated the evaluation to support the allegations inserted in the warning notice, giving no recognition to any of her achievements during the previous year. A few weeks later, as Jones was entering the cubicle area, she accidentally brushed against her supervisor. He accused her of assaulting him. Jones, at least a foot shorter in height and 150 pounds lighter in weight, was no match for him, and although the accusation obviously was spurious, she was fired the following day.

Once these facts were assembled, a clear picture of retaliation emerged. The four basic elements of a retaliation claim were present. The evidence clearly established that for several years Jones had satisfactorily performed her job functions. Once she engaged in a protected activity—the filing of a discrimination charge with the EEOC—her employer ordered adverse employment actions against her. The causal connection was apparent in the close proximity in time—two weeks—between her filing of the EEOC charge and the first adverse action taken against her. In addition, the sudden change in her employer's attitude toward her—in the past her personal idiosyncrasies, if not applauded, had at least been tolerated—as well as its subsequent pattern of adverse conduct provided us with convincing evidence of a causal connection between the filing of the EEOC charge and the ensuing adverse actions, including her termination.

Ultimately, Jones's case was settled for a figure equal to more than seven years of her salary—a sum far in excess of my original evaluation of her case. Undoubtedly the strength of the retaliation charge was a significant factor in the employer's decision to settle the case rather than proceed to trial. If the case had not been settled, we might very well have met defeat on the age and sex discrimination charges, but the retaliation charge appeared solid. The employer was unwilling to let a jury decide that issue.

As noted earlier in this chapter, in order to succeed in a retaliation case, the claimant need not prove that her employer actually discriminated against her; she is required only to show that when engaged in a protected activity, she had a reasonable, good-faith belief that the behavior she complained about was discriminatory. Even though the court may not be convinced that the claimant had actually been victimized by acts of discrimination, she may still prevail on her retaliation charge as long as she possessed a good-faith belief that her employer's acts were discriminatory. Establishing the existence of a good-faith belief has proved to be the downfall of more than a few claimants alleging retaliation.

Sherry Kantar worked as a telemarketer sales representative for the Baldwin Cooke Company, a purveyor of office supplies. Throughout her employment she maintained that her supervisor subjected her to a pattern of derogatory and offensive remarks relating to her religion and that he sexually harassed her by inquiring about her sex life. When a vice president of the company interviewed Kantar to ascertain more specifically the nature of her complaints, the only matter Kantor referred to was a single occurrence where a group of three workers were heard to be joking about people of the Jewish faith.

Subsequently Kantar's complaints became a bit more specific when she informed company officials that certain coworkers had made inappropriate jokes and comments in her presence. In an effort to resolve those complaints, her employer moved Kantar's desk to a place where she was unable to hear the conversations of coworkers. Interpreting this move as a form of retaliation, Kantar began to keep a moment-to-moment diary of occurrences she believed were discriminatory or retaliatory, recording each instance of what she thought to be improper behavior on the part of her fellow workers. These workers felt they were being spied upon. Office morale fell, company sales diminished, and some workers threatened to quit. Eventually conditions grew so bad that management concluded it had no alternative but to terminate Kantar.

She later alleged she had been subjected to acts of religious and sex discrimination, thus forcing her to endure a hostile work environment. From the perspective of the court that later reviewed her claims, it appeared more likely that she had had personality conflicts with her supervisor and coworkers, which could not reasonably be interpreted as amounting to a hostile work environment. Although she claimed that the company had retaliated against her, she could not show she had at any time participated in a protected activity. She had been discharged not because she complained about the discriminatory actions of her supervisor and coworkers but because she had engaged in a course of conduct that undermined the morale of other office workers and was generally detrimental to the company's operations.

Baldwin Cooke neither discriminated nor retaliated against Kantar. As the court that ruled on her Title VII claims noted,

> Like any good law, Title VII has been subjected to its share of abuse. In particular, plaintiffs all too often interpret the law as protecting them from any offensive comment or adverse action by their supervisors or co-workers. Plaintiff Sherry Kantar is one such plaintiff.[7]

The court dismissed her claims.

Before concluding this chapter, we must examine a 2006 Supreme Court decision that broadened the concept of retaliatory conduct. As noted above, almost all courts have ruled that any materially adverse change in a worker's terms and conditions of employment may provide the basis for a retaliation charge. In its 2006 decision, the Supreme Court ruled that Title VII's ban on retaliation is not limited to actions adversely affecting a worker's terms and conditions of employment, but rather provides for a much broader protection. Although this case involved claims of sex discrimination, the Supreme Court made it clear that its newly formulated definition of retaliatory conduct applies to cases involving all categories of discrimination, including religious discrimination.

Sheila White, the only woman working in the Maintenance of Way Department of the Burlington Northern & Santa Fe Railway, operated a forklift. Her supervisor was not happy with her in that position, and he repeatedly told her that the department was no place for a woman. He also made insulting and inappropriate remarks to her in the presence of her male coworkers. White complained, and after company officials conducted an internal investigation, Burlington suspended the supervisor and ordered him to attend sexual harassment training sessions.

Immediately afterward, Marvin Brown, another member of Burlington's supervisory staff, removed White from forklift duty and assigned her to track laborer tasks, explaining that her reassignment reflected coworker complaints that "a more senior man" should have the "less arduous and cleaner job" of forklift operator. Now White was unhappy. She filed a complaint with the EEOC claiming that her reassignment amounted to sex discrimination and retaliation for having complained about her supervisor. A few days after this, she had an argument with another supervisor, and later that day Brown charged her with insubordination and suspended her without pay. White invoked internal grievance procedures, and these led to her reinstatement with back pay for the thirty-seven days of her suspension.

Subsequently she filed another retaliation charge with the EEOC, later commencing litigation against Burlington on the ground that its decisions to change her job responsibilities and suspend her without pay constituted acts of retaliation in violation of Title VII. A jury found in her favor, and that verdict was affirmed on appeal. When the case reached the Supreme Court, Burlington argued that employment actions prohibited by the antiretaliation provisions of Title VII should be limited to those that affect an employee's "compensation, terms, conditions, or privileges of employment," and since White's wages and hours were not affected by her reassignment, she did not suffer an adverse employment action as that term is understood in the law. The Court disagreed, ruling that acts of retaliation extend beyond those that affect a worker's compensation, terms, conditions, or privileges of employment, since an employer can effectively retaliate against an employee by taking actions not directly related to her employment, even by causing her harm outside the workplace.

A reassignment to a more difficult, dirtier, and less prestigious job is no less retaliatory because it does not result in a diminishment in pay or benefits. Similarly, a thirty-seven-day suspension without compensation is no less retaliatory because in the end the worker is fully compensated, since many employees would find a five-week period without a paycheck to be a material hardship.

How much harm need be done before an employer's conduct is considered retaliatory? Not much, responded the Supreme Court—the action against the worker must be sufficient to dissuade a reasonable worker from charging the employer with discriminatory conduct. The Court deliberately phrased the standard to be applied in general terms, since the significance of any given act of retaliation often depends upon particular circumstances:

The real social impact of workplace behavior often depends on a constellation of surrounding circumstances, expectations, and relationships which are not fully captured by a single recitation of the words used or the physical acts performed.... A schedule change in an employee's work schedule may make little difference to many workers, but may matter enormously to a young mother with school age children.... A supervisor's refusal to invite an employee to lunch is normally trivial, a non-actionable petty slight. But to retaliate by excluding an employee from a weekly training lunch that contributes significantly to the employee's professional advancement might well deter a reasonable employee from complaining about discrimination.

The job to which White was reassigned was considered less prestigious and its duties more arduous and dirtier than those of a forklift operator. Such a reassignment of responsibilities would have been considered materially adverse to a reasonable worker, sufficient to dissuade her from charging the employer with discriminatory conduct.

White's suspension without pay led the Court to the same conclusion. She and her family had to live thirty-seven days without income, not knowing whether she would ever be allowed to return to work. An employee facing a choice between retaining her job and filing a discrimination complaint might well choose the former, since the prospect of an indefinite suspension without pay could very well act as a deterrent to choosing the latter.

White chose to charge Burlington with discriminatory conduct and retaliation. In allowing her to do both, the Supreme Court greatly expanded those circumstances in which workers may charge their employers with retaliation.[8]

Since the enactment of Title VII, its anti-retaliation provisions have given employees a powerful tool to challenge employers set on acting adversely to a worker who dares to allege discriminatory conduct. The Supreme Court has now rendered that tool even more potent. Human resources personnel and company counsel, through their training, are generally aware that acts of retaliation against a worker engaged in a protected activity are unlawful. Apparently that awareness is not always assimilated by management employees, who frequently are all too quick to order acts of retaliation in response to claims of discrimination. An angry and emotional retaliatory response to allegations of employment discrimination only multiplies the problems confronting an employer charged with employment discrimination.

19

Some Additional Issues

It remains for us to examine certain miscellaneous issues that commonly appear in cases involving the religious rights and responsibilities of employers and employees.

Employer Awareness of an Employee's Religious Beliefs

An employer cannot be held liable for violating a worker's religious beliefs if it is unaware that the worker holds such beliefs. A worker who challenges an employment decision adverse to his interests must demonstrate that the decision was made by someone in the employ of the defendant employer who had knowledge of the worker's religious beliefs.

Steven Lubetsky applied for a correspondence analyst position with Applied Card Systems with operations in Florida. He interviewed with Debbie Gracia, a recruiter in the employ of Applied Card. He performed well during the course of the interview, and Gracia extended him an offer of employment, conditioned upon a credit check. After accepting the offer, Lubetsky advised Gracia that he was Jewish and asked her about the company's leave policy regarding the observance of religious holidays. A discussion of that policy then ensued.

Gracia notified John Bardakjy, manager of the correspondence department, that she had made a conditional offer of employment to Lubetsky. Bardakjy recognized the name as that of a person he had recently met at a job fair, and he recalled that the individual had behaved aggressively and rudely after being informed that Applied Card was hiring only applicants with previous experience. On the basis of those recollections, Bardakjy directed Gracia to rescind the offer of employment.

Gracia telephoned Lubetsky at his home and falsely notified him that because of an office mix-up she had made him an offer when the position had already been promised to another applicant. Two weeks later, Lubetsky saw a newspaper advertisement soliciting applications for the position he had applied for and had been told was filled. He immediately filed a complaint with the EEOC alleging that the job offer had been withdrawn because of his religion.

During the course of the EEOC investigation that followed, Bardakjy testified that he did not learn that Lubetsky was Jewish until he read his complaint filed with the EEOC, and that the decision not to hire him rested solely on his recollection of the aggressive and rude behavior Lubetsky had exhibited at the job fair. Gracia admitted she had lied to Lubetsky about the reason for withdrawing the job offer but only to spare his feelings by not drawing attention to what Bardakjy perceived as his character flaws. After the EEOC concluded its investigation, Lubetsky filed a complaint in federal court alleging that Applied Card had rescinded its offer of employment solely because he was Jewish, thus engaging in religious discrimination.

In the end, the court ruled against Lubetsky. During the course of the proceedings conducted by the trial court, Lubetsky failed to present any evidence that Bardakjy, who made the decision not to hire him, knew of his religion. Gracia of course was aware of it, but she testified she had not informed Bardakjy that Lubetsky was Jewish. Lubetsky failed, therefore, to demonstrate that the challenged employment decision was made by a person possessing knowledge of his religious beliefs, and thus the court had no alternative but to dismiss his case.[1]

It is also incumbent upon a worker to provide his employer with details of his religious beliefs sufficient to allow it to formulate a proposal to accommodate them. If the worker fails in that regard, again his case will be dismissed.

Anheuser-Busch periodically tested its employees for the presence of illegal drugs. Employees were granted sixty days' advance notice of a test and were required to sign a consent form allowing the company to proceed with it. Employees' written consents were necessary because the company's independent test-sampling service required it. An employee who failed to authorize the test was subject to immediate discharge. Ned Cary was given notice of a test but refused to sign the consent form. He explained that as an ordained Baptist minister he was prohibited "from exhibiting my own personal assent to duress." Company officials asked him to provide information pertaining to the prohibitions he claimed prevented him from proceeding with the test, but he refused to comply with that request. Anheuser-Busch then fired Cary, and he filed suit.

The primary issue before the court related to the extent of Anheuser-Busch's knowledge of Cary's religious beliefs. Had Cary given his employer information concerning those beliefs sufficient to activate the company's legal responsibility to offer him an appropriate accommodation? Despite the company's requests for additional information, Cary had persisted in offering only the vaguest explanation of his objections to taking the test. The court noted that it was impossible to discern what Cary was objecting to when he stated that inasmuch as he was an ordained Baptist minister he was prohibited "from exhibiting my own personal assent to duress":

> Surely plaintiff must be required to put forth more...before the employer can fairly be found to have notice of a bona fide religious objection.... The court holds that where an employee states vaguely that his beliefs prevent him from signing a required document, and then further refuses attempts to clarify the employee's belief, the employer has no information to rely on to attempt to accommodate the employee, and therefore cannot be held to have violated Title VII.[2]

Before a worker initiates legal action against his employer, he would be well advised to make certain that he has appropriately apprised his employer of the existence and nature of his religious beliefs, as well as the manner in which the employer's workplace decisions will adversely affect his practice of those beliefs. If he fails to pursue that course, his legal claims may very well be dismissed.

Stray Remarks, Casual Commentary, and Discriminatory Animus

Anti-Semitism and other types of discriminatory animus often appear in the workplace in the form of coworker commentary and angry remarks. A single comment or remark, without other evidence of discriminatory animus, is most often insufficient to prove discriminatory conduct. But on occasion, it may rise to a level where no other evidence is required to establish the existence of a hostile work environment.

In a discrimination case that reached the New York Court of Appeals, the complainant, a mother of three who at the time was also attending graduate school, worked weekends as a waitress at the Imperial Diner in New York City. On two consecutive weekends she was assigned to work behind the counter, an assignment considered less desirable than a table position, and she complained to one of the diner's owners. At first he ignored her, but later responded to her complaints with an obscene anti-Semitic remark, that she thought she was something special because she was Jewish, "just like all the other f_ _ _ _ing Jewish broads around here." She demanded that he apologize, and when he refused, she left the diner and went home to her children.

Several days later she returned to the diner to collect her pay. The owner asked her to return to work. "If you apologize, I will," she said. "Never," he replied. Again she walked out of the diner, this time not to return. At that point, the New York State Division of Human Rights took up her cause and sued the diner owners, alleging violation of New York's Human Rights Law, a statute similar to Title VII.

When the case came before the Court of Appeals, the court observed that a person intent on discriminating against another ordinarily does not declare or announce his purpose. Rather, it is far more likely he will pursue his discriminatory practices in devious ways, using subtle and elusive methods. But there was nothing subtle or elusive in the diner owner's response to the complainant's objections to her work assignments. His contempt for the complainant and other Jewish employees was proclaimed openly and crudely. This act alone—an act vilifying the complainant's religion in a matter that was related to her working conditions—was sufficient to prove that the diner owners were engaged in unlawful discriminatory practices.[3]

Some, but not all, religiously biased comments or remarks are admissible as evidence in support of a worker's discrimination claim. The rule of admissibility applicable to these types of remarks requires that they be made by a person who made the employment decision adversely affecting the worker or by a person who in some way was involved in making that decision. Remarks made by non-decision makers or persons not in any way involved in the decision-making process are classified as "stray remarks" and are generally not admissible to support a discrimination claim.[4]

Abstract comments also are generally inadmissible. Facetious remarks are usually labeled "abstract" and are thus incapable of raising an inference of discrimination. Comments that are merely condescending or inappropriate in the circumstances also are generally rejected by the courts. But statements evidencing blatant bias, made in direct reference to a decision affecting a worker, provide that worker with strong evidence of discriminatory intent.

Leon Weiss, a Jew, was employed as a warehouseman in a New Jersey distribution center. (Also see discussion in chapter 4.) When a vacancy occurred in a position designated as the "warehouse lead person," the manager of the distribution center interviewed several employees, including Weiss, for the position. Although it was generally known throughout the facility that Weiss was the best-qualified candidate, the manager selected another worker. When a coworker angrily confronted the manager regarding his rejection of Weiss, the manager responded in anger: "As long as I'm the manager, no Jew will run the warehouse for me."

When Weiss sued the warehouse owners for religious discrimination, he was required to show that the reasons advanced by the company for failing to promote him were pretextual and that he had been denied the promotion only because of his religion. In light of the manager's anti-Semitic remark that no Jew would ever run the warehouse on his watch, the court had little difficulty in ruling that the reasons advanced by the company were indeed pretextual. "There may exist a more unequivocal way to express an intent to exclude [a Jewish person] from consideration for promotion, but none comes readily to mind." The manager's single discriminatory remark was sufficient to support a verdict in Weiss's favor.[5]

Opposition to Homosexuality Based on Religious Principles

Evelyn Bodett, a quality assurance manager for CoxCom, supervised thirteen employees, including Kelley Carson. Bodett was an evangelical Christian, Carson a homosexual. Bodett was aware of Carson's sexual orientation because Carson was openly gay. When Carson first came under Bodett's supervision, Bodett immediately informed her that homosexuality was condemned by the religious principles that guided her life.

Shortly after her assignment to Bodett's unit, Carson broke up with her female partner and was, as described by Bodett, in "a state of emotional distress." Bodett told Carson that her homosexual relationship was probably the source of the turmoil in her life, that it was contrary to God's design and was sinful. When Carson informed Bodett's supervisor that she had grown uncomfortable with Bodett's attitude toward her sexuality, an internal investigation of Bodett's treatment of Carson ensued, and in the end Bodett was discharged for having violated CoxCom's sexual harassment policy.

Bodett claimed, contrary to appearances, that she had been terminated not because she had violated the company's sexual harasssment policy but solely on account of her religion. She argued that she had opposed Carson's homosexuality on religious grounds, but that if she had opposed it on any other grounds, she would not have been terminated. She was unable, however, to show that a supervisor who treated Carson as she had, but for reasons other than religious, would not also have been terminated. Since she could not prove that she would have been treated differently absent her religious convictions, her religious discrimination claim was dismissed.[6]

Workers who oppose homosexuality on religious grounds generally end up in a great deal of trouble. Although homosexuality does not fall within the protections of Title VII, homosexuals are often protected by their employers' sexual harassment policies, as was Carson. Workers who violate those policies for religious reasons are likely to be subjected to disciplinary action. Moreover, unlike federal law, the laws of many states and municipalities render workplace harassment of homosexuals illegal, and thus an employee's harassment of a homosexual coworker may subject the employer to liability under those laws.

On the other side of the issue, homosexuals have at times attempted to use religion as a weapon to gain protection from those who oppose homosexuality. Alicia Pedreira, a lesbian, attempted to circumvent Title VII's lack of protection for homosexuals by claiming that her termination had been motivated by religious rather than homosexual considerations.

Pedreira worked as a family specialist at the Spring Meadows Children's Home, a facility owned and operated by Kentucky Baptist Homes for Children (KBHC). At the time she was hired, she was not known to be homosexual. Once it became known that she was a lesbian, KBHC officials ordered her termination because they believed that her homosexual lifestyle was antithetical to the facility's core values, thus making it impossible for her employment to continue. As a matter of policy, KBHC required all its employees to "exhibit values in their professional conduct and personal lifestyles that are consistent with the Christian mission and purpose of the institution." This policy, it maintained, prohibited the employment of homosexuals.

Pedreira filed a Title VII action challenging (1) her termination and (2) KBHC's adoption of antihomosexual policies, claiming that each of those actions constituted an act of religious discrimination. She argued that KBHC perceived an employee's homosexual lifestyle as a failure to embrace its religious beliefs and practices. She did not contest KBHC's position that it did not require its employees to attend religious services or become members of any religious denomination, but she maintained that an employee's professional conduct and personal lifestyle were not deemed acceptable by KBHC unless the employee conformed to its Christian mission and purpose. She further argued that the requirement that an employee live a lifestyle consistent with KBHC's religious beliefs imposed those religious beliefs upon her as a condition of her employment.

The fallacy in Pedreira's position lay in her failure to allege that her lifestyle was premised upon any particular religious principles. She did not state whether she accepted or rejected Baptist beliefs or the beliefs of any other religious denomination. Since she had not adopted any religious beliefs, she could not claim that KBHC policies violated them. The court therefore ruled that "there is no religious discrimination in an employment policy which does not require and does not inhibit the practice of or belief in any faith." Because Pedreira's religious freedoms had not been impaired by KBHC employment requirements, the court dismissed her complaint.[7]

Using the White House Guidelines in the Private Sector

In 1994 the EEOC proposed new rules pertaining to workplace harassment, including religious harassment. When religious groups and some members of Congress complained that the proposed rules defined religious harassment too broadly, the EEOC withdrew them. Subsequently a group of religious and legal organizations assembled by the Clinton administration prepared a set of guidelines for use by federal agencies in connection with the religious practices of their employees. The product of their work is entitled "White House Guidelines on Religious Exercise and Religious Expression in the Federal Workplace."[8] Although designed for the federal workplace, these guidelines have at times proved useful in analyzing workplace disputes occurring in the private sector. The remainder of this chapter is devoted to a review of those portions of the guidelines that appear particularly applicable to private-sector workplaces.

Religious Expression

Employees should be permitted to engage in private religious expression in the workplace to the same extent that they may engage in nonreligious private expression. Examples:

1. An employee may keep a Bible or Quran in her work area and read it during breaks.
2. An employer may restrict the size and placement of religious art but cannot single out such art for preferential or harsher treatment than nonreligious art.

Employees should be permitted to engage in religious expression with fellow employees to the same extent that they engage in nonreligious expression. Religious expression should not be restricted unless it interferes with workplace efficiency. Employees may attempt to persuade fellow employees to adopt their religious views but must cease such initiatives if the other employees indicate that discussions of that type are unwelcome. Examples:

1. An employee engages a fellow employee in a religious discussion, urging her to embrace his faith. She disagrees but is willing to continue the discussion. Under those circumstances, no reason exists for the employer to intercede to halt the discussion.

2. An employee invites a coworker to attend services at her church, though she knows that the coworker is a devout adherent of another religion. The coworker is angered by the invitation and asks that it not be repeated. If the matter comes to the attention of the employer, it should make certain that no further invitations are issued.

3. A nonsupervisory employee hands another employee a religious tract urging her to convert to another religion lest she be condemned to eternal damnation. If nothing further is said, the employer should not intercede.

If the discussions in any of the three cited examples are part of a larger pattern of verbal attacks on fellow employees, such speech, by virtue of its harassing nature, may constitute religious harassment or create a hostile work environment. In these circumstances, the employer must intervene.

Because supervisors possess the power to fire, promote, or otherwise alter conditions of employment, employees may perceive their supervisors' religious expression as coercive even if it is not intended to be such. Supervisors must be careful, therefore, to ensure that their words and actions are not perceived as directed to coercing religious or nonreligious behavior.

Religious Discrimination

Whether particular conduct gives rise to a hostile environment or constitutes religious harassment generally depends upon its frequency or repetitiveness and its severity. The use of derogatory language, if severe or invoked repeatedly, may constitute religious harassment, and a single incident, if sufficiently abusive, may also. Examples:

1. An employee repeatedly makes derogatory remarks to other employees about their faith or lack of faith. Such conduct constitutes religious harassment.

2. In the heat of an angry exchange, one employee makes a derogatory remark about the other's religion. The comment is not repeated. Unless the remark

is sufficiently severe or pervasive to alter the conditions of the insulted worker's employment, this is not religious harassment.

3. During lunch, certain employees gather in an unoccupied room for prayer or Bible study. Even if other employees feel excluded, this is not religious harassment.

Accommodation

Although an employer need not accommodate a worker's religious beliefs or practices that result in more than a de minimis cost, that cost must be real, not speculative or hypothetical. An accommodation cannot be denied if the employer regularly offers similar accommodations for nonreligious purposes. Examples:

1. An employer must adjust work schedules to accommodate a worker's Sabbath observance if a substitute worker is available or the employee's absence would not impose an undue hardship on the employer.
2. An employee must be permitted to wear religious attire unless it unduly interferes with the functioning of the workplace.
3. An employee should be excused from a particular assignment if it contravenes his or her religious beliefs, provided the employer would not suffer undue hardship in reassigning the employee.

Establishment of Religion

Supervisors and employees must not engage in religious activities in such manner that a neutral observer would interpret those activities as being endorsed by their employer. Examples:

1. At the conclusion of weekly staff meetings, where attendance is required, an employee leads the group in prayer. The prayer should be permitted, provided it is clear that it is not endorsed by the employer.
2. At Christmas, a supervisor places a wreath over the entrance to the main office. This activity should be permitted.

Guiding Legal Principles—Religious Expression

Many religions encourage their adherents to spread the faith at every opportunity. As a general matter, proselytizing in the workplace is entitled to the same protection as other forms of speech. Employee proselytization, however, may be halted if it impairs workplace discipline, has a detrimental impact on close working relationships, interferes with the efficient operation of the employer's enterprise, or prevents the proselytizing employee from performing his duties adequately.

Guiding Legal Principles—Hostile Work Environment and Harassment

A hostile working environment need not originate with the employer or its supervisors, as fellow employees may create a hostile environment through their own words and actions. It is not created by the bare expression of speech with which others disagree. Rather, it must be sufficiently severe or pervasive to alter a worker's conditions of employment. Whether conduct may stand as the predicate for a finding of religious harassment depends on the totality of the circumstances, such as the nature of the conduct in issue and the context in which it occurred.

Guiding Legal Principles—Accommodation

Although an employer need not incur more than a de minimis cost in providing an accommodation, its hardship must be real rather than speculative. If an employer regularly permits accommodations for nonreligious purposes, it may not deny comparable accommodations for religious purposes.

The White House Guidelines respond to questions frequently asked by employers and employees. The generality of the responses at times stands in stark contrast to the specificity of judicial responses to similar issues arising in the course of the litigation of workplace religious disputes. As a consequence, some of the court rulings cited in this book may seem to stand at odds with these guidelines. In such instances, judicial determinations always trump guidelines, even those issued under the authority of the president of the United States.

RELIGION AND THE LAW IN THE
WORKPLACE OF THE FUTURE

Five million Muslims and an equal number of Jews now live in the United States along with 157 million members of various Christian denominations. If tomorrow morning a small portion of those adherents of the Muslim, Jewish, and Christian faiths were to arrive at their places of work with the intention of converting fellow employees to their religious beliefs, the American workplace would be overwhelmed by the chaos that would ensue.

It appears certain that great numbers of workers will continue to insist upon practicing their religion in America's twenty-first-century workplace. As in the past, employers and their workers will confront complex issues that commonly occur in the struggle to protect the rights of those who wish to exercise their religious beliefs while also securing the rights of those who elect not to participate in workplace religious activities. Thus, on the one hand, it becomes incumbent upon those who insist on bringing their religious beliefs and practices to the workplace to develop a heightened understanding of the responsibilities they assume in subjecting others to those beliefs and practices. On the other hand, those who are determined to work in an environment free of religious beliefs and practices must endeavor to develop an equally heightened understanding of the responsibilities they assume in opposing the introduction of their fellow workers' beliefs.

Since its adoption in 1964, Title VII has been the primary tool employed in resolving workplace disputes involving religious issues. Workplace disputes are primarily resolved in the administrative processes of the EEOC or through litigation in the courts. Are these the best methods for resolving those issues? Are they the most efficient ways of working through those disputes? Is an EEOC investigator or a judge better equipped to resolve those disputes than the parties themselves? We look for enlightenment in a case involving an employer's failure to accommodate the Sabbath observance of one of its workers.

Home Depot hired Bradley Baker in March 2001, assigning him to a full-time sales position in the floor and wall department in its store in Auburn, Massachusetts. Thereafter, Baker frequently traveled to Rochester, New York, to be with his fiancée, with whom he often attended church services at the Gospel Fellowship Church in nearby Belmont. During the course of premarital counseling by the pastor of that church, Baker became "fully aware of the importance of the Sabbath" and the Bible's commandment not to work on that day. Ultimately he fully accepted the teaching of the Gospel Fellowship Church that Sunday is a day of rest and meditation and that strict observance of the Sabbath is essential for salvation.

Just prior to marrying his fiancée, Baker moved to the Rochester area and applied for a position with Home Depot's store in Henrietta, New York. At the time of his interview he informed the store manager that he would be unable to work on Sundays because of his religious convictions but that he could work any other day at any time. Baker also discussed the matter with his prospective supervisor, who said there would be no problem in formulating a schedule that provided him with Sundays off. During the following twelve months, several changes in store personnel resulted in various supervisory staff becoming involved in scheduling Baker's work hours, but Home Depot continued to accommodate his request not to work on Sunday.

After Baker had been working in the Henrietta store for a little more than a year, management appointed a new store manager. About one month later, the new manager called him to her office and inquired about his request not to work on Sundays. When Baker explained that his religious beliefs foreclosed any labor on Sunday, she informed him that he "needed to be fully flexible and if [he] could not work on Sundays, then [he] could not work [for Home Depot]."

In the previous thirteen months, six members of the store's supervisory staff had reviewed Baker's request not to work on Sundays, and each of them, without hesitation, had accommodated his request. In contrast, the newly installed store manager, after giving the matter little or no thought, dismissed Baker's religious convictions as if they were of no consequence and ordered him to work on Sundays. The fact that the store management had been able to accommodate Baker for a period of more than a year was a fact that the new manager found irrelevant and of no significance either to Baker or to Home Depot.

Thereafter, the manager scheduled Baker to work on a Sunday. On that day, he called the store, reporting that he would be unable to work because of religious reasons. Two days later, the manager questioned him about his absence from work on the preceding Sunday. Baker once again reiterated the reasons for his absence, and the manager again rejected those reasons and insisted that he work on Sundays.

She asked Baker whether he attended church services, and when he responded that he did, she offered to place him on a work shift that would allow him to work later in the day, thus permitting him to attend church services. Baker rejected the offer, again emphasizing that his religious convictions required him to abstain from all work on Sunday.

The manager also offered Baker the option of part-time employment, whereby he would have Sundays off, but then he would have neither a guaranteed forty-hour week nor health and other benefits he had had as a full-time employee. Baker's wife was then pregnant; full-time employment and its attendant benefits were now essential for him and his family, and thus he could not accept the part-time offer. He asked the manager not to force him to choose between his religion and his job.

The following week Baker was again scheduled for Sunday work. When he did not appear for work, his employment was terminated, purportedly on account of unexcused absences. Baker filed a Title VII action against Home Depot, thus initiating litigation between the parties that would extend over a period of several years. In the end, Baker prevailed. The court held that each of the manager's proposals failed to eliminate the conflict Baker confronted each time he was scheduled for Sunday work. An accommodation cannot be considered reasonable if it does not eliminate an employee's conflict between job and religious practice.[1]

Was all this litigation necessary? From the perspective of Home Depot, did its store manager act in its best interests when she refused to excuse Baker from Sunday work? If the previous store manager had been able to accommodate Baker's religious convictions by not scheduling him for Sunday work, why could the new manager not have done so also? Apparently she wanted to make a point: no employee on her watch was to be excused from Sunday work. In adopting that position, she subjected her employer to several years of litigation and all its attendant costs. In terminating Baker, she also subjected him, his wife, and his family to untold suffering. Why? Why could the parties to this dispute not have resolved it without resorting to litigation?

Dealing with religious matters in the workplace requires common sense, good business practices, and a continuing attitude of respect for all parties involved.[2] Many of the workplace disputes reviewed in this work could have been resolved without the involvement of the EEOC or the courts if goodwill had been exercised by all parties to the dispute. Sadly, goodwill often appears to be in short supply whenever a religious dispute arises in the workplace. Instead, emotional responses, leading to the assumption of entrenched positions, are more likely to be found in those situations.

Workers have a greater interest than their employers in resolving these disputes before they reach the litigation stage. In litigation, the burden of proof lies with the employee. Intentional discrimination, along with many other matters common to litigation of this nature, is difficult to prove, and as a consequence, many a case has gone down to defeat merely because the worker did not have at hand the proof necessary to establish an essential point in the litigation. Accordingly, the employee more often than not fails to prevail in these cases. Resolving the dispute before a legal complaint is filed is often the better path for the employee to pursue.

It may not always be practical to sue. Litigation is a time-consuming, emotion-draining, nerve-racking, and often deeply frustrating process. Before electing to sue, a worker must carefully consider the emotional stress and pain he and his family will probably be forced to endure during a drawn-out, bitterly contested battle. But in addition, he and his attorney must assess the chances of achieving a successful conclusion and whether the likely final result warrants the efforts involved in attaining it.

If the employee has been terminated and has been unable to find another comparable position, the decision to proceed to litigation is not a difficult one. There may be no alternative but to sue. If, however, the dispute remains unresolved and the worker retains his employment status, the decision is far more complex. If he sues, during the course of the litigation—a process that will probably last several years—his employment responsibilities will require him to associate daily with those persons he has charged with discriminatory conduct, a difficult situation indeed. And even if the litigation ultimately culminates in a resolution of the dispute in his favor, he must still consider whether, after an acrimonious proceeding, there exists any likelihood of future career advancement with this employer.

Employers are also motivated to settle religious disputes without litigation where circumstances allow because litigation engenders court costs, attorney's fees, disruption in the workplace and, on occasion, a public relations nightmare. A poorly thought-out decision, such as the one made by the Home Depot manager, may cause far greater problems for the employer than would accommodating the religious demands of an employee.

Litigation is surely not the ideal way for an employer or an employee to cope with hostile and offensive work environment problems. In the end, however, it is the only practical approach currently available. On the plus side, litigation enlightens: it provides employers and employees with a broad awareness of the types of workplace religiously oriented conduct that are acceptable and those that are not. Accordingly, more litigation today may diminish its need tomorrow. Some time in the future perhaps, these disputes will be resolved fairly, equitably, efficiently, and—most important—amicably.

NOTES

Introduction

1. Jay A. Conger, ed., *Spirit at Work: Discovering the Spirituality of Leadership* (San Francisco: Jossey-Bass, 1994), 1.

2. George Gallup, Jr. and Michael D. Lindsay, *Surveying the Religious Landscape: Trends in U.S. Beliefs* (Harrisburg, PA: Morehouse, 1999), 2.

3. Steve Frakas, Jean Johnson, and Tony Foleno, *For Goodness' Sake: Why So Many Want Religion to Play a Greater Role in American Life* (New York: Public Agenda, 2001), 21.

4. Douglas A. Hicks, *Religion and the Workplace: Pluralism, Spirituality, Leadership* (New York: Cambridge University Press, 2003), 102.

5. Georgette F. Bennett and Myrna Marofsky, *Religion in the Workplace: A Guide to Navigating the Complex Landscape* (New York: Tanenbaum Center for Interreligious Understanding, 2003), 7.

6. Ibid., 12.

7. Hicks, *Religion and the Workplace,* 106.

8. Equal Employment Opportunity Commission Charge Statistics first published on June 17, 2009, and made available at http://www.eeoc.gov/stats/religion. The number of charge filings increased from 1,709 to 3,273 between 1997 and 2008.

9. *Religious Bias in the Workplace* (New York: Tanenbaum Center for Interreligious Understanding, 2001), 14–15.

1. Is There a Place for Religion in the Workplace?

1. Walter Rauschenbusch, *Christianity and the Social Crisis* first published by Macmillan, New York, 1907, and reissued by Harper, New York, in 1964 and Westminster/John Knox Press,

Louisville, in1991. This work was again reissued, along with the commentaries of eight current religious thinkers, under the title *Christianity and the Social Crisis in the 21st Century,* ed. Paul Raushenbush (New York: Harper One, 2007).

2. Walter Rauschenbusch, *Christianizing the Social Order* (New York: Macmillan, 1919).

3. Ibid., 67–68.

4. Elizabeth Balanoff, "Norman Thomas: Socialism and the Social Gospel," *Christian Century,* January 30, 1985, 101–102.

5. Walter Rauschenbusch, *Christianizing the Social Order,* 99.

6. Ibid., 41–42.

7. Ibid., 36, 125.

8. Ibid.,111.

9. Steve Farkas, Jean Johnson, and Tony Foleno, *For Goodness' Sake: Why So Many Want Religion to Play a Greater Role in American Life* (New York: Public Agenda, 2001), 32.

10. Ibid.

11. Ibid.

12. David J. Bosch, *Transforming Mission: Paradigm Shifts in Theology of Mission* (Maryknoll, N.Y.: Orbis Books, 1991).

13. David W. Miller, *God at Work: The History and Promise of the Faith at Work Movement* (New York: Oxford University Press, 2007), 6, 10, 11, 24, 25.

14. Ibid., 106.

15. Ibid., 74.

16. Ibid., 77–78.

17. Georgette F. Bennett, *Religion in the Workplace: A Guide to Navigating the Complex Landscape* (New York: Tanenbaum Center for Interreligious Understanding, 2003), 19.

2. What Is Religion as Defined by Law?

1. *Peterson v. Wilmur Communications, Inc.,* 89 FEP Cases 148 (E.D. Wis. 2002).

2. 42 U.S.C. § 2000e et seq.

3. *Africa v. Pennsylvania,* 662 F.2d 1025 (3d Cir. 1981).

4. *Employment Division, Department of Human Resources of Oregon v. Smith,* 494 U.S. 872 (1990).

5. *United States v. Seeger,* 380 U.S. 163 (1965).

6. *Thomas v. Review Board of the Indiana Employment Security Division,* 450 U.S. 707 (1981).

7. *Welsh v. United States,* 398 U.S. 333 (1970).

8. *Slater v. King Soopers, Inc.,* 809 F. Supp. 809 (D. Colo. 1992); *Bellamy v. Mason's Stores, Inc.,* 368 F. Supp. 1025 (E.D. Va. 1973), *aff'd,* 508 F.2d 504 (4th Cir. 1974).

9. *Peterson v. Wilmur Communications, Inc.*

10. *Frazee v. Illinois Employment Security Department,* 489 U.S. 829 (1989).

11. *Thomas v. Review Board of the Indiana Employment Security Division.*

12. EEOC Guidelines: 45 Fed. Reg. 72,611 and 72,610.

13. EEOC Guidelines: 29 C.F.R. § 1605.1.

14. *United States v. Seeger,* 380 U.S. 163.

15. *Philbrook v. Ansonia Board of Education,* 757 F. 2d 476 (2d Cir. 1985); *rev'd and remanded on other grounds,* 479 U.S. 60 (1986).

16. *Cooper v. Oak Rubber Co,* 15 F.3d 1375 (6th Cir. 1994).

17. *EEOC v. IBP, Inc.,* 61 FEP Cases 1351 (C.D. Ill. 1993).

18. *Hansard v. Johns-Mansville Products Corp.,* 5 FEP Cases 707 (E.D. Tex. 1973).

19. *Shpargel v. Stage Co.,* 71 FEP Cases 1739 (E.D. Mich. 1996).

20. *Tiano v. Dillard Department Stores,* 139 F.3d 679 (9th Cir. 1998).

3. Religious Discrimination and the Civil Rights Act of 1964

1. 42 U.S.C. § 2000e et seq.

2. Neal Learner, "Employers Attempt to Balance Work and Religion," *Christian Science Monitor,* April 12, 2004.

3. Ibid., referring to EEOC Charge Statistics for years 1993–2003.

4. Ibid., citing Georgette Bennett, president of the Tanenbaum Center for Interreligious Understanding.

5. Georgette F. Bennett, *Religion in the Workplace: A Guide to Navigating the Complex Land-scape* (New York: Tanenbaum Center for Interreligious Understanding, 2003), 20.

6. *Weiss v. United States,* 595 Fed. Supp. 1050 (E.D. Va. 1984).

7. *Rosen v. Thornburgh,* 928 F.2d 528 (2d Cir. 1991).

8. *McDonnell Douglas Corp. v Green,* 411 U.S. 492 (1973). Twenty years later, the Supreme Court further developed this procedure in *St. Mary's Honor Center v. Hicks,* 509 U.S. 502 (1993).

9. *Furnco Construction Corp. v. Waters,* 438 U.S. 567 (1978).

10. *Reeves v. Sanderson Plumbing Products, Inc.,* 530 U.S. 133 (2000).

11. *Binder v. Long Island Lighting Co.,* 57 F.3d 193 (2d Cir. 1995).

12. *McDonnell Douglas,* 411 U.S. 492.

13. *Furnco,* 438 U.S. 567.

14. *Sattar v. Motorola, Inc.,* 138 F.3d 1164 (7th Cir. 1998).

15. *Nielson v. AgriNorthwest,* 82 FEP Cases 893 (Wash. Ct. App. 1999).

16. Raymond F. Gregory, *Age Discrimination in the American Workplace: Old at a Young Age* (New Brunswick, N.J.: Rutgers University Press, 2001) 35, 139.

17. *Lambert v. Condor Manufacturing Inc.,* 768 F. Supp. 600 (E.D. Mich. 1991).

18. *Meritor Savings Bank v. Vinson,* 477 U.S. 57 (1986). Although this case involved allegations of sexual harassment, the principles enunciated by the Supreme Court are applicable to religious harassment and hostile environment cases.

19. *Harris v. Forklift Systems, Inc.,* 510 U.S. 17 (1993).

4. Religious Discrimination at Various Stages of the Employment Relationship

1. EEOC, "Religion-Based Charges: 1997–2008," http://www.eeoc.gov/stats/religion. Over that twelve-year period the number of no-cause findings was consistently high, varying between 58 and 65 percent.

2. *EEOC v. WilTel, Inc.,* 81 F.3d 1508 (10th Cir. 1996).

3. *McDonnell Douglas Corp. v. Green,* 411 U.S. 492 (1973).

4. *Weiss v. Parker Hannifan Corp.,* 747 F. Supp. 1118 (D.N.J. 1990).

5. EEOC, "Brink's to Pay $30,000 to Peoria Area Woman for Failure to Accommodate Religious Beliefs," news release, January 2, 2003 (citing *EEOC v. Brink's, Inc.,* 1:02-cv-01111 (C.D. Ill. 2002)).

6. *Karriem v. Oliver T. Carr, Co.,* 38 FEP Cases 882 (D.D.C. 1985).

7. *Carter v. Bruce Oakley, Inc.,* 849 F. Supp. 673 (E.D. Ark. 1994).

8. *McGlothin v. Jackson Municipal Separate School District,* 829 F. Supp. 853 (S.D. Miss. 1992).

9. *Citron v. Jackson State University,* 456 F. Supp. 3 (S.D. Miss. 1977).

10. *Rodriguez v. City of Chicago,* 69 FEP Cases 993 (N.D. Illinois 1996).

11. *Singh v. Bowsher,* 609 F. Supp. 454 (D.D.C. 1984).

12. *Simmons v. Sports Training Institute,* 52 FEP Cases 1322 (S.D.N.Y. 1990).

13. *Krulik v. Board of Education of the City of New York,* 781 F.2d 15 (2d Cir. 1986).

14. *Opuku-Boateng v. State of California,* 93 F.3d 1461 (9th Cir. 1996).

15. *Mann v. Milgram Food Stores, Inc.,* 730 F.2d 1186 (8th Cir. 1984).

5. Religious Discrimination Claims Arising Out of the Termination of Employment

1. *Beasley v. Health Care Service Corp.,* 940 F.2d 1085 (7th Cir. 1991).

2. *Evans v. Bally's Health and Tennis, Inc.,* 64 FEP Cases 33 (D. Md. 1994).

3. *Venters v. City of Delhi,* 123 F.3d 956 (7th Cir.1997).

4. *Henn v. National Geographic Society,* 819 F.2d 824 (7th Cir. 1987).

5. *EEOC v. University of Chicago Hospitals,* 276 F.3d 326 (7th Cir. 2002).

6. *Young v. Southwestern Savings and Loan Association,* 509 F.2d 140 (5th Cir. 1975).

7. *Gannon v. Narragansett Electric Co.,* 777 F. Supp. 167 (D.R.I. 1991).

6. Employee Proselytization

1. Douglas A. Hicks, *Religion in the Workplace: Pluralism, Spirituality, Leadership* (New York: Cambridge University Press, 2003), 103.

2. *Chalmers v. Tulon Co. of Richmond,* 101 F.3d 1012 (4th Cir. 1996).

3. *Cary v. Anheuser-Busch, Inc.,* 53 FEP Cases 955 (E.D. Va. 1988).

4. *Wilson v. U.S. West Communications,* 58 F.3d 1337 (8th Cir. 1995), *aff'g* 65 FEP Cases 200 (D. Neb. 1994).

5. *Helland v. South Bend Community School Corp.,* 93 F.3d 327 (7th Cir. 1996).

6. *Spratt v. County of Kent,* 621 F. Supp. 594 (W.D. Mich. 1985), *aff'd,* 810 F.2d 203 (6th Cir. 1986).

7. *Banks v. Service America Corp.,* 73 FEP Cases 173 (D. Kans. 1996).

8. *Johnson v. Halls Merchandising,* 49 FEP Cases 527 (W.D. Mo. 1989).

9. *Banks,* 73 FEP Cases at 176.

7. Employer Proselytization

1. *Minnesota v. Sports & Health Club, Inc.,* 370 N.W.2d 844, 37 FEP Cases 1463 (Minn. 1985).

2. *EEOC v. Townley Engineering & Manufacturing Co.,* 859 F.2d 610 (9th Cir. 1988).

3. *EEOC v. Preferred Management Corp.,* 88 FEP Cases 1363 (S.D. Ind. 2002).

8. Employer Liability for Employee Acts of Religious Harassment

1. Raymond F. Gregory, *Unwelcome and Unlawful: Sexual Harassment in the American Workplace* (Ithaca: Cornell University Press, 2004), 17–18.

2. *Kantar v. Baldwin Cooke Co.,* 69 FEP Cases 851 (N.D. Ill. 1995).

3. *Weiss v. Ren Laboratories of Florida,* 81 FEP Cases 73 (S.D. Fla. 1999).

4. *Turner v. Barr,* 65 FEP Cases 909 (D.D.C. 1993).

5. *Powell v. Yellow Book USA, Inc.,* 445 F.3d 1074 (8th Cir. 2006).

6. *Sarin v. Raytheon Co.,* 69 FEP Cases 856 (D. Mass. 1995).

7. *Johnson v. Spencer Press of Maine, Inc.,* 364 F.3d 368 (1st Cir. 2004).

9. Workplace Discrimination and Certain Religious Groups

1. *Religious Bias in the Workplace* (New York: Tanenbaum Center for Religious Understanding, 2001), 15, 19.

2. *Young v. Southwestern Savings and Loan Association,* 509 F.2d 140 (5th Cir. 1975).

3. J. H. Oldham, *Life Is Commitment* (New York: Association Press, 1959), 48.

4. Douglas A. Hicks, *Religion and the Workplace: Pluralism, Spirituality, Leadership* (New York: Cambridge University Press, 2003), 95, 106.

5. Michelle Boorstein,"Federal Panels Order NIH to Reinstate Priest," *The Washington Post,* March 2, 2007.

6. *Skorup v. Modern Door Corp.*, 153 F.3d 512 (7th Cir. 1998).

7. *Lawson v. State of Washington*, 296 F.3d 799 (9th Cir. 2002).

8. *Thomas v. Review Board of the Indiana Employment Security Division*, 450 U.S. 707 (1981).

9. *Shanoff v. State of Illinois Department of Human Services*, 258 F.3d 696 (7th Cir. 2001).

10. *Gordon v. MCI Telecommunications Corp.*, 59 FEP Cases 1363 (S.D.N.Y. 1992).

11. *Shapolia v. Los Alamos National Laboratory*, 992 F.2d 1033 (10th Cir. 1993).

12. *Religious Bias in the Workplace*, 14.

13. Susan Sachs, "A Nation Challenged: For Many American Muslims, Complaints of Quiet but Persistent Bias," *New York Times*, April 25, 2002.

14. Mary Beth Sheridan, "Bias Against Muslims Up 70%," *Washington Post*, May 3, 2004.

15. Michelle Boorstein, "Surge in Anti-Muslim Incidents Reported," *Washington Post*, September 19, 2006.

16. "Muslim Pilot Fired Due to Religion and Appearance, EEOC Says in Post 9/11 Backlash Discrimination Suit," EEOC, news release July 17, 2003.

17. *EEOC v. Trans States Airline, Inc.*, 462 F.3d 987 (8th Cir. 2006).

18. Public Law No. 282, Pa. Cons. Stat. § 11–1112.

19. *United States v. Board of Education of the School District of Philadelphia*, 911 F.2d 882 (3d Cir. 1990).

20. Laurie Goodstein, "Islamic Emblem of Faith Also Trigger for Bias," *New York Times*, November 3, 1997.

21. *Fraternal Order of Police v. City of Newark*, 170 F.3d 359 (3d Cir. 1999).

22. *Karriem v. Oliver T. Carr Co.*, 38 FEP Cases 882 (D.D.C. 1985).

23. Kelley Holland, "Office Space: Under New Management; When Religious Needs Test Company Policy," *New York Times*, February 25, 2007.

24. Ibid.

25. *Campos v. City of Blue Springs, Missouri*, 289 F.3d 546 (8th Cir. 2002).

26. *Hobbie v. Unemployment Appeals Commission of Florida*, 480 U.S. 136 (1987).

10. Religion in the Public-Sector Workplace

1. *Bollenbach v. Board of Education of Monroe-Woodbury Central School District*, 43 FEP Cases 1205 (S.D.N.Y. 1987).

2. *Brown v. Polk County, Iowa*, 61 F.3d 650 (8th Cir. 1995).

3. *Berry v. Department of Social Services, Tehama County*, 447 F.3d 642 (9th Cir. 2006).

4. *Marchi v. Board of Cooperative Educational Services of Albany, Schoharie, Schenectady, and Saratoga Counties*, 173 F.3d 469 (2d Cir. 1999).

5. *Palmer v. Board of Education of the City of Chicago*, 603 F.2d 1271 (7th Cir. 1980).

6. *Hobbie v. Unemployment Appeals Commission of Florida*, 480 U.S. 136 (1987).

7. *Thomas v. Review Board of the Indiana Employment Security Division*, 450 U.S.707 (1981).

8. *Vander Lann v. Mulder*, 178 Mich. App. 172, 50 FEP Cases 1242 (1989).

9. *Kelly v. Municipal Court of Marion County*, 852 F. Supp. 724 (S.D. Ind. 1994), *aff'd*, 97 F.3d 902 (7th Cir. 1996).

10. White House Guidelines on Religious Exercise and Religious Expression in the Federal Workplace, August 14, 1997. The guidelines were not promulgated as an Executive Order but as a policy statement.

11. Proselytizing in the Public-Sector Workplace

1. *Baz v. Walters*, 782 F.2d 701 (7th Cir. 1986).

2. *Bishop v. Aronov*, 926 F.2d 1066 (11th Cir. 1991).

3. *Peloza v. Capistrano Unified School District*, 37 F.3d 517 (9th Cir. 1994).

4. *Knight v. State of Connecticut Department of Public Health*, 275 F.3d 156 (2d Cir. 2001).

5. *Lumpkin v. Brown,* 109 F.3d 1498 (9th Cir. 1997).

6. *Tucker v. California Department of Education,* 97 F.3d 1204 (9th Cir. 1996).

12. Exemptions from the Discrimination Laws Granted to Religious Organizations

1. Title VII, § 702(a), 42 U.S.C. § 2000e-1(a).

2. Title VII, § 703(e)(2), 42 U.S.C. § 2000e-2(e)(2).

3. *DeMarco v. Holy Cross High School,* 4 F.3d 166 (2d Cir. 1993).

4. *Tomic v. Catholic Diocese of Peoria,* 442 F.3d 1036 (7th Cir. 2006).

5. *Rayburn v. General Conference of Seventh-day Adventists,* 772 F.2d 1164 (4th Cir. 1985).

6. *Killinger v. Samford University,* 113 F.3d 196 (11th Cir. 1997).

7. *Lemon v. Kurtzman,* 403 U.S. 602 (1971).

8. *EEOC v. Fremont Christian School,* 781 F.2d 1362 (9th Cir. 1986).

9. *Little v. Wuerl,* 929 F.2d 944 (3d Cir. 1991).

10. *Gosche v. Calvert High School,* 997 F. Supp. 867 (N.D. Ohio 1998), *aff'd without opinion,* 181 F.3d 101 (6th Cir. 1999).

11. Title VII, 703(e)(2), 42 U.S.C. § 2000e-2(e)(2).

12. *EEOC v. Kamehameha Schools,* 990 F.2d 458 (9th Cir. 1993).

13. *Feldstein v. Christian Science Monitor,* 555 F. Supp. 974 (D. Mass. 1983).

14. Title VII, § 703(e)(1), 42 U.S.C. § 2000e–2(e)(1).

15. *Pime v. Loyola University of Chicago,* 803 F.2d 351 (7th Cir. 1986).

16. *Vigars v. Valley Christian,* 805 F. Supp. 802 (N.D. Cal. 1992).

17. *Piatti v. Jewish Community Centers of Greater Boston,* 63 FEP Cases 942 (Mass. Super. Ct. 1993).

18. *Dothard v. Rawlinson,* 433 U.S. 321 (1977).

19. *Kern v. Dynalectron Corp.,* 577 F. Supp. 1196 (N.D. Tex. 1983), *aff'd,* 746 F.2d 810 (5th Cir. 1984).

13. The Ministerial Exception

1. *McClure v. Salvation Army,* 460 F.2d 553 (5th Cir. 1972), quoting *Sherbert v. Verner,* 374 U.S. 398 (1963).

2. *Rayburn v. General Conference of Seventh-day Adventists,* 772 F.2d 1164 (4th Cir. 1985).

3. *EEOC v. Catholic University of America,* 83 F.3d 455 (D.C. Cir. 1996).

4. *Maguire v. Marquette University,* 627 F. Supp. 1499 (E.D. Wis. 1986), *aff'd on other grounds,* 814 F.2d 1213 (7th Cir. 1987).

5. *Alicea-Hernández v. The Catholic Bishop of Chicago,* 320 F.3d 698 (7th Cir. 2002).

6. *EEOC v. Southwestern Baptist Theological Seminary,* 651 F.2d 277 (5th Cir. 1981).

7. *Stouch v. Brothers of the Order of Hermits of St. Augustine,* 836 F. Supp. 1134 (E.D. Pa. 1993).

8. *Weissman v. Congregation Shaare Emeth,* 38 F.3d 1038 (8th Cir. 1994).

9. *Bollard v. California Province of the Society of Jesus,* 196 F.3d 940 (9th Cir. 1999).

14. Questionable Applications of the Ministerial Exception

1. Diana B. Henriques "Where Faith Abides, Employees Have Few Rights," *New York Times,* October 9, 2006.

2. The facts recited here are based on those set forth in various court documents filed in the United States District Court, Northern District of Ohio, Western Division, Docket No. 3:02CV7171, for *Rosati v. Toledo, Ohio Catholic Diocese,* 233 F. Supp. 2d 917 including the Affidavit of Mary Rosati, the Affidavit of Dr. Candilee Butler, the Affidavit of Sister Sharon Elizabeth

Gworek, and Plaintiff's Memorandum in Opposition to Defendants' Motion for Summary Judgment.

3. Rosati Complaint, filed in the action cited in the preceding note.

4. Defendants' Memorandum in Support of Motion for Summary Judgment, filed in the action cited in note 2.

5. Plaintiff's Memorandum in Opposition to Defendants' Motion for Summary Judgment, filed in the action cited in note 2.

6. Defendants' Reply Memorandum in Support of Motion for Summary Judgment, filed in the action cited in note 2.

7. *Rosati v. Toledo, Ohio Catholic Diocese,* 233 F. Supp. 2d 917 (N.D. Ohio 2002).

8. *Petruska v. Gannon University,* 462 F.3d 294 (3d Cir. 2006).

9. *Petruska, v. Gannon University,* supra.

10. *Petruska v. Gannon University,* supra.

11. 42 U.S.C. § 2000bb(b). In 1997, the Supreme Court declared the Religious Freedom Restoration Act unconstitutional as applied to the states. *City of Boerne v. Flores,* 521 U.S. 507 (1997).

12. *Hankins v. Lyght,* 441 F.3d 96 (2d Cir. 2006).

13. "Where Faith Abides, Employees Have Few Rights," *New York Times,* October 9, 2006.

15. General Principles of Accommodation

1. *EEOC Guidelines on Discrimination Because of Religion,* 29 C.F.R. § 1605.1 (1967).

2. Title VII, § 701(j), 42 U.S.C. § 2000e(j).

3. *Trans World Airlines, Inc. (TWA) v. Hardison,* 432 U.S. 63 (1977).

4. Ibid. (Marshall, J., dissenting).

5. *EEOC Guidelines on Discrimination Because of Religion,* 29 C.F.R. § 1605 (1980).

6. *Proctor v. Consolidated Freightways Corp. of Delaware,* 795 F.2d 1472 (9th Cir. 1986).

7. *Toledo v. Nobel-Sysco, Inc.,* 892 F.2d 1481 (10th Cir. 1989).

8. *Anderson v. U.S.F. Logistics (IMC), Inc.,* 274 F.3d 470 (7th Cir. 2001).

9. *Brener v. Diagnostic Center Hospital,* 671 F.2d 141 (5th Cir. 1982).

10. *Ansonia Board of Education v. Philbrook,* 479 U.S. 60 (1986). This decision appears to undermine EEOC Guidelines that provide that when there is more than one means of accommodating an employee's religious beliefs and practices, the employer must offer the alternative with the fewest disadvantages to the employee being accommodated.

11. Josh Schopf, "Religious Activity and Proselytization in the Workplace: the Murky Line Between Healthy Expression and Unlawful Harassment," *Columbia Journal of Law and Social Problems* 31 (1997): 39, 43.

12. David L. Gregory, "The Role of Religion in the Secular Workplace," *Notre Dame Journal of Law, Ethics & Public Policy* 4 (1990): 749.

13. *Smith v. Pyro Mining Co.,* 827 F.2d 1081 (6th Cir. 1987).

16. Accommodation in Practice

1. *Virts v. Consolidated Freightways Corp. of Delaware,* 285 F.3d 508 (6th Cir. 2002).

2. *Shelton v. University of Medicine & Dentistry of New Jersey,* 223 F.3d 220 (3d Cir. 2000).

3. *Bruff v. North Mississippi Health Services, Inc.,* 244 F.3d 495 (5th Cir. 2001).

4. *Eversley v. MBank Dallas,* 848 F.2d 172 (5th Cir. 1988).

5. *EEOC Guidelines on Discrimination Because of Religion,* 29 C.F.R. § 1605.2(e)(1).

6. *Protos v. Volkswagen of America, Inc.,* 797 F.2d 129 (3d Cir. 1986).

7. *Wangsness v. Watertown School District,* 541 F. Supp. 332 (D. S.D. 1982).

8. *EEOC v. Ilona of Hungary, Inc.,* 108 F.3d 1569 (7th Cir. 1997).

17. Accommodation in Out-of-the-Ordinary Circumstances

1. *Cloutier v. Costco Wholesale Corp.,* 390 F.3d 126 (1st Cir. 2004).

2. *Kalsi v. New York City Transit Authority,* 78 FEP Cases 1705 (E.D.N.Y. 1998).

3. *Daniels v. City of Arlington, Texas,* 246 F.3d 500 (5th Cir. 2001).

4. *EEOC v. University of Detroit,* 904 F.2d 331 (6th Cir. 1990).

5. *EEOC v. American Federation of State, County and Municipal Employees, AFL-CIO,* 937 F. Supp. 166 (N.D.N.Y. 1996).

6. *EEOC Guidelines on Discrimination Because of Religion,* 29 C.F.R. § 1605.2(d).

7. National Labor Relations Act, 29 U.S.C. § 169. One court has declared this act unconstitutional because it limits the religious beliefs entitled to protection to "established and traditional tenets or teachings of a bona fide religion, body, or sect which has historically held conscientious objections to joining or financially supporting labor organizations." *Wilson v. National Labor Relations Board,* 920 F.2d 1282 (6th Cir. 1990).

18. Religious Discrimination and Retaliation

1. 42 U.S.C. § 2000e-3 (a).

2. Equal Employment Opportunity Commission Charge Statistics FY 1997 Through FY 2009, available at www.eeoc.gov/eeoc/statistics/enforcement/charges.cfm.

3. *Firestine v. Parkview Health System, Inc.,* 388 F.3d 229 (7th Cir. 2004).

4. *Hertz v. Luzenac America, Inc.,* 370 F.3d 1014 (10th Cir. 2002).

5. *Mandell v. County of Suffolk,* 316 F.3d 368 (2d Cir. 2003).

6. Raymond F. Gregory, *Age Discrimination in the American Workplace: Old at a Young Age* (New Brunswick, New Jersey: Rutgers University Press, 2001), 102–107.

7. *Kantar v. Baldwin Cooke Co.,* 69 FEP Cases 851 (N.D. Illinois 1995).

8. *Burlington Northern & Santa Fe Railway Company v. White,* 548 U.S. 53 (2006). The case was first reported in the 6/23/2006 edition of the *New York Times.*

19. Some Additional Issues

1. *Lubetsky v. Applied Card Systems, Inc.,* 296 F.3d 1301 (11th Cir. 2002).

2. *Cary v. Carmichael,* 908 F. Supp. 1334 (E.D. Va. 1995), *aff'd,* 116 F.3d 472 (4th Cir. 1997).

3. *Imperial Diner v. State Human Rights Appeal Board,* 52 N.Y.2d 72 (1980).

4. *Price Waterhouse v. Hopkins,* 490 U.S. 228 (1989).

5. *Weiss v. Parker Hannifan Corp.,* 747 F. Supp. 1118 (D.N.J. 1990).

6. *Bodett v. CoxCom, Inc.,* 366 F.3d 736 (9th Cir. 2004).

7. *Pedreira v. Kentucky Baptist Homes for Children, Inc.,* 86 FEP Cases 417 (W.D. Ky. 2001).

8. White House Office of the Press Secretary, news release, August 14, 1997.

20. Religion and the Law in the Workplace of the Future

1. *Baker v. Home Depot,* 455 F.3d 541 (2d Cir. 2006).

2. Georgette F. Bennett and Myrna Marofsky, *Religion in the Workplace: A Guide to Navigating the Complex Landscape* (New York: Tanenbaum Center for Interreligious Understanding, 2003), 34.

Cases Discussed in the Book

Africa v. Pennsylvania, 662 F.2d 1025 (3d Cir. 1981).

Alicea-Hernandez v. Catholic Bishop of Chicago, 320 F.3d 698 (7th Cir. 2002).

Anderson v. U.S.F. Logistics (IMC), Inc., 274 F.3d 470 (7th Cir. 2001).

Ansonia Board of Education v. Philbrook, 479 U.S. 60 (1986).

Baker v. Home Depot, 455 F.3d 541 (2d Cir. 2006).

Banks v. Service America Corp., 73 FEP Cases 173 (D. Kans. 1996).

Baz v. Walters, 782 F.2d 701 (7th Cir. 1986).

Beasley v. Health Care Service Corp., 940 F. 2d 1085 (7th Cir. 1991).

Bellamy v. Mason's Stores, Inc., 368 F. Supp. 1025 (E.D. Va. 1973), *aff'd,* 508 F.2d 504 (4th Cir. 1974).

Berry v. Department of Social Services, Tehama County, 447 F.3d 642 (9th Cir. 2006).

Binder v. Long Island Lighting Co., 57 F.3d 193 (2d Cir. 1995).

Bishop v. Aronov, 926 F.2d 1066 (11th Cir. 1991).

Bodett v. CoxCom, Inc., 366 F.3d 736 (9th Cir. 2004).

Bollard v. California Province of the Society of Jesus, 196 F.3d 940 (9th Cir. 1999).

Bollenbach v. Board of Education of Monroe–Woodbury Central School District, 43 FEP Cases 1205 (S.D.N.Y. 1987).

Brener v. Diagnostic Center Hospital, 671 F.2d 141 (5th Cir. 1982).

Brown v. Polk County, Iowa, 61 F.3d 650 (8th Cir. 1995).

Bruff v. North Mississippi Health Services, Inc., 244 F.3d 495 (5th Cir. 2001).

Helland v. South Bend Community School Corp., 93 F.3d 327 (7th Cir. 1996).

Henn v. National Geographic Society, 819 F. 2d 824 (7th Cir. 1987).

Hertz v. Luzenac America, Inc., 370 F.3d 1014 (10th Cir. 2002).

Hobbie v. Unemployment Appeals Commission of Florida, 480 U.S. 136 (1987).

Imperial Diner v. State Human Rights Appeal Board, 52 N.Y.2d 72 (1980).

Johnson v. Halls Merchandising, 49 FEP Cases 527 (W.D. Mo. 1989).

Johnson v. Spencer Press of Maine, Inc., 364 F.3d 368 (1st Cir. 2004).

Kalsi v. New York City Transit Authority, 78 FEP Cases 1705 (E.D.N.Y. 1998).

Kantar v. Baldwin Cooke Co., 69 FEP Cases 851 (N.D. Ill. 1995).

Karriem v. Oliver T. Carr, Co., 38 FEP Cases 882 (D.D.C. 1985).

Kelly v. Municipal Court of Marion County, 852 F. Supp. 724 (S.D. Ind. 1994), *aff'd*, 97 F.3d 902 (7th Cir. 1996).

Kern v. Dynalectron Corp., 577 F. Supp. 1196 (N.D. Tex. 1983), *aff'd*, 746 F.2d 810 (5th Cir. 1984).

Killinger v. Samford University, 113 F.3d 196 (11th Cir. 1997).

Knight v. State of Connecticut Department of Public Health, 275 F.3d 156 (2d Cir. 2001).

Krulik v. Board of Education of the City of New York, 781 F.2d 15 (2d Cir. 1986).

Lambert v. Condor Manufacturing Inc., 768 F. Supp. 600 (E.D. Mich. 1991).

Lawson v. State of Washington, 296 F.3d 799 (9th Cir. 2002).

Lemon v. Kurtzman, 403 U.S. 602 (1971).

Little v. Wuerl, 929 F.2d 944 (3d Cir. 1991).

Lubetsky v. Applied Card Systems, Inc., 296 F.3d 1301 (11th Cir. 2002).

Lumpkin v. Brown, 109 F.3d 1498 (9th Cir. 1997).

Maguire v. Marquette University, 627 F. Supp. 1499 (E.D. Wis. 1986), *aff'd on other grounds*, 814 F.2d 1213 (7th Cir. 1987).

Mandell v. County of Suffolk, 316 F.3d 368 (2d Cir. 2003).

Mann v. Milgram Food Stores, Inc., 730 F. 2d 1186 (8th Cir. 1984).

Marchi v. Board of Cooperative Educational Services of Albany, Schoharie, Schenectady, and Saratoga Counties, 173 F.3d 469 (2d Cir. 1999).

McClure v. Salvation Army, 460 F.2d 553 (5th Cir. 1972).

McDonnell Douglas Corp. v Green, 411 U.S. 492 (1973).

McGlothin v. Jackson Municipal Separate School District, 829 F. Supp. 853 (S.D. Miss. 1992).

Meritor Savings Bank v. Vinson, 477 U.S. 57 (1986).

Minnesota v. Sports & Health Club, Inc., 370 N.W.2d 844, 37 FEP Cases 1463 (Minn. 1985).

Nielson v. AgriNorthwest, 82 FEP Cases 893 (Wash. Ct. App. 1999).

Opuku-Boateng v. State of California, 93 F.3d 1461 (9th Cir. 1996).

Palmer v. Board of Education of the City of Chicago, 603 F.2d 1271 (7th Cir. 1980).

Pedreira v. Kentucky Baptist Homes for Children, Inc., 86 FEP Cases 417 (W.D. Ky. 2001).

Peloza v. Capistrano Unified School District, 37 F.3d 517 (9th Cir. 1994).

Peterson v. Wilmur Communications, Inc., 89 FEP Cases 148 (E.D. Wis. 2002).

Petruska v. Gannon University, 462 F. 3d 294 (3d Cir. 2006).

Philbrook v. Ansonia Board of Education, 757 F.2d 476 (2d Cir. 1985), *rev'd and remanded on other grounds*, 479 U.S. 60 (1986).

Piatti v. Jewish Community Centers of Greater Boston, 63 FEP Cases 942 (Mass. Super. Ct. 1993).

Pime v. Loyola University of Chicago, 803 F.2d 351 (7th Cir. 1986).

Powell v. Yellow Book USA, Inc., 445 F.3d 1074 (8th Cir. 2006).

Price Waterhouse v. Hopkins, 490 U.S. 228 (1989).

Proctor v. Consolidated Freightways Corp. of Delaware, 795 F.2d 1472 (9th Cir. 1986).

Protos v. Volkswagen of America, Inc., 797 F.2d 129 (3d Cir. 1986).

Rayburn v. General Conference of Seventh-day Adventists, 772 F.2d 1164 (4th Cir. 1985).

Reeves v. Sanderson Plumbing Products, Inc., 530 U.S. 133 (2000).

Rodriguez v. City of Chicago, 69 FEP Cases 993 (N.D. Ill. 1996).

Rosati v. Toledo, Ohio Catholic Diocese, 233 F. Supp. 2d 917 (N.D. Ohio 2002).

Rosen v. Thornburgh, 928 F.2d 528 (2d Cir. 1991).

Sarin v. Raytheon Co., 69 FEP Cases 856 (D. Mass. 1995).

Sattar v. Motorola, Inc., 138 F.3d 1164 (7th Cir. 1998).

Shanoff v. State of Illinois Department of Human Services, 258 F.3d 696 (7th Cir. 2001).

Shapolia v. Los Alamos National Laboratory, 992 F.2d 1033 (10th Cir. 1993).

Shelton v. University of Medicine & Dentistry of New Jersey, 223 F.3d 220 (3d Cir. 2000).

Sherbert v. Verner, 374 U. S. 398 (1963).

Shpargel v. Stage Co., 71 FEP Cases 1739 (E.D. Mich. 1996)

Simmons v. Sports Training Institute, 52 FEP Cases 1322 (S.D.N.Y. 1990).

Singh v. Bowsher, 609 F. Supp. 454 (D.D.C. 1984).

Skorup v. Modern Door Corp., 153 F.3d 512 (7th Cir. 1998).

Slater v. King Soopers, Inc., 809 F. Supp. 809 (D. Colo. 1992).

Smith v. Pyro Mining Co., 827 F.2d 1081 (6th Cir. 1987).

Spratt v. County of Kent, 621 F. Supp. 594 (W.D. Mich. 1985), *aff'd,* 810 F.2d 203 (6th Cir. 1986).

St. Mary's Honor Center v. Hicks, 509 U.S. 502 (1993).

Stouch v. Brothers of the Order of Hermits of St. Augustine, 836 F. Supp. 1134 (E.D. Pa. 1993).

Thomas v. Review Board, Indiana Employment Security Division, 450 U.S. 707 (1981).

Tiano v. Dillard Department Stores, 139 F.3d 679 (9th Cir. 1998).

Toledo v. Nobel-Sysco, Inc., 892 F.2d 1481 (10th Cir. 1989).

Tomic v. Catholic Diocese of Peoria, 442 F.3d 1036 (7th Cir. 2006).

Trans World Airlines, Inc. (TWA) v. Hardison, 432 U.S. 63 (1977).

Tucker v. California Department of Education, 97 F.3d 1204 (9th Cir. 1996).

Turner v. Barr, 65 FEP Cases 909 (D.D.C. 1993).

United States v. Board of Education of the School District of Philadelphia, 911 F.2d 882 (3d Cir. 1990).

United States v. Seeger, 380 U.S. 163 (1965).

Vander Lann v. Mulder, 178 Mich. App. 172, 50 FEP Cases 1242 (1989).

Venters v. City of Delhi, 123 F.3d 956 (7th Cir.1997).

Vigars v. Valley Christian, 805 F. Supp. 802 (N.D. Calif. 1992).

Virts v. Consolidated Freightways Corp. of Delaware, 285 F.3d 508 (6th Cir. 2002).

Wangsness v. Watertown School District, 541 F. Supp. 332 (D.S.D. 1982).

Weiss v. Parker Hannifan Corp., 747 F. Supp. 1118 (D.N.J.1990).

INDEX